THE MERCY OF THE SKY

THE MERCY OF THE SKY

THE STORY OF A TORNADO

HOLLY BAILEY

VIKING

VIKING
An imprint of Penguin Random House LLC
375 Hudson Street
New York, New York 10014
penguin.com

Map illustrations by Sarah Schumacher

ISBN 978-0-525-42749-0

Printed in the United States of America
1 3 5 7 9 10 8 6 4 2

For my mother

MOORE, THE PATH OF THE STORM

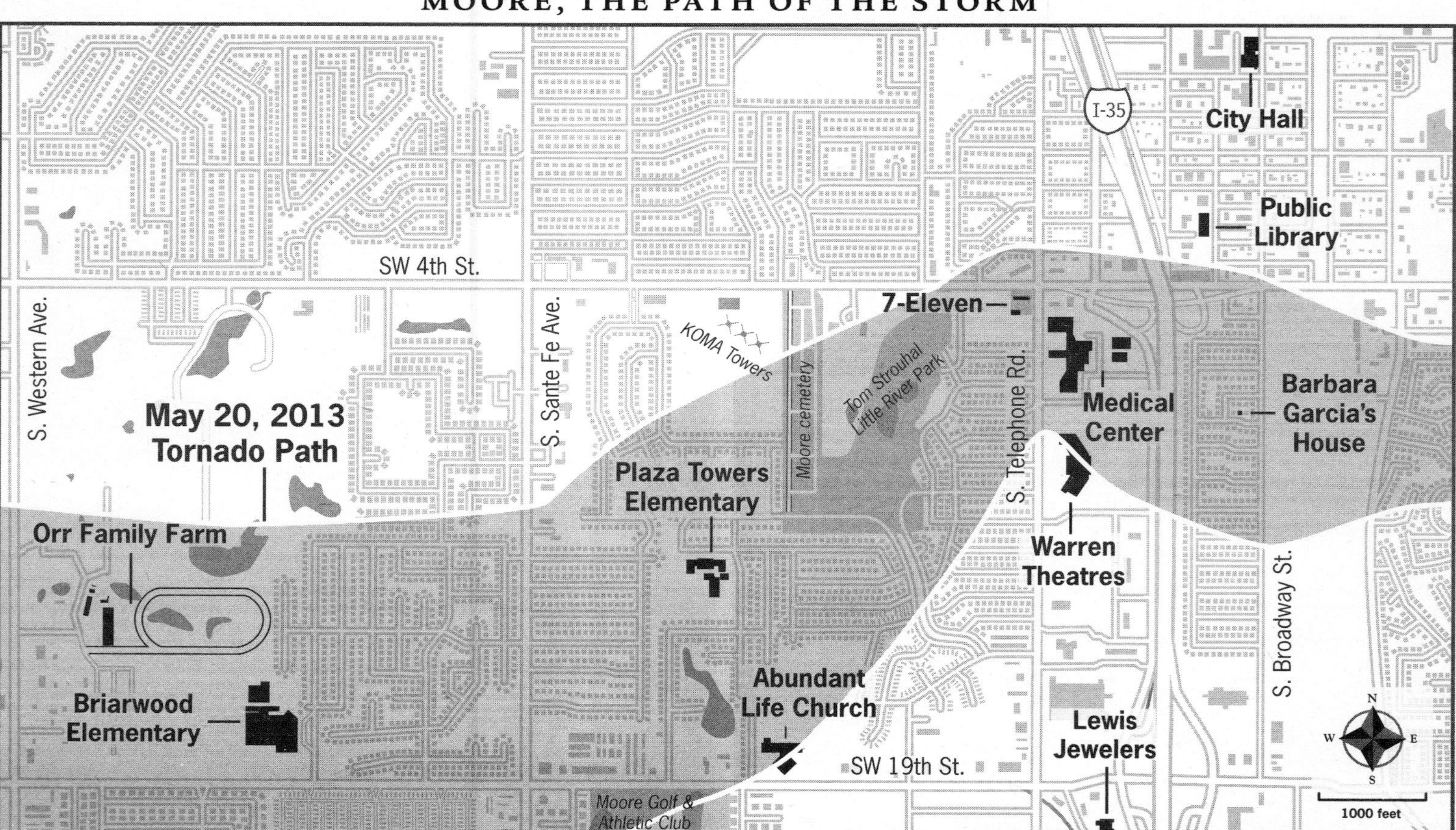

OKLAHOMA CITY AND THE THREE TORNADOES

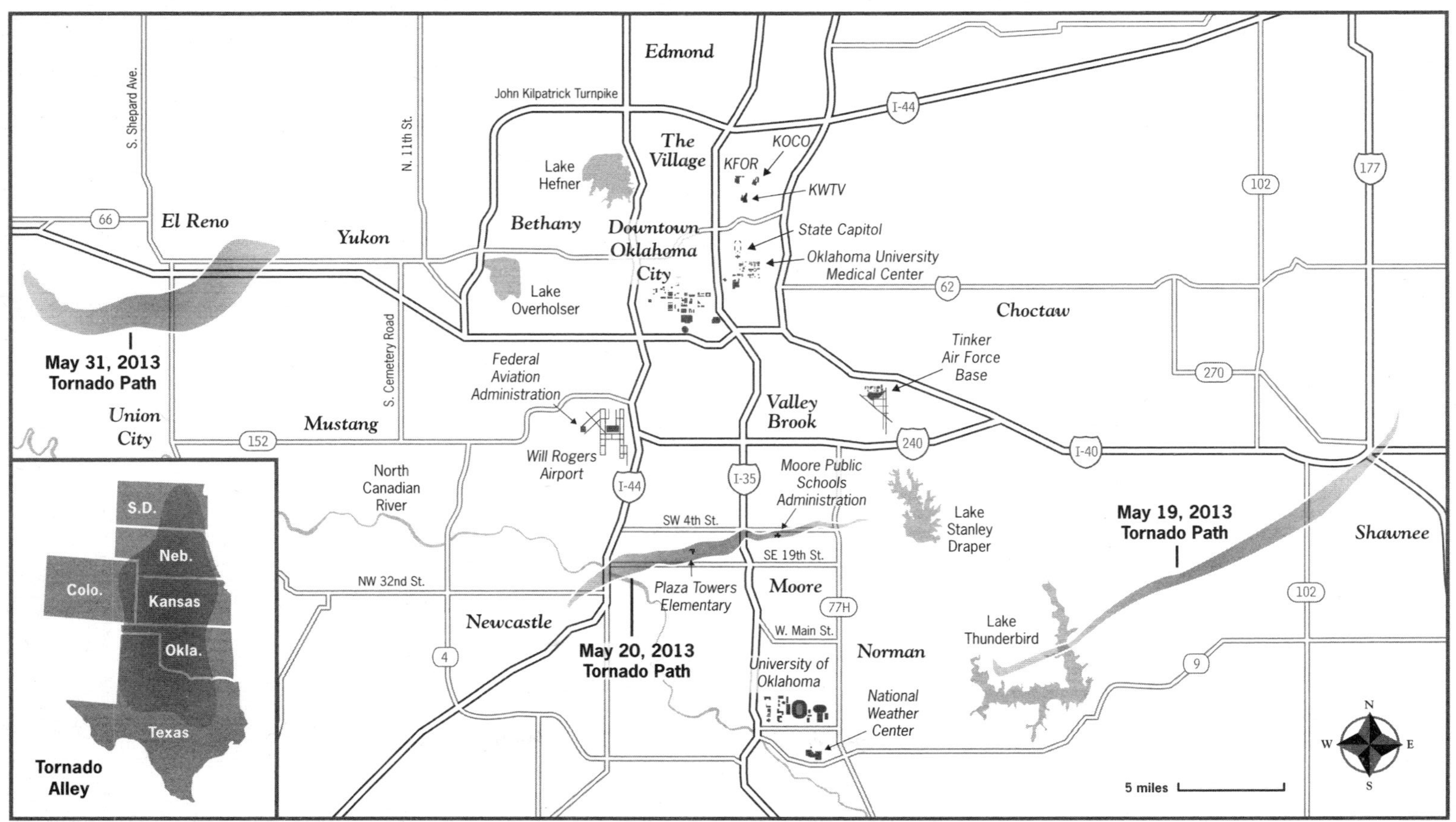

THE
MERCY
OF THE
SKY

INTRODUCTION

Central Oklahoma has long been known as "tornado alley," and anyone watching the news knows why. In May 2013 two of the strongest tornadoes on record hit the ground there in less than two weeks. On May 20 a milewide twister packing winds in excess of 200 miles per hour tore through the center of Moore, a quiet suburb south of Oklahoma City, killing twenty-five people and injuring several hundred. Among the dead were seven third graders at Plaza Towers Elementary, who died when their school building collapsed on top of them. It was the fifth tornado in fifteen years to sweep through Moore, a town that has been so unlucky with the weather that many locals refer to it as the "tornado alley of tornado alley."

I spent most of my childhood in Moore. Though I lived a few miles away in south Oklahoma City, I went to school in Moore until I was fourteen, right on SW Fourth Street, a few blocks north of Plaza Towers. Many members of my family have called Moore their home over the years. Some still do, residing a mile north of where the May 20 tornado hit. Knowing their city's track record with the weather, they jumped in their car that Monday and fled the storm, looking in their rearview mirror and praying that they would have a home to come back to when dark clouds had passed. It wasn't the first time they'd had to run, and given Moore's history, it probably won't be the last.

The May 20 storm bore eerie similarities to a tornado that had slammed into Moore almost exactly fourteen years earlier. That storm, which hit on May 3, 1999, was so devastating that many Oklahomans still refer to it by its date alone—like their own version of 9/11. The May 3 twister was another milewide monstrosity that killed thirty-six people as it cut a deadly diagonal from just south of Oklahoma City through Moore. More than five hundred people were injured, some so horrifically it was a miracle they survived. The storm caused more than $1 billion in damage. In Moore alone it wiped out several entire subdivisions on the west side of town, reducing them to ruins.

The May 3 storm remains the strongest tornado ever recorded in the nearly one hundred years since scientists have been trying to understand the mysterious phenomenon of the tornado. At one point its winds clocked in at 302 miles per hour—the highest wind speed ever measured near the surface of the earth. The storm may in fact have been stronger, but nobody could get close enough to measure it at the epicenter. Meteorologists studying tornadoes have been forced to keep a safe distance from their subjects. The 1999 storm was so destructive it prompted the National Weather Service to rethink how it measured tornadoes on the Fujita scale, which was launched in the 1970s to categorize storms by size and wind speed. In 2007 scientists adopted the Enhanced Fujita scale, which factors in the damage left in a tornado's wake to more accurately gauge how strong it was—though so much is still a guessing game.

In 2013 some neighborhoods that had been rebuilt after 1999 were hit again—a destructive second act that has never happened to any other city. But just when it seemed it might be an exact replay of May 3, the May 20 tornado turned slightly to the east, taking aim at the heavily populated central part of Moore. At points it became wider and moved more slowly than the previous storm, becoming what is known as a "grinder" as it took its time chewing neighborhoods into tiny bits. The storm left behind more than $2 billion in damage, giving it the dubious distinction of being one of the most costly tornadoes in history. The May 3 tornado had been ranked as an F5—the highest rating under the original Fujita scale. The tornado that hit fourteen years later was categorized as an EF5—the highest possible rating on the updated scale. Moore was suddenly one of the only cities in the world to have been hit twice, in almost exactly the same spot, by two maximum-strength tornadoes.

Before Moore had a chance to fully digest its latest unlucky bout with the weather, the storm sirens sounded again. Just eleven days later, on May 31, an even larger storm developed to the west of the city. A tornado that was at least 2.6 miles wide—bigger than the width of Manhattan—touched down in nearby El Reno, a few miles west of Oklahoma City, not long after Friday-evening rush hour. The El Reno storm, as it came to be called, is now the widest tornado on record. Fortunately, the tornado hit the ground in wide-open farm country, where houses were few and far between. Just as it began to aim east toward the more heavily populated city of Yukon, whose main road into town is named after its most famous son, the country singer Garth Brooks, and beyond that to Oklahoma City, it lifted, sparing Moore from another devastating hit. But it left behind irreparable damage. People still jittery over the May 20 tornado had jumped in their cars and tried to flee the storm at the last minute, clogging the roads as the twister approached. Four people—including a mother and her infant son, born just seventeen days earlier—died when the storm sucked their vehicles off the roads on and near Interstate 40, where the tornado's nearly 300-mile-per-hour winds picked up 18-wheelers and twisted them like tinfoil.

The twister had been moving straight east, but out of nowhere it quickly changed direction several times, erratically veering northeast, then heading due north as it grew into one of the most violent storms in history. It then literally made a loop over Interstate 40, turning around to hit land it had already hit. It swerved west, then southwest, then south, then southeast and east again, covering several miles in just minutes. Nobody had ever seen a storm like it, and as it unpredictably danced all over the landscape, the tornado was so gargantuan that no one on the ground realized it was changing direction. It was so massive it had multiple vortices swirling around inside it—monsters within the monster—though you couldn't see them until you were right up on it, at which point you were too close to escape. With no warning, the massive twister turned on people who had been chasing the storm, including crews from the local television stations and The Weather Channel, who were sending live video feeds when the tornado began raining debris down on them. Some were picked up in their cars and hurled off the road. Many had spent their careers warning people to avoid the path of a dangerous tornado, and now they found themselves unexpectedly discovering the consequences firsthand.

Three veteran storm chasers died that night. Their white Chevy Cobalt was found half a mile from where it was lifted up by the storm, crushed like a crumpled-up soda can, and dropped in the middle of a canola field. Still buckled in the passenger seat was fifty-four-year-old Tim Samaras, one of the most respected tornado scientists in the world. But even Samaras, who was not a risk taker in his pursuit of the strange monsters he had devoted his life to studying, was caught off guard by the El Reno twister, a weather system so destructive that someone later said it seemed as if it had been designed specifically to kill storm chasers.

Samaras's car was so mangled—its engine and front two tires ripped away—that a state trooper on patrol almost didn't recognize it was a vehicle when he saw it from the road. Inside he found Samaras dead, still strapped in the passenger seat. His shirt, shoes, and a single sock had been inhaled by the storm, but somehow his wallet containing his identification was in his pocket. Peering into the car, the officer saw the seatbelt in the driver's seat was still buckled, but the seat itself was empty. Carl Young, a forty-five-year-old meteorologist and Samaras's longtime chase partner, had been sucked away. His body was found half a mile to the west, facedown in a creek swollen by flash flooding. The next morning, just after dawn, officers found Samaras's son Paul, who was twenty-four, a few yards away in the same creek, his body revealed only after the floodwaters had subsided.

When the El Reno storm hit, I was nearly 1,500 miles away at a concert in New York City, but I knew almost instantly that a twister had touched the ground. My iPhone lit up with a text message from a recent ex-boyfriend, a photojournalist living in California who was already booking a flight to Oklahoma because it looked like disaster was about to strike again. I ran outside and called my mother, who lived in south Oklahoma City—right in the storm's path. She didn't pick up, which wasn't like her, and I began to worry. I flagged down a cab and headed home, pulling up live video of the storm on my iPhone from KWTV, the CBS affiliate in Oklahoma City that was renowned as the longtime home of Gary England, the weatherman who had gotten me through every storm as a kid. Every few minutes, I'd try to call my mother again. But there was no answer as the storm inched ever closer to her home.

It was a routine we went through almost every spring—bad weather would pop up in Oklahoma, and I would call to check in. But this time was different. Only days earlier I had gone back to Moore to cover the aftermath of the May 20 storm, and even though I had grown up around severe weather and at one point had even dreamed of being a meteorologist, it wasn't until that trip home that I had realized in a visceral way how truly horrific and ruthless tornadoes could be.

By then I hadn't lived in Oklahoma for fourteen years. I had left Oklahoma City in early 1999, bound for Washington, D.C., where I covered politics for various news outlets until I landed a gig at *Newsweek*. As the magazine's youngest White House correspondent, I traveled to several war zones, including trips to Baghdad with President Obama and to Kabul with Vice President Cheney. I hadn't even had a passport before I joined the White House beat, and suddenly I found myself in the same time zone as Osama bin Laden twice in the span of a few months. I was stunned by the pure devastation I saw in the volatile places we went, as motorcades sped past shelled buildings and landscapes so bombed out they resembled the moon.

In 2005, I witnessed a war zone closer to home when I was among the small pool of reporters who accompanied President George W. Bush on his first trip to the Gulf Coast to survey the devastation in the aftermath of Hurricane Katrina. In helicopters and later on the ground, we saw New Orleans, one of America's most beautiful old cities, submerged under several feet of dark, swampy water. It was a sight and smell that none of us on that trip—Bush included, I'm sure—will ever forget. At one point the heat, humidity, and smell were so overwhelming that a reporter turned and vomited. And we were only visitors. In a few hours we would get back on *Air Force One* and fly back to Washington. I couldn't imagine what the people of New Orleans, who couldn't escape the disaster around them, were going through.

Yet none of that prepared me for what I found when I returned to Moore on May 21, 2013—less than twenty-four hours after the tornado had hit. As I steered my rental car along SW 149th, a street I had driven down countless times before, the landscape around me was unrecognizable. Under dark, ominous skies I passed large electrical transformers that had once stood as high as six-story buildings but were now bent and twisted into the ground. Every tree as far as the eye could see was shorn of its branches, its trunk whittled down to a giant slingshot. In the mostly rural farmland all around me, there were large swaths where tall grass had been literally sucked from the ground—bald spots that revealed the red, muddy earth below. In the fields where vegetation remained, the mix of grass and weeds seemed permanently bent toward the east—as if every blade had been sprayed into place with a thick coat of Aqua Net.

As I approached May Avenue, I began to see the outlines of familiar neighborhoods, but many homes were simply gone, wiped clean off their concrete slabs. I could see tiny figures picking through piles of debris in the distance, and with the road ahead blocked by downed trees and power lines, I pulled over, got out, and began to hike through a muddy field strewn with the confetti of people's lives—photos, shoes, clothes, books, and toys, all carelessly tossed about. I even saw a child's rudimentary drawing of a smiling blond woman, the pink construction paper tattered and wet but still somehow firmly tacked to a corkboard that had been blown off a wall somewhere. The oak trees that lined May Avenue were sheared off and covered in debris. They resembled grotesque Christmas trees, decorated in jagged pieces of metal and pink insulation that hung from their maimed branches. A king-sized mattress was impaled on one like a sick version of a holiday angel. The remains of a crushed car were wrapped around the trunk of one tree so closely that they looked like a discarded piece of chewing gum stuck to a pole by someone too lazy to throw it in a garbage can.

Even along the Gulf Coast after Katrina, I had never seen devastation like this. The fact that it was my city, my hometown, made the devastation that much more shocking. Standing there, a terrible odor hit me. It was the smell of death—worse than New Orleans after the hurricane. To my immediate right was a giant dead cow, bloodied and still, its eyes wide open as if in terror. About a dozen yards behind it were several dead horses that were being slowly pushed into a pile by a man in a gas mask driving a forklift. As I stood there in the middle of May Avenue, several residents gathered near me to watch, holding their noses and looking shell-shocked as thunder boomed in the distance and it began to rain. The horses had lived there, one man told me, but the cow he had never seen before, a terrible gift left behind by a tornado that had taken almost everything.

It was things that remained that surprised him. While his house was gone, reduced to a pile of scrap wood, he pointed to a home across the street—totally obliterated except for a chimney and a closet, where the missing door revealed clothes still on their hangers, just as they had been before the storm. The only sign something was amiss was a few spots of mud, spit out by the storm and splattered on a jacket sleeve as innocuously as dots of tomato sauce after a spaghetti dinner.

Farther into Moore, I found more signs of how strong, but also how peculiar, the storm had been. The local bowling alley had taken a direct hit that wiped out the entire building. But in the middle of the rubble, a line of bowling pins stood in precise formation on one of the dusty lanes. How had they not been knocked down by a storm so fierce that it destroyed almost everything in its path and shook the ground like a tiny earthquake? In some neighborhoods entire blocks were decimated by the tornado's winds, reducing most houses to nothing but sticks, while on the next street some homes were unscathed except for a missing shingle or two and a coat of mud on the windows. One resident told me how her entire kitchen had been blown apart, her refrigerator sucked out and deposited onto a jungle gym at a playground down the block. But her vintage Fire King dishware, so old she rarely used it, had been left untouched in a nearby cabinet, without a crack or a scratch. "I guess the tornado didn't like tulips," she said matter-of-factly, referring to the red and yellow flowers adorning her dinnerware.

The peculiar behavior of tornadoes was no mystery to me. I have been fascinated by storms ever since I was a kid, when I would watch them rumble past my house, scary but beautiful at the same time. I grew up during the oil bust in Oklahoma, and we didn't have much money, so my mom entertained me by taking me to the public library, where we went spent hours at a time. Aside from poring over the Sweet Valley High series (which is what made me want to become a journalist, as one of the twins worked for the school paper), I didn't waste much time with young-adult books. Instead, I checked out every volume I could find about storms and tornadoes, and what the library didn't have I somehow persuaded my mom to buy, even on our limited income. I was probably the only nine-year-old kid in my neighborhood with a scientific field guide to storm clouds.

Despite my obsession with tornadoes, I had never seen one in person (and still haven't). On many occasions when I was older, I'd drive toward threatening storms, hoping to catch a glimpse of a funnel cloud, though I never got too close. You never knew when one would turn on you, and when it did, size didn't matter. "A tornado is a tornado," my mother often told me. "No matter how big it is, it can kill you." I even enrolled in a storm-chasing class when I was at the University of Oklahoma, entertaining the idea that, as a journalist, I might want to write about storms someday. But I dropped out after I was offered an internship at the *Chicago Tribune*'s Washington bureau for a semester, an opportunity that was too good to turn down—especially for someone who had never lived outside Oklahoma and longed to get away. When I moved to the East Coast for good after college to pursue my journalism career, I missed the storms. But the weather that began to roll through Oklahoma was unlike anything I'd experienced in my childhood.

Starting with the 1999 tornado, the storms back home seemed to be getting bigger and more violent. They were nothing like the tornadoes I remembered as a kid—storms I found to be absolutely terrifying were a tenth of the size of the twisters that have rumbled through Oklahoma in recent years. Some have attributed the dark turn in the weather to climate change, but the truth is, even the scientists who know more about tornadoes than anybody aren't sure how to explain it. And that is what is fascinating about tornadoes. They hit so often, but scientists still know so little about what causes them and what is happening inside them that makes them so deadly. As one meteorologist told me, a tornado is like an iceberg, where the funnel is only a small glimpse, less than 10 percent, of the entire storm. People know more than they did thirty years ago, when the only warning that a tornado was coming was the neighbor's roof blowing away. On May 20 the storm sirens sounded sixteen minutes before the tornado hit the ground—an eternity in tornado science—and the weather community is desperately working to expand that time.

There are some things about tornadoes that scientists will never understand. One of these is the unique relationship that people in central Oklahoma have with the bad weather that torments them every spring. No region in the country has been ravaged more frequently by killer tornadoes, yet people there would never dream of living anywhere else. During the May 3, 1999, tornado, my mom's younger sister Betty lost her home. By then she and my Uncle Dale and their kids were living on a farm near Shawnee—east of Oklahoma City—but they had kept their first home in Moore, and it was wiped from the slab when the tornado moved through. Fourteen years later, on the night before the May 20 tornado, they were struck again. An EF4 twister with winds gauged at 166 miles per hour approached their farm, and Aunt Betty could see it moving across the valley right toward her. Up close the tornado looked nothing like she had expected. It was a giant wedge of a cloud that looked, she told me later, "like a column of boiling black water."

As it drew close, she raced around the house gathering what she could to take to the basement. Important papers were already in the safe, but for some reason, as she ran around her bedroom, she grabbed a bottle of Versace perfume that she and my mother had found on an antiquing trip a few months before. Later, as she recounted the story, she couldn't explain why that perfume had been so important, why she had suddenly been so determined to save it: a discontinued bottle of perfume from the 1990s, which she used only sparingly. "I guess your mom could have put a few drops on my dead body," she said, with a laugh. "No tornado is going to take my fancy perfume."

Her youngest son, Gordon, lived nearby but was in Oklahoma City that afternoon. He had tried to get to her before the storm hit, but she had urged him to stay away. She didn't want him to get caught up in the storm trying to drive to the house, and on the phone he had started to cry, telling her that he didn't want her to die. As the storm passed, the tornado ripped the roof off her house, destroyed several barns, and completely demolished Gordon's home nearby. Fortunately, my aunt was safely sheltered in their basement, and she emerged to see not only the damage but also the puzzling things the storm did as it moved over their land. Several of their cows and horses were picked up by the tornado in the south pasture and carried nearly half a mile away to the north pasture. The animals were pretty scraped up, but amazingly none died.

My aunt has now been through two killer storms in fourteen years, not including all the near misses in between, when she watched tornadoes skirt her land. But not once has she considered leaving, not for a second. Instead, as she and Uncle Dale battled with the insurance company over the cost of rebuilding their home, she tried to find the humor in the situation. Things could always be worse, she pointed out. She could be dead. And the tornado hadn't been totally ungracious. The storm had deposited on her doorstep a skinny, one-eyed calico cat, which followed her around, rubbing against her legs as she yelled into the phone at her insurance agent. She had no idea where the cat had come from.

While my aunt's home was partially destroyed, the tornado left her neighbor's home across the street completely untouched. But in a bizarre twist, a fierce lightning storm came through the next morning and struck that pristine house and burned it to the ground. Another sign, she said, that things could be much worse.

My mother's attitude toward storms was no different. On the night of that terrible El Reno tornado, I finally reached her as the storm seemed to be redeveloping due west of her house. She was in an underground shelter across the street from her home at my Aunt Mary's house—crowded with several of Mary's kids, their children, and their dogs. The storm sirens were blaring, and it was raining and "blowing like the dickens," she told me. Her phone was dying, and she told me she would call me later. A few miles to the west, a small EF1 tornado, with winds measured at 100 miles per hour, blew off part of the roof at the Oklahoma City airport and traveled east across the city before lifting. It was followed by intense flash flooding that killed thirteen people in Oklahoma City. Among the dead was an entire family that had crowded into a drainage ditch to take cover from the tornado and been washed away.

I tried to reach my mom again later that night and the next day, but her phone went straight to voicemail. I knew the power was out in her neighborhood and that she was probably okay, but the next day my ex-boyfriend, on the ground to cover the damage, asked for her address so he could go check. He texted me a picture of her house—a little windblown but still standing. When I finally reached her, she sounded weary but was almost blasé about her close call. She told me about driving through her neighborhood the morning after the storm and seeing roofs damaged and trees ripped apart. Around the corner from her house, she looked up and saw a giant trampoline impaled on a tree. "This is why I always say you should never buy a trampoline," she told me, "because in Oklahoma, you are always going to end up owning one, even if you didn't buy it." I knew that her dispensing of random folksy advice was her strange way of coping, and all I could do was laugh.

The way my mom and her sister reacted to those two terrible storms perfectly encapsulates the attitude most Oklahomans have about living in an area so prone to deadly weather. They are resilient survivors, stubborn in their refusal to let nature get the best of them. It seems to be a spirit passed down through the generations, dating back to the days of the Dust Bowl, when a severe drought ravaged the land in unspeakable ways and forced many Oklahomans to migrate west. Those who survived—and, surprisingly, many did—wore it as a badge of pride, a sign that somehow they had triumphed over the worst Mother Nature had to offer. If only they had known what she would throw at their descendants in the decades to come.

That sense of satisfaction in surviving the elements is no different in Oklahoma today. Despite the fact they are smack-dab in the middle of the most dangerous tornado zone in the country, most Oklahomans never think about leaving or moving somewhere else. They argue that they are no crazier than Californians who suffer the constant threat of earthquakes or people in New Orleans, New York, or Miami who know that one giant hurricane could wipe out parts of their beloved city for good. "I could never leave," my aunt told me. "You stay and you rebuild."

And many have, even in Moore, where people have lost their homes, all of their belongings, even their loved ones to the killer storms that have taken aim at the city again and again. So many have chosen to stay, praying they might be spared from the next storm. Everybody agrees there will be one; the only unknown is when. People in Oklahoma describe it as living "at the mercy of the sky," a saying I first heard my grandmother use when I was barely old enough to understand what storms were. Over the years, people in Moore and elsewhere in central Oklahoma have become amateur meteorologists as they have adapted to life in the danger zone of storms, attuned to clues of when bad weather is on approach.

When I was in Moore talking to survivors of the May 20 tornado, I couldn't help but think of one of the most terrifying nights of my childhood. I was ten years old when a tornado swept through north of Oklahoma City. I still remember how a sunny afternoon suddenly turned into a dark and threatening evening. Moisture clung to the air, a wetness you feel only when a tornado is brewing. Jagged bolts of lightning lit up the sky, which was the color of an ugly bruise. The scariest part was how calm it was. That's what you are taught to fear the most, a storm that is suddenly quiet, because that's when the twister is about to hit. Unlike hurricanes or typhoons, which can spend weeks swirling and gathering strength over the ocean before landfall, tornadoes are still largely unpredictable. They appear and disappear, large or small, with little warning beyond signs that the weather conditions might be ripe. No one knows what's going to happen or when, although the National Weather Service and others in the weather community have invested untold millions in money and manpower trying to figure that out.

On that night back in 1986, the tornado struck two housing additions in Edmond, a suburb of Oklahoma City, destroying nearly 40 homes and severely damaging 150 others. Fifteen people were injured, but no one died. I later found out the storm was two hundred yards wide—just over one tenth of a mile. To put that in perspective, the tornado that tore through Moore on May 20, 2013, was more than ten times its size and the El Reno tornado that followed eleven days later was thirty times larger. Had the funnel not lifted before it headed toward the more populated center of town, the level of destruction could have been reminiscent of an atomic bomb.

Meteorologists now believe these bigger storms are part of a larger trend, not anomalies, but they don't know the cause. The tornadoes are not only getting bigger but also showing up at random times of the day and the year. It used to be that tornadoes would hit mostly in the springtime, in the early evening when the ground had warmed from a full day of sun, causing the warm surface air to rise and collide with the unstable air above. But two years ago Oklahoma was hit by a tornado in January, and there have been an increasing number of storms in the fall, around October—a "second spring," as some locals joke. The May 20 tornado that hit Moore took place hours earlier than usual, in the middle of the afternoon, when kids were still at school.

When I arrived in Moore the day after the tornado, the stories of incredible bravery and horror were just beginning to be told—how teachers had thrown their bodies on top of their students to shield them from the storm, at great risk to themselves. How young mothers had done everything they could to shield their tiny babies whose lives had barely begun. One mother survived to tell the tale of how her seven-month-old baby girl had been sucked from her arms and killed. Another mother died cradling her four-month-old son in the tiny bathroom of a 7-Eleven where she had rushed to take cover when the storm hit. The store took a direct hit, and rescue workers who spoke of digging through the rocks and debris began to sob uncontrollably at what had been lost. But then there were miracles too, like what happened at Briarwood Elementary, where the entire building was leveled but no one died.

Within hours of the tornado, Moore, which had been through this routine so many times before, was already on the job of picking up the pieces. The city began hauling debris away and repairing the damage even before people could come to grips with the horrible scar that had been left on their city. That same day, the owner of the liquor store on SW Fourth Street, just four blocks north of where homes had been blasted away by the tornado, went outside and replaced the letters on his marquee that had been sucked away by the storm. His previous sign had been famous around town for its witty messages, but this one was simple. "We'll be okay," it read.

It was at that moment I knew I wanted to tell the longer story of what had happened here. As a native, I knew how people felt about the weather, how they loved it and feared it all at the same time. I wanted to know what it was like being in the path of a tornado that seemed bigger than life itself as it bore down on the city from the west. I knew I had to chronicle the story of those who survived one of the worst tornadoes in history—and those who didn't make it. And I wanted to tell the larger story of how unique Oklahoma is because of the weather, the often crazy lengths to which the local media go in trying to cover the storms in a state where local meteorologists are more famous than celebrities.

This book is a story of Oklahoma's relationship with the weather as told through the lens of what happened in Moore. It's a story of that disaster, the hours leading up to the tornado, the suspenseful minutes during the heart of the storm, and the painful hours of reckoning afterward. It's about the victims, the survivors, and the people who tried to help, all of them working tirelessly to tackle this horrifying natural disaster. It's a story of death and destruction but also of survival and resilience. It is the story of the people of Oklahoma, who choose to live at the mercy of the sky in a part of the country where you can lose everything—your home, your business, even your life—in one unpredictable, violent storm.

CHAPTER 1

4:00 A.M., MAY 20

Gary England rarely sleeps in the springtime, and even though he was dead tired, with an aching fatigue that seemed to penetrate his bones, he had spent another night tossing and turning. All he'd hoped for was a little bit of shut-eye, a few hours of peace. But the sleep he so desperately needed had eluded him again, as it so often did at this time of the year, when tornadoes are most likely to embark on their destructive dance.

Lying in bed in his house on the northern outskirts of Oklahoma City, painfully tired but awake, England felt like a zombie. Worse than that, he was a zombie with tornadoes whirling through his head. It was like this every spring: When he would shut his eyes at night, terrible storms would rumble through his mind—conjuring horrible memories of death and destruction—only to collide head-on with the agonizing question of when the next one would hit. That's what kept him up on nights like this: the trepidation that the next round of bad weather was about to begin.

That Monday he felt more unsettled than usual. Staring at the ceiling, he couldn't shake the feeling that something really bad was going to happen, and every time he drifted off to sleep for even a few seconds, he was suddenly jolted awake by an overwhelming feeling of dread. It was like an alarm he couldn't shut off that just kept sounding again and again. Bad weather had been in the forecast for a week. But how bad? He desperately needed to sleep, but his mind was too busy thinking, planning, worrying. How bad would this storm be? Would people be ready? Was he ready?

Well before dawn, England finally gave up and crawled out of bed, trying not to wake Mary, his wife of fifty-two years, who slept beside him. He padded down the hall to his computer, which was still on from when he'd left it a few hours before, its screen showing a radar image of Oklahoma. He looked at the small clock in the corner of the screen. It was just after 4:00 A.M. He had been in bed less than three hours. He was tired, but the adrenaline was already starting to kick in, or maybe it hadn't really subsided from the day before.

May 19 had been a late night at KWTV-9, Oklahoma City's CBS affiliate, where Gary England had been forecasting the weather since 1972. His title was "chief meteorologist," but he was more than just a weatherman. Yes, he did the daily forecasts, and yes, he was on television five days a week—sometimes more. But at seventy-three he was considered to be something of a weather god in Oklahoma, the most famous meteorologist in a state that has raised forecasting to an art.

It was the apex of storm season, and that Sunday had been particularly destructive. Two tornadoes had swept through the Oklahoma City metro, carving their way through the heart of England's viewing area. One had hit just north of the city, in the suburb of Edmond, not far from the KWTV studio. An even stronger twister, a massive stovepipe of a storm with winds measuring at least 160 miles an hour, had touched down along the southeastern part of the metro area. It was stalked on live television from every possible angle by dozens of storm chasers on the ground and in the sky as it churned through the Oklahoma countryside, furiously devouring everything in its path.

England had been on air until almost midnight, directing the chasers linked to KWTV and monitoring the severe weather as it moved to the east. When the storms eventually petered out, the radar went quiet, and he headed home, the twisters continued to dance in his head, tormenting him with the dark questions that had increasingly come to consume him: How many people had died that night? Could he have done more to save them?

Late March to June is prime tornado season in Oklahoma, a time when the most dangerous thunderstorms of the year rumble across the plains, though they've been known to hit as early as January and as late as November. The threat of tornadoes has come to be a key part of Oklahoma culture and lore—the equivalent to watching Sooner football on a crisp fall Saturday or going to church on Sunday mornings. Football, Jesus, and tornadoes: That was Oklahoma. It was a fact of life, and everybody knew and accepted it when I was growing up.

Gary England was right at the center of that culture, a human warning system who had become synonymous with bad weather in a state that took a degree of pride in its designation as the epicenter of the nation's "Tornado Alley." Over the last thirty-five years, four of the most dangerous tornadoes on record had hit Oklahoma, and England had been on air for every one of them, not to mention the thousands of other twisters he had covered—both large and small. People often asked him how many tornadoes he'd been through as a meteorologist, but he had long ago lost count. "I've dealt with thousands of tornadoes," he would say, with a weary grin. "And I feel like it too."

Short and slight, with wheat-colored blond hair that had grown thinner over the decades, he did not look or act like the grandfather he was. He was known to sprint through the studio at prime moments of weather drama, thanks in part to the running shoes he'd taken to wearing with his suit since the camera never showed his feet. But he increasingly felt his age—especially during storm season, when the station would interrupt its regular programming to track bad weather as it moved across the state. Like other television stations in Oklahoma City, KWTV would sometimes go for hours without a commercial break during particularly dangerous storms, coverage that weather-crazy viewers around the state had come to expect. England was the star of the show, fueled by little more than pure adrenaline and the occasional sip of Diet Sprite—since tornadoes don't tend to pause for bathroom breaks.

He would stare into the camera, talking to viewers for hours on end about the approaching storms while micromanaging the show around him. He directed the storm chasers out in the field and monitored as many as a dozen live video feeds from cameras mounted on cars and on the station's helicopter, which flew into the storm to give viewers at home a bird's-eye view of the weather. Behind him was a tiny army of young meteorologists, many recent graduates of the University of Oklahoma's weather school, who had grown up watching him on TV. They now worked in his shadow, hoping to learn everything they could from the man who was revered as the godfather of weather coverage among storm junkies.

Since joining KWTV in 1972, he had pushed every boundary of television weather coverage. Some weathermen thought nothing of relying simply on data and radar information from the National Weather Service, but England considered himself as more than just a meteorologist. He was a soldier on the front lines who did whatever possible to keep his viewers safe from Mother Nature's wrath, even if it meant violating protocol.

People still talked about a storm that had hit Union City in 1973, when England had broken into programming and declared a tornado warning minutes before the National Weather Service had. He had done so again and again over the years, much to the chagrin of scientists who criticized England as brash and reckless. A few years later, after reading an article that suggested Doppler radar could be a major advance in tracking tornadoes, England persuaded Channel 9 to invest in its own Doppler—even when it was unclear whether the technology really worked. England helped invent the tiny map at the bottom of a television screen that warned of coming storms, and under his guidance KWTV became the first station to deploy its helicopter to chase tornadoes. But it was his friendly folksiness and his tendency to be right about the weather that kept people tuned in. Sometimes it seemed he had a direct line up into the sky.

Over the years, KWTV, looking to spice up its coverage, had given him new toys to play with. For the 2013 storm season, it was a touch-screen radar that operated like a giant iPad, which at first mystified England, who had thought of himself as tech savvy. "Uh, all righty," he said, as he poked at the screen trying to figure out how to zoom in and out during its first night on air. But in truth, none of the toys mattered. He himself was the star attraction—the hero of a generation of Oklahomans who either credited him with saving their lives or thought of him as the best source of entertainment in a state obsessed with storm coverage.

Long before The Weather Channel introduced tornado spotting as an adventure sport to most of America, weather coverage had become a tense and obsessive form of reality TV in Oklahoma, with local meteorologists and storm chasers playing key supporting roles in Mother Nature's unpredictable script. England was the most famous and enduring character of this strange drama. On most days he had the stage presence of a small-town boy made good, with a folksy demeanor and deep Oklahoma twang that would be a career killer for most broadcast journalists today.

But his sunny presence on television could shift in an instant when he detected a storm brewing. Over his decades on air, viewers had come to know that when he took off his suit jacket and got serious, things were going to be bad, really bad. When he told people to take cover or to get out of the path of a storm, there was no question that they had better do it—or they could very well die. England had unfortunately been proved right again and again over his career.

In 2010 a popular Oklahoma City blog called *The Lost Ogle* conducted a poll of its readers to gauge the most powerful person in Oklahoma. England came in first, followed by Jesus in second place. From then on, the blog jokingly referred to him as "Lord England"—a nickname that to many wasn't so far from the truth.

While KWTV's ratings went up and down over the years, it was hard to think of anyone in Oklahoma who was more known or revered. His rivals at other stations sometimes beat him in the ratings, but no one came close to his stature. Elected officials privately cringed in fear that he might get the political bug someday and put them out of a job. After every big storm, lawmakers—from the governor to members of the state legislature—were quick to tell their constituents that they had consulted with Gary England about the weather, seeking his advice on storm preparations. In most cases he had far more credibility than they did.

But after forty-one years on the air, he was bigger than politics. He was a living legend, immortalized in newspaper cartoons as something of an antitornado superhero. His office was crowded with artwork that people from all over the state had gifted him at meet-and-greets. One painted him as a grinning hero in a cowboy hat wrangling an ominous, wild twister. Another cast him as a robed Obi-Wan Kenobi from *Star Wars*—Oklahoma's "only hope" against dangerous weather. At the station's front desk, visitors passed by a giant bronze bust of a smiling Gary England that had been given to the meteorologist in 2007, when he was named one of Oklahoma's "100 Heroes and Outlaws" as part of the state's centennial celebration. The selection committee, England liked to joke, had somehow mistaken him for a hero.

England had mixed feelings about the bust, which he passed on his way into the studio most days. He was flattered, but he was also a little embarrassed. He knew how lucky he was—a boy from a tiny town in northwestern Oklahoma who'd considered being a pig farmer until he'd caught the weather bug. He'd been recognized by the state for doing a job he absolutely loved. Sometimes the sculpture seemed a little too much like a memorial. Despite the ambitious meteorologists waiting in the wings in anticipation that he'd soon retire, England wasn't done yet. He loved his job. He loved his viewers, and they loved him. And he was obsessed with finding ways to keep them safer from storms that seemed only to be getting bigger and deadlier every year.

He saw his job as more than being a local weatherman. It was a public duty, a calling, to keep people safe, and he wasn't ready to walk away from that responsibility just yet. Some days, he did wonder if it wasn't starting to be too much. It wasn't the physical demands of the job, the hours on air, the giving up of any semblance of personal life for weeks on end every spring. It was the burden he felt to protect people, both viewers and his staff in the field. In the end, he knew he was just one man pitted against the elements, but knowing that didn't make it easier when people died. He had dedicated his life to trying to prevent mass casualties from tornadoes like those that had hit towns around him when he was a kid—he'd never forgotten the storm in 1947 that wiped out Woodward, Oklahoma, killing more than one hundred people. But in recent years the pressure he felt to save people's lives had started to consume him.

To his viewers and even many of his closest friends, family, and coworkers, he was his usual cheerful, folksy self—at least when the weather wasn't bad. But privately he was haunted by storms. He couldn't understand how in a state where people were so obsessed with weather, where local media was saturated with warnings, so many people continued to die. He constantly worried about whether he had done everything within his power to protect people. Had he said the right words or issued the warnings fast enough for people to take shelter? What more could he have done?

He had always been a bit of a worrier, consumed by thoughts like these. But his anxiety intensified after May 3, 1999, when a milewide twister wiped out parts of Moore and south Oklahoma City. That storm had changed his life. For the first time in his long career, England had essentially narrated live a nearly two-and-a-half-hour trail of destruction as KWTV's helicopter hovered in the sky capturing every second of the monster storm churning its way into some of the most heavily populated parts of his viewing area. He was stunned as he saw debris from homes and cars flying through the air, carried like Matchbox toys. In his most calm but stern voice, he'd warned people they should get below ground or they would very likely die. But many hadn't listened.

Thirty-six people had died—the biggest death toll in the state from a tornado in decades. With more than 10 miles of neighborhoods completely wiped off the map, many believe the death toll would have been far higher had it not been for the local weather coverage. In the days after the storm, state and local officials praised Oklahoma City's weathermen for their handling of the storm. England was lauded for saving lives with his specific warnings pinpointing exactly where the tornado's trajectory would take it and calling out street names in an urgent attempt to clear out the neighborhoods before it was too late. Many survivors credited him with protecting them that day. As the massive cleanup began, some spray-painted messages on whatever remained of their wiped-out homes. "Gary England saved my life," one message, scrawled on a mangled garage door, read. "Thank you, Gary England!" said another.

In response, he smiled and somewhat bashfully accepted the praise. When asked about it, he agreed that things could have been far worse, but inside he was torn apart in a way that he had never been by the hundreds of storms he had seen in his career. Even as the state moved on, rebuilding as it always did, he obsessed over the people who had been killed that day. Why had they died? Did they not know the storm was coming? Had they not taken cover? What could he have done to reach them more effectively?

"Tornadoes can be very majestic when they are out in the fields somewhere, when no one is around," he often told people. "But my god, when you put them in a populated area, it is terrifying." As Oklahoma City expanded and cities like Moore built out into the rural farmland tornadoes were known to frequent, the potential scale and scope of the devastation was growing.

Back in 1999, a few weeks after the May 3 storm, England took an afternoon off work and pulled the coroner's reports on the people who had been killed that day. It was the beginning of a dark tradition he would secretly pursue over the next decade after every deadly tornado as he embarked on a desperate search to understand how people had died and maybe learn how he could save more lives the next time disaster struck.

England was horrified by the injuries he read about in the coroner's reports. Some victims had tried to run from the tornado and been sucked up and spit out, their bodies literally pulverized by the storm. Others had been killed when they were hit in the head by flying debris. He quietly talked to doctors about the injuries of those who had survived—and was amazed and shocked by what he heard. He was told about people whose skin had almost been sandblasted off by the storm—leaving their bones and tendons exposed. One man's eyeball had literally exploded when he was hit by debris, but he lived too. Another victim had been impaled in the throat by a two-by-four.

He didn't tell anyone what he had done. He felt it was too morbid, too dark. But on air he began issuing unusual decrees for subsequent storms. In addition to his usual mantra urging people to "take your safety precautions" and "get below ground," he started telling people to wear helmets and shatterproof goggles, along with heavy, long-sleeved clothing. He told them to dress as if they were going to war. He suspected some of his fellow meteorologists might think he had gone off the deep end. He was encouraging his viewers to do something that even the National Weather Service hadn't endorsed. But he didn't care. "Twenty percent of those killed on May 3 died of brain injuries," he said. "I'm from Seiling, Oklahoma, and that to me says wear a helmet."

Fourteen years later, in 2013, the National Weather Service began issuing similar directives about helmets and clothing—which made England feel somewhat vindicated. But by then he had grown more obsessive in other ways about his responsibility to his viewers. KWTV had given him a "lifetime" contract to stay on air until he felt like he wasn't, as the station's owner put it, "having fun" anymore. And more and more, the joy he had found in his job was vanishing, erased by the suffocating burden of protecting people from the erratic whims of Mother Nature. Since the 1999 tornado, England had felt intense pressure to get everything exactly right—his words, his mannerisms. Over the years, he had grown more and more worried that any innocent misstep—such as the mistakes that had plagued some of his weather rivals at the other local stations—could result in death. He had always reviewed the tapes of coverage after the storms, but he began to take it a step further.

During every major weather event, he not only had the station tape the live coverage on air. He asked that another camera roam throughout the studio to film him and his staff at work. Afterward, he went over the tapes again and again, watching and listening carefully to everything he or anyone else—his storm trackers, his colleagues in studio—had said. He was like a football coach looking for any weakness in his team as he tried to plan the perfect plays against an enemy that was largely unpredictable. He would review the tapes dozens of times—sometimes that very night, in part because he couldn't sleep. It was a routine he'd long ago gotten used to—the sleepless nights in the springtime, the nightmares of what the season would have in store. Sitting at his computer on May 20, he was plagued by questions that had come to haunt him after every major storm: How many people had died, and what could he have done to save them?

When he had left the station after midnight, the extent of casualties had still been unknown. But he had been unnerved by the footage of what he'd seen of the storm to the southeast of Oklahoma City—cars demolished and swept off the road and homes wiped clear of their foundations. A grandmother had been rescued from a bathtub that had been lifted from her home and lodged in a tree. It was a miracle, and he hoped there would be others, but deep down he always assumed the worst. How many people had died? The question haunted him as he made his fifteen-minute commute home, where his wife was still awake and waiting for him as she did after almost every storm.

They'd met at Southwestern Oklahoma State University fifty-three years earlier. England had just left the navy, and though he was in school pursuing his dream of being a weatherman, he'd spent more time studying girls in his first semester than hitting the books. He was on a date with another girl when he saw her walking between two cars—a tiny strawberry-blonde cheerleader with the most beautiful blue eyes he'd ever seen. As she passed directly in front of him, he reached out, grabbed her arm, and pulled her into a kiss. It was love at first sight. His date punched him and stormed away, and England grinned at the stunned cheerleader. Her name was Mary, and even though she thought he was a bit of a rascal, they were inseparable after that. Soul mates, they said. A year later they were married. They had one daughter, Molly, who now lived in Southern California with her husband and two daughters—far away from the wild weather of Oklahoma.

As he kissed Mary good night, his mind was elsewhere. Checking his computer one last time, he saw that there was still no word on fatalities. Climbing into bed he was tired—but it was the kind of tired where you can't sleep. How many people had died? The question wouldn't go away.

Now, wide awake and back at his computer, he still had no

answers. As he began poring over weather data for the day, he could see that the storms were likely to be as bad as or worse than Sunday's. The projection maps suggested the worst weather would be to the south of Oklahoma City—which would be a relief, if true, since that was mostly open farmland. But looking at the current radar, England noticed that there was a line of moisture positioned right over the city—a hint that trouble might be brewing closer to home.

In his gut he knew there was only one way to tell how bad it would be that day. He stood up and walked to his front door. It was almost 5:00 A.M., and the dark sky was just starting to lighten, with flecks of gold to the east, where the sun would soon rise. As he opened the door, he was hit by a blast of air so salty and warm and moist it felt as though the Gulf of Mexico, hundreds of miles to the south, were at his doorstep. He was instantly reminded of the last time he had felt air so unstable this early in the morning: It was on May 3, 1999.

His heart pounding, he quickly went back to his computer and sent out an e-mail to the entire KWTV staff, putting the station on "priority one"—the highest alert level possible. It was all hands on deck. He warned that it was likely there would be tornadoes that day directly to the west of Oklahoma City, heading right toward the metro area.

Within minutes, it was clear he wasn't the only one who'd had a sleepless night. Many of his staff, including his roster of storm chasers, replied to his e-mail almost as soon as he'd sent it, asking what their role should be in the coverage that day. But as England began to respond to them and organize their war plan, at the back of his mind that haunting question presented itself again and again: How many people would die that day? And what could he do to save them?

CHAPTER 2

6:00 A.M., MAY 20

The alarm went off too early, as it always did. Amy Simpson had never been a morning person. Not when she was a kid and certainly not now, just weeks after her forty-second birthday. All she wanted to do was roll over and go back to sleep, cuddled next to the love of her life, her husband, Lindy, but responsibility called. Her two children, Scarlet, seven, and Roarke, twelve, needed to be woken up and fed and shuttled off to school. And she had to be at work early too, a couple of miles away at Plaza Towers Elementary in Moore, where she was wrapping up her third year as head principal.

Resisting the urge to sleep a few minutes more, Simpson forced herself out of bed, still half asleep but her mind alert enough to begin going through her mental to-do list. She already knew it would be a busy day, the very last Monday of the school year. And as she quickly glanced at her phone, she saw confirmation of what the local news had been predicting for almost a week: Monday would be a day of bad weather. A 100 percent probability of severe storms, the forecast said. Hail and high winds and a strong chance of tornadoes in the afternoon, some likely in the Oklahoma City metro area.

It sounded like a typical May afternoon in Oklahoma, Simpson thought as she began to get ready for work. She wasn't being indifferent. It was just the way it was, the way it had always been. Born and raised in Moore, Simpson simply couldn't recall a single May in her entire life that hadn't been interrupted by the rumble of thunderstorms and the threat of twisters. For her and many others in central Oklahoma, Mother Nature's springtime wrath was as routine as the leaves changing colors in the fall. And while the weather could be scary—and on many days in the late spring, it was—storms were something that she'd been raised to live with, like an annoying relative you couldn't disown. Oklahoma didn't cancel school for severe thunderstorms. If it did, there would simply be no classes for much of the spring.

For as long as Amy Simpson could remember, one of the first things she had done when she went outside was look up at the sky to see what it was doing. She couldn't remember how the habit had started; it seemed to be instinctual, something everybody did. She had long ago discerned the differences between "the good clouds and the bad clouds," as she put it, something she was teaching her own children the way her parents had taught her. It was all part of what people here called being "weather aware." The storms could blow up in an instant, and kids were taught from the moment they could grasp a clear thought to pay attention to the sky and to follow the weather reports, even when there wasn't a cloud to be seen. But as cautious as she was on storm days, Simpson also knew that life had to go on, no matter what the forecast was. And just as she'd gotten used to the crash of thunder and flash of lightning, her own kids were adapting to it too. Such was life on the plains of stormy Oklahoma.

Outside, the streets of Moore were quiet and still except for the occasional whine of the 18-wheelers going up and down Interstate 35, which cut a straight line, north to south, through the center of town. The sun was still a few minutes away from rising, but it was light enough to see a hazy blue peeking through dense pockets of scattered clouds. One needed only to feel the air to know a storm was coming. A thick blanket of humidity hung over the city like an invisible fog—so steamy car windows glistened with drops of moisture that shimmered like tiny rhinestones as they were illuminated by the glow of passing headlights. It smelled as if the rain might explode from the heavens at any second—a sweet, refreshing scent that was almost intoxicating to people who had grown up around the warm rainstorms of the Oklahoma spring. But while there were a few showers in the surrounding areas, Moore was still in the clear, at least on the radar—though the heavy, moist air suggested it wouldn't be for long.

All over town people were waking up and seeing the same thing. It had been like this for almost a week: stormy days and stormy nights, threatening skies, with warnings of more bad weather to come. Sometimes at this time of year it seemed the weather was just on one endless, stormy loop. Most people in Oklahoma had learned to love the spring storms—finding a strange beauty in the clouds and the awesome majesty of the storms as they moved across the landscape. But the residents of Moore appreciated in ways few others did how truly brutal Mother Nature could be.

Four times since 1998 Moore had been hit by tornadoes—destructive funnels that dropped from the sky and wiped out large swaths of the city as they moved from west to east. None was more devastating than the one that hit on May 3, 1999, a storm that flattened neighborhoods on the west side of town like an atomic bomb as it cut a 38-mile path across central Oklahoma. Fourteen years later, it was still the storm that people who had lived through it talked about, the one every storm since had been compared with.

At the time, like her neighbors, Simpson thought that May 3 was "the storm of the century," as people put it, that incredible once-in-a-lifetime tornado that people would tell their grandkids about. She'd been in Oklahoma City when the storm hit, at a teacher's banquet, and she hadn't even known about it until she'd tried to get back to Moore. Unlike many others, her family had been spared, but she still remembered the fear and worry she'd felt when she couldn't immediately reach them. She never wanted to go through an experience like that again.

But four years later, on an early Thursday evening in May 2003, Moore was hit again, in almost exactly the same spot, by a tornado with winds nearing 200 miles per hour that struck a neighborhood that had just been rebuilt. Until then, many people around Moore had clung to that old adage that lightning doesn't strike twice in the same spot. But not only was that not true—lightning actually could strike twice and often did in Oklahoma, where homes regularly burned to the ground during the electrical storms that accompanied the rains—it almost certainly didn't apply to tornadoes. They threatened Moore again and again, the thunderheads furiously rotating in the sky above but never quite touching the earth. By the time another large funnel hit the ground—on May 10, 2010—people both in and outside Moore had started to question what it was about the city that made it so unlucky with the weather. Why did the worst storms Oklahoma had ever seen always seem to hit Moore?

There was no sign or memorial marking where the May 3 tornado had hit—the leveled neighborhoods had long ago been rebuilt, and the young trees planted to replace the ones killed by the storm were now leafy and fully grown. On the streets where people had died or been critically injured sheltering from a storm that reduced their homes to toothpicks and sucked away everything they owned, things were back to normal. The houses weren't old, but they no longer looked brand-new. The paint had faded ever so slightly, and the driveways no longer had that look of freshly poured concrete. The yards out front had spots of crabgrass blending in with the replanted sod. The neighborhoods looked comfortable and well lived in, as though nothing had ever been amiss. Life moved on, and only someone like me, who knew Moore before the storms, could really tell the difference.

But more than a decade later, May 3 lived on in the memories of the people who had survived that dreadful day. The damaged areas might have been rebuilt, but the tornado's impact on the psyche took longer to heal, if it ever really did. Stories of past storms and all the terrible, incredible, and peculiar things they had done were passed down through the generations in Oklahoma like stories of war, and it was no different around here.

Residents of Moore who had been around for the '99 tornado still remembered as though it were yesterday the way the sky had grown dark and ominous, how the air had been sticky with moisture. They recalled how the tornado had sounded, like a roaring freight train, as it indiscriminately chewed up everything in its path. They spoke of how it had smelled—like moist, tilled earth and freshly cut lumber—and how the ground had shaken as it swept through the city, a massive, dark cloud that seemed to swallow the entire sky. And when they retold the story of what it had been like on that Monday, they sometimes found it hard to breathe thinking of that sick helplessness they'd felt as it hit and after it had passed, leaving miles and miles of the city smashed to bits. They wondered how they would ever recover. But somehow they did—physically at least. And they did it again two more times after that. Still, every time thunderclouds rose up in the west aiming toward Moore, many in town wondered with a tinge of anxiety: Would this be another May 3?

It was a thought that ran through Steve Eddy's mind almost every time severe weather exploded on the landscape west of town. As city manager of Moore, a nonelected position second in power only to the mayor and the city council, Eddy was in charge of making sure the city ran smoothly. Part of his job was to anticipate disaster—or at least plan for it and do what he could to keep the city in business. On this Monday, even before the sun was up, Eddy already had the wheels in motion, preparing for the bad weather that had been forecast for days—coming on that same familiar path from the west.

Almost every employee of the city government in Moore was on alert. The entire police and fire departments were on standby; the public works employees were ready to deploy. On the first floor of City Hall, the emergency management office had been a hive of activity all weekend, as severe storms pounded the region again and again. Just twelve hours earlier a tornado warning had been issued for Moore, but as Eddy, his deputy Stan Drake, and Gayland Kitch, the city's emergency manager, had nervously monitored the radar and the wall-to-wall coverage on local television, the storm had stayed just to the south of town as it moved to the northeast, a narrow but fortunate miss.

Eddy had gone to bed that night grateful his town had been spared, but he knew he'd have to go through it all again the next day. For days meteorologists at the National Weather Service had warned him and other city officials in the region that radar patterns suggested Monday's weather could be treacherous—possibly worse than the storms that had hit on preceding days, and those had been pretty bad. On Sunday he'd watched on television as a giant stovepipe of a funnel dropped to the ground about 15 miles east of Moore. For all the study that had gone into the storms that ravaged Oklahoma, weather was still an unpredictable game of luck and chance. While meteorologists had gotten incredibly skilled at forecasting the conditions that could spawn tornadoes, it was still a mystery where and when the funnel would drop, and when it did, there was little those in its path could do except take cover or get out of the way. One shift in the wind or a tweak in any of the other mysterious components that forced a funnel to the ground and that tornado would have hit Moore, and Eddy knew it.

As the city stirred to life outside his window, Eddy saw that the forecast hadn't changed—in fact, it seemed to have grown worse overnight, and that concerned him. Meteorologists were forecasting that the storms would fire up in the midafternoon—not the early evening, when bad weather usually hit. He worried they could have an impact on schools, where classes didn't let out until around 3:00 P.M. or later, and on rush-hour traffic, as residents drove home after work. Scanning his e-mail, Eddy learned from a colleague that the Weather Service had scheduled a conference call for later that morning to go over what it was expecting. Although it was a routine call, he felt a twinge of dread. Eddy wished that storm season were over. Lately, bad weather wasn't exclusive to the spring, but May was still the month when the worst seemed to roll through, the four weeks of the year he dreaded the most.

Eddy was a realist, but there was part of him that held out hope that Moore would be lucky and that whatever storms developed would stay to the north or the south. Part of him felt guilty for even having those thoughts. Knowing firsthand how horrific storms could be, he never wanted to wish bad weather on anybody. But he couldn't help but hope that if storms did develop, Moore would somehow be spared. His town had seen its fair share of tornadoes. It didn't need another.

At fifty-seven, Eddy had been working for the city government in Moore for almost half of his life. Like Simpson, he was a "lifer," as people often refer to those who grew up in Moore and never left. While some moved away, to other cities in Oklahoma or out of the state altogether, many people in Moore stayed put, drawn in by something they couldn't quite explain. Maybe that was why Moore still felt like a small town, even though it had transformed into a larger city over the years. Or maybe it was simply the people, how friendly they were and how resilient.

Eddy had moved to Moore when he was in second grade, and a few people in town still called him "Stevie," as he was known back in grade school. Moore was barely a blip on the map when he and his parents arrived in town in the early 1960s, drawn by the ability to buy a nice house cheaply and the quiet allure of suburban life. As a child, Eddy had watched the new city slowly rise up around him, with new buildings, new schools, new homes, and a flood of new residents. In a single decade the population had jumped from a little under two thousand residents in 1960 to nearly nineteen thousand in 1970, a surge driven by an influx of families who liked the idea of living in a small town, but one that was still an easy commute to Oklahoma City and to the region's other major employers—including the University of Oklahoma in nearby Norman and Tinker Air Force Base in Midwest City. But like other parts of Oklahoma, Moore was hard hit when the bottom suddenly fell out of the surging energy market in the early 1980s. It was the worst economic hit in Oklahoma since the days of the Great Depression, and tens of thousands of people lost their jobs in a matter of months, including many in Moore. The tiny suburb, once booming, suddenly went stagnant as businesses closed and some residents were forced to move to other states to look for work. But Eddy never gave up on his hometown.

Watching Moore rise and evolve around him as a child had made Eddy dream about helping to run a city someday, and when he came back to his hometown after college, he began working his way up through City Hall. In many ways it was a dream job for him. It wasn't just a career. It was personal. He was serving the town he loved, helping it grow into the thriving city he'd always known it could be. He'd always known that the weather would be a factor in the job. The city had been battered by severe storms for as long as he could remember—windstorms that uprooted trees and torrential rains that caused flooding in parts of town. The tornado sirens had gone off once or twice when he was growing up, but nothing serious had ever hit, just a tiny spout here and there. Some in town still talked about a tiny funnel that had touched down on the football field at Moore High School during a practice one afternoon in the late 1960s—a slender funnel that slunk down from the dark clouds above and zipped back up so quickly some wondered if what they'd witnessed had really happened.

Like the managers of other cities in central Oklahoma, Eddy and his colleagues had planned for a tornado—contemplating how the city would respond if one ever hit. But Eddy never imagined, not even once, how terrible and devastating the storms that began to roll through Moore would be.

Eddy was assistant city manager when the first big tornado hit in October 1998—ripping off roofs and knocking down fences as it moved north along Santa Fe Avenue on the city's west side. Compared with the storms since, that twister was nothing—a third of a mile wide, with winds measured at about 100 miles per hour. But every tornado, no matter its size, is dangerous, and he remembered how worried he had been for the people of his town as he watched the storm develop. He never imagined that only seven months later Moore would be in the crosshairs of another tornado, a funnel more than three times the size that would go down as one of the most destructive in history. Like others in Moore, Eddy had a vivid memory of that night, the terrible shock he felt as he stood in the middle of one of those flattened neighborhoods looking at unimaginable destruction as far as the eye could see.

By then Eddy was widely regarded around the city as a calm and steady hand in tense moments, exactly the kind of person you wanted in charge when the bad times hit. Quiet and matter-of-fact, he was not someone who felt the need to talk when words didn't need to be spoken. He wasn't someone who got "excitable," as he often put it. Like many Oklahomans, he didn't spend time debating why the storms had happened. Eddy saw his job as keeping the city going, no matter what had happened. He was determined to act quickly and get things back on track. But even he couldn't help but be stunned by the enormity of the May 3 storm. While he was outwardly calm and collected, Eddy's mind raced with questions, and though he didn't dare voice them, he had doubts just as everyone did about what the storm meant for his city's future. How could they recover? How would they deal with all this debris? Millions of tons of destroyed houses and the evidence of the lives within them blown across town by the most ruthless storm he'd ever known. Where would they even begin?

Put in charge of overseeing the city's cleanup, Eddy filed his doubts away and got to work. It was what he had been hired to do, and the people around him did the same, eager to restore what sense of normalcy they could. Within three weeks the city had hired an outside contractor to begin carting the debris away. And mindful that other storms could hit, Moore city officials, at Eddy's urging, approved a preexisting contract with the same company for future storms, so that the city could get to the task of rebuilding far more quickly if something like this were to happen again. "Nothing good happens until all of that crap is gone," Eddy bluntly told his colleagues. It turned out to be an incredibly insightful decision—as more storms followed. Suddenly, government officials from all over the country descended on Moore, this tiny little town that few people had ever heard of, to study how Eddy and his colleagues had helped their city bounce back. Eddy took it all in stride. "We were just doing our jobs," he told people. He wasn't being modest. It was what he really believed.

Over the years, Eddy, who ascended to city manager a few months after the May 3 tornado, came to be regarded across the country as a leading expert on how to respond to tornadoes. Many were specific tasks that could be replicated, but some things simply couldn't—including the attitude of people in Moore. Outsiders marveled at the town's resilience, but to Eddy that was simply the way people here were, the way they had been raised. If you were knocked down, you got back up. It was what you did. But he did acknowledge the small-town nature of Moore had helped in the darkest days.

Some of the relationships between people at City Hall dated back decades, to long before they worked for the government. Eddy had known Glenn Lewis, the mayor, and Stan Drake, the assistant city manager, since they were students at Moore High School. They were the same age, and all had graduated the same year: 1973. They knew one another as well as they knew anybody, and that familiarity, personal history, and mutual trust came in handy not only in the storm recovery but also as the city underwent a major transformation in the aftermath of the storm.

To Eddy and other lifers, there was the Moore before the tornadoes and the Moore that existed afterward. Like everyone, he wished that his town had never known what it was like to go through a horrific twister—much less three of them. But at the same time, Eddy looked for the good in what had happened. The storms had sparked a dramatic revitalization in Moore—as if the twisters, as terrible as they were, had been some strange natural conduit for urban renewal. The wiped-out neighborhoods, rebuilt with brand-new homes, sparked a string of new development and investment that Moore hadn't experienced since the days before the oil bust. Suddenly, a city that had been long been viewed as something of a no-man's-land—a few unremarkable exits off Interstate 35 that people passed as they were driving between Oklahoma City and Norman—was reconsidered as an undiscovered paradise for the suburban working class. Young families who wanted to send their kids to good schools in a place where they could still afford to buy a home in a good neighborhood flocked to Moore, and businesses that saw an opportunity to make money followed.

Between 1990 and 2000 Moore's population lingered at just over 40,000 people—a number impacted by the number of people displaced after the 1999 tornado. But by 2010 the population had jumped to more than 55,000—a number that continued to steadily increase. Developers couldn't keep up with the demand for homes, and the landscape of Moore began to shift from a quiet, mostly rural bedroom community to a suburban boomtown.

People who had left Moore and came back to visit were

astonished at how much their hometown had changed in such a short time. And even natives like Amy Simpson, who had never left, sometimes couldn't believe it either. She and her family lived a little south of Nineteenth Street in a housing addition that was not even five years old. She was old enough to remember when this part of Moore had been mostly empty farmland, miles and miles of nothing but trees and grassy fields and the occasional bored cow, which tilted its head up and stared at cars cruising the narrow back roads, rough and bumpy, that hadn't been repaved in years because they saw so little traffic.

When I was growing up, anything south of Nineteenth Street in Moore was considered "out in the country." But what had been a simple two-lane country road was now a four-lane thoroughfare, one of the busiest stretches in town, lined on both sides with shopping centers that had been built a few years earlier but still looked brand-new. It used to be that people in Moore would have to drive 10 miles south to Norman or north to Oklahoma City to do their shopping, but now big-box retailers were right here on Nineteenth Street: Target, Walmart, Home Depot. The only Starbucks in town was on the corner, next door to the perpetually crowded Chick-fil-A, where the drive-through window would open for breakfast and remain swamped until closing time, as cars wrapped around the building in endless want of a chicken sandwich. It was hard to believe that less than twenty years earlier there hadn't even been a traffic light on the block—just stop signs that drivers often floated through because there was nobody around to yield to.

When Simpson was a student at Moore High School, most of the kids in town spent their Friday nights cruising in slow circles around the city like a scene out of *American Graffiti*, talking and listening to music and rolling down their windows to yell to friends in other cars. They went up Twelfth Street, down Eastern Avenue in front of the high school, and all the way back down Fourth Street, past the three towering antennas of KOMA, one of the oldest radio stations in the state. Back then the towers were the closest thing Moore had to a landmark, their red and white lights blinking a slow, mesmerizing code that could be seen as far as 20 miles away across the flat landscape. The only other iconic symbol of Moore was the local water tower, which for decades had been painted with a gigantic American-flag smiley face before it was replaced with the town's name in the mid-1990s.

Now the biggest landmark in town and the major hangout was the Warren Theatres, a massive seventeen-screen cinema a few blocks north of Nineteenth Street that was widely regarded as the best movie house in the entire state. Outfitted with an IMAX theater, it was easily one of the biggest buildings in town, eclipsing the forty-five-bed hospital next door. Many in the area had been shocked when the theater chose to locate in Moore, a town that had for years been snootily regarded by its neighboring cities as a mostly unremarkable city that wasn't even worth pulling off the highway for.

Moore had expanded so much that it was growing hard to tell where the town ended and the neighboring cities began—especially on the west side, which bordered Oklahoma City. In recent years new homes had cropped up on the landscape like unstoppable weeds. There weren't enough houses to meet the demands of families who wanted to send their kids to the public schools in Moore, a district that included part of south Oklahoma City. Developers offered big money to farmers willing to sell off their land. While some signed their property over, many still hung on, unwilling to give in to the suburban sprawl.

Running out of space on the west side, Moore had started to

expand south toward Norman, a bustling college town of 118,000 that housed the University of Oklahoma, where I went to college, like so many other kids who grew up in Moore. New housing additions and retail developments began to replace the empty countryside along Interstate 35. To people who hadn't been paying close attention, Moore seemed to have transformed overnight from a sleepy suburb into a boomtown, a city that seemed to be thriving even when the national economy wasn't.

But Moore's rebirth was accompanied by nervousness. Many in town cast a wary eye toward the west, wondering if Mother Nature would come and take it all away. A town reborn in part because of a tornado had now expanded into an even bigger target. Around town there was an odd dynamic: People didn't want to believe God could be callous enough to send another tornado to Moore. But at the same time many believed it would almost certainly happen.

Just a few months earlier a town-hall meeting had been organized by a pair of meteorologists from the University of Oklahoma who had partnered with the National Weather Service to find out what people believed about the weather. The idea was to study superstitions and myths about storms in Oklahoma as a way of understanding how to better communicate the risks of bad weather. At the meetings many old wives' tales resurfaced. In nearby Norman residents told researchers they felt their city had been spared by storms because the town had been built on an old Native American burial ground. The spirits, they said, had kept the storms away. It was a story that had circulated for generations, though there was little evidence to back it up. Only a few months earlier a small tornado had gone right past the University of Oklahoma, forcing even meteorologists at the National Weather Service, located on the south side of campus, to take cover.

But it was the people in Moore the scientists found most interesting. Around forty people showed up at the local community center—about three times the turnout in other towns. And for more than an hour, residents young and old took turns speculating aloud as to what it was about Moore that made it so unlucky when it came to the weather. Many had shown up not only to share what they thought about the weather but also to find out what others thought—searching for answers to a mystery that baffled even the scientists who knew more about tornadoes than anyone.

One woman, whose home had been destroyed in 1999 and then again in 2003, asked whether it was something about the elevation of the city. Others wondered if it was the city's location east of the South Canadian River that somehow made it vulnerable. All of the tornadoes that had hit Moore over the years had formed just south of the river, near Newcastle, before moving to the northeast toward Moore. People wondered if it wasn't something about the mostly dry riverbed that channeled the storms their way, and as they speculated, they looked at the scientists, longing for answers. But there were none. Even they didn't know why Moore was so unlucky.

At the end of the night, as they had at all their meetings, the scientists asked participants to list the city they believed was most at risk of being hit by future storms. Residents of other cities had been unanimous: It would be Moore. And in Moore the answer was the same: Moore would be hit again. It was only a matter of when. The researchers were caught off guard by how resigned people seemed to their fate. They didn't sound defeated—just accepting. "They happen, and they happen to us," one man said.

It was an attitude that Eddy understood. He'd heard it from plenty of people over the years. After the tornadoes he'd worried that people might move away from Moore, concerned about living in a town that had been hit by storms that had followed eerily similar paths. But while some did move away, others stayed put—and new residents joined them, hoping and praying the storms would stay away. Eddy knew his job wasn't to try to understand the whys and hows of the storms. But there were moments when he couldn't help himself, and he'd quizzed meteorologists about the theories he'd heard over the years. Nobody knew. It all seemed to be just bad luck.

As he left his house that morning to head to his office, Eddy felt that familiar feeling in the air. He knew another storm was coming, and there was nothing he could do to stop it. All he could do was prepare for the worst and hope God or luck would be on Moore's side.

CHAPTER 3

8:00 A.M., MAY 20

The sun was barely up when Rick Smith reached his desk at the National Weather Service in Norman. It felt like he had never left. His computer was still on, and he thought he could feel a hint of warmth in his chair, though he knew that was just in his head. His wife sometimes teased him about her missing husband. "Have you seen him?" she'd ask with a mischievous smile. She knew as well as he did that this was just the way it was in the stormy month of May. It's how it had always been in the twenty years since he'd joined the National Weather Service as a meteorologist—and even before that, when he was just a kid staring up at the clouds above Memphis. He'd always been watching and waiting for the perfect storm.

Smith had turned forty-nine a few months earlier. His once-dark-blond hair had grown thinner and was almost white now, giving his skin a pinkish glow. Behind his wire-rim glasses one could detect a few more lines around his blue eyes, signs of a life well lived. But even as the calendar ticked forward, he still felt like that kid looking up at the sky. The mystery was as compelling to him now as it had been when he was just a boy. Early on in his career, he'd been out in the field spotting storms for the Weather Service, chasing tornadoes along the back roads of Tennessee, Arkansas, and occasionally Oklahoma. But now he mostly followed the storms through a bank of computer screens and on television, and though he sometimes missed that smell and how the sky looked as it transformed everything around him, it wasn't any less of a thrill.

He'd started out as a forecaster, but over the years he had become something of a do-it-all at the Weather Service. He trained storm spotters. He dealt with the media. His official title was "warning coordination meteorologist," which meant it was his job to talk to emergency services and other government officials in cities that were likely to be hit, getting out as much advance warning as possible. Recently he'd taken on another increasingly important task: He ran the agency's Twitter and Facebook feeds when things heated up.

While most people in Oklahoma watched storm coverage on television, Smith agonized over how to reach those who didn't—those who had no television or had become blasé because there were so many storms. People always said they were afraid of getting hit by a tornado, but the truth was many didn't actually believe it could happen to them. Those were the people Smith worried about the most—the ones who had grown used to the weather and had stopped taking it seriously. Social media, he hoped, might be a way of getting warnings out to them.

The night before, he had been at the office almost until midnight. It had been a day of unusually high drama at the Weather Service, which was saying something. Oklahoma had been in the midst of a severe-weather outbreak for days, as massive storms meandered through the central part of the state. Spring was often like this, endless hours on duty, living on coffee and Diet Coke and whatever else the vending machines downstairs offered, waiting and wondering what Mother Nature would do.

Just before 5:00 P.M., things had gotten weird. A cloud had popped up on radar just to the west of the office and then exploded into a large, rotating thunderstorm—known in weather terms as a supercell. The ominous storm began to suck the air and energy from everything around it as it crouched down and grew wider on the landscape. Inside the forecasting center one of the meteorologists calmly issued a tornado warning for the storm almost directly above their heads, maintaining such a cool and steady focus one might have been forgiven for thinking it was all happening hundreds of miles away.

There was no panic or yelling—beyond the voice of a frantic storm chaser echoing from one of the giant monitors that would stream the local television stations on bad-weather days. While it was Armageddon on television—and outside the window too—the Weather Service was a quiet hum of activity, like a bank on payday.

On particularly bad-weather days, forecasters will sometimes get a little edgy, but this is only really apparent to people who know them well enough to notice the chink in their calm veneer. Over the years, Smith had become adept at reading their body language. He monitored the radars and absorbed the data just like everyone else, but he was also able to detect that slight difference in temperament, the way someone's jaw would tense or brow furrow, or that hint of something in the voice. It was his gauge of how bad a severe-weather day was likely to be. If they were nervous, he was nervous. And on that day you could slice the tension with a knife.

The National Weather Service offices are located on the second floor of the sprawling National Weather Center, at the southern end of the University of Oklahoma campus in Norman. Only a decade before, the area had been mostly empty farmland, but the NWC, as it was known, had quickly transformed the landscape when it opened in 2006, a gleaming, nearly 300,000-square-foot glass-and-brick monument to the study of weather. You could see it from more than a mile away, especially at night, when, lit up like a giant cathedral, it stood out sharply against the dark woods of Highway 9.

That it looked like a church seemed fitting. If tornadoes were something of a religion for those who followed them, central Oklahoma was the holy land, and this building was a sacred place that drew in those who were most captivated by the mystery of the storm. Virtually every major weather agency in the country could be found here. Down the hall from the National Weather Service were two sister agencies: the Storm Prediction Center, an arm of the Weather Service that does severe-weather forecasting for the entire country, and the National Severe Storms Laboratory, which leads research into the genesis of storms and seeks to develop technology to better predict them. Upstairs on the fifth floor were the offices and classrooms of the University of Oklahoma's School of Meteorology, widely considered the Ivy League of weather programs, where some of the nation's leading scientists were training the next generation of meteorologists.

Over the years, the NWC had become a weather mecca, drawing pilgrims from around the country. In the surrounding few blocks the university had built out roads leading to office buildings that were so brand-new there was no grass on the lawns out front, just freshly raked dirt. Inside, offices were rented to private companies in the weather business eager to be as close as possible to the scientists with whom they partnered on projects like improving radars and coming up with new and better ways of presenting weather data. Already there wasn't enough space to meet the demand.

On the east side of the burgeoning weather campus was a giant white dome with diamond-shaped indentations that, sitting high on stilts in the trees above Highway 9, resembled a gigantic golf ball teed up for play. It was the radar that changed everything about weather forecasting. The Doppler radar was first employed by the air force to track enemy positions during World War II, but military officials soon noticed that the short pulses of radio waves emitted by the radar were also picking up details about storms. The Doppler could measure the intensity of precipitation within a storm as well as its development and movement. But it wasn't until decades later, in the 1950s, that it was officially adopted as a weather-forecasting tool.

Doppler radars now dot the landscape of central Oklahoma—there are at least four in Norman alone, positioned to capture the storms that regularly roll up from the southwest—but in 1969, when the Severe Storms Lab relocated its offices from Kansas City, the first Doppler radar to be used for weather purposes was installed just outside its offices along Interstate 35 in Norman. It was surplus equipment handed over by the air force. Back then the locals eyed the giant golf ball–shaped radar with curiosity, wondering how something so weird looking could possibly help them understand the freak, killer storms that hit with almost no notice.

Four years later the radar proved its usefulness. In May 1973, when a giant F4 tornado blew through Union City, about 30 miles west of Oklahoma City, the Doppler radar in Norman captured for the first time the entire life cycle of a twister. It was a breakthrough that changed the science of weather forecasting forever. For the first time scientists could see how a tornado had come to life, how it had picked up in intensity and then, just as suddenly, faded away. The radar had revealed signs of a possible tornado developing long before it actually hit the ground—proving that it might be possible to expand warning times exponentially for potentially deadly storms. It was the official beginning of decades of research into storms that nobody really understood.

Over the last forty years researchers have become increasingly skilled at detecting and forecasting the environment most prone to creating tornadoes. In the beginning there is usually a thunderstorm that, in the simplest terms, erupts when warm and cool air fronts collide. The warm air rises, pushed up by the cooler air, and as its temperature drops, it releases moisture, generates energy, and causes instability. Sometimes the outcome is just rain and lightning, a result of the energy created when frozen raindrops collide in the upper echelon of the clouds. But in Oklahoma the base ingredients are more volatile. Intensely moist air from the Gulf of Mexico will often collide with cool, dry air wafting down from Canada over the Rockies, and the two forces are further churned together by the jet stream, a fast-moving current that flows west to east directly over the state. Scientists have observed that the jet stream causes the warm, sticky air to rise more quickly, in what is called an updraft, and the cool, dry air to fall in a downdraft.

When the elements are particularly unstable—when, for instance, one finds significantly varied temperatures and moisture levels—those crosscurrents will sometimes coalesce in a supercell. That is when tornadoes are sometimes produced. Supercells are longer lasting and more dangerous than other storms because their updraft of warm air is often ever so slightly tilted, feeding more surface moisture into the storm. This causes the winds to rotate ever more furiously and to form a vortex of air known as a mesocyclone, which is visible on radar if not to the naked eye. It is the next step that most baffles meteorologists: In some storms the vortex narrows and lengthens, dropping out of the clouds and aiming for the ground. As it does so, its spin becomes still more furious and lethal. And yet, even if the conditions are ripe, not every supercell will produce a tornado. Scientists still have no idea why that is. Some speculate that it has something to do with the temperature of the air wrapping around the mesocyclone within the storm, but the truth is they simply do not know. Tornadogenesis, the scientific term for how tornadoes are born, remains a frustratingly incomplete science.

One of the simple reasons for this is the difficulty of amassing reliable data. Who could ever hope to penetrate the eye of a storm and emerge to tell the tale? Even if you could build a strong enough gadget, how could you position it in the right path? The Doppler did not fully resolve the mystery, but it did increase our understanding of the conditions that might lead to the formation of tornadoes and thereby significantly increased warning times. On May 19 the meteorologists at the National Weather Service saw the possible tornado coming almost fifteen minutes before it nearly hit them—an eternity in forecasting terms—thanks to their Doppler radar.

As emergency sirens began to wail, nonessential staff rushed downstairs to a partially underground theater, where live coverage of the storm from the local television stations was being projected on screens. Gary England was on—as were his counterparts at the other stations: KFOR's Mike Morgan and KOCO's Damon Lane. At one point there was an odd moment when the researchers and students in the room found themselves staring at three separate live pictures of the sky literally right outside their door as increasingly frantic storm chasers raced down the back roads of Norman trying to stay ahead of the storm. It wasn't just chasers working for the local television stations; there were amateurs out there too, whose vehicles were outfitted with cameras that recorded their surroundings. It had a bit of the feel of a bad disaster movie. There was an edge in the room, but no one panicked. Some were actually disappointed. The students in the room who had come to OU to study storms like this itched to get outside or go on the roof of the building, to the open-air classroom where on certain days they were invited to sit at desks and study the sky around them. But that day they were told it was too dangerous: They would have to wait for another storm.

Upstairs, top officials at the Weather Service were considering what would happen if they were to take a direct hit. In anticipation of Oklahoma's wild weather, the facility had been built out of bulletproof glass and the walls reinforced with Kevlar. They were said to be able to withstand winds of 250 miles per hour, and a backup power generator could supposedly keep the building running for three days. But nobody knew if this was actually true. It had yet to be tested. Though a few small twisters had hit in the seven years since the building had been erected, the worst storms had bypassed Norman, either heading to the north, toward Moore, or staying south.

Smith and his colleagues calmly went over the backup plan, reviewing how they would relocate their staff to the Weather Service's old headquarters on the north side of town near the airport. Satellite agency offices around the region were on standby to take over operations if the worst happened. Still, it was hard to fathom a direct hit. Smith could hardly believe a storm capable of producing a tornado was literally in their backyard, taking aim at the people whose job it was to warn and protect the public. Mother Nature had one sick sense of humor.

The National Weather Service issued an official warning, telling everyone in Norman to take cover—a point Smith reiterated on Twitter. "DO NOT look for it," he tweeted. "Take cover right now!" In Oklahoma people will sometimes stay out in their front yards to watch approaching storms, their curiosity and awe trumping any natural sense of fear. The country singer Toby Keith, who grew up in Moore, had even written a song about the phenomenon—"Trailerhood"—which poked fun at people who, when the storm sirens blare, race outside with "a six pack and a lawn chair" waiting for the tornado to come. Even meteorologists aren't immune. As they warned people to take cover and move into shelters or relocate to interior rooms, some of the scientists in the office left their cubicles and ran to the windows to watch the storm taking shape just west of the building. It was a rare opportunity for people who spent their professional lives tracking twisters on radar to physically see one with their own eyes unfolding before them. Smith was right there with them—watching the storm with the same curiosity and fear that had captivated him as a kid.

One of his earliest weather memories was of being frozen in fear at claps of thunder so loud they shook his house. He ran to his parents, terrified by the darkening clouds that seemed as if they were out to get him. But that fear soon turned into fascination, and the next thing he knew, he was standing outside as the storm approached, looking up at the sky, unable to tear his eyes away. That fascination—the awe of what Mother Nature could do—was what had driven him to become a meteorologist. He wanted to understand what was happening in the sky around him. Almost everybody who worked in weather for a living had a similar story—the storm that had hooked them for life.

As precarious as Sunday's storm had appeared, the tornado had stayed in the clouds as it passed over Norman, sparing the Weather Service a direct hit. It had touched the ground a short while later northeast of town, in the wide-open farmland east of Moore, rapidly increasing to an EF4 tornado with winds approaching 200 miles per hour. It had wiped out a mobile-home park and heavily damaged or destroyed dozens of homes before crossing Interstate 40, where it picked up several tractor-trailer trucks and slammed them to the ground, shattering them into pieces. Among the farmhouses it had hit was one belonging to my aunt.

As night fell and the storms finally fizzled out, Smith and his colleagues had watched local coverage of the tornado damage, accompanied by terrifying up-close footage of the giant twister captured from different angles by storm chasers on the ground and by the local news stations' helicopters, which had followed it in the air. They had wondered about the death toll—which still hadn't been released—and considered their own narrow miss. Why had it spared them but not others?

They'd had little time to stop and ponder the storm's trajectory. Forecasters on staff were already predicting that another round of storms was on its way Monday—even worse than what they'd seen in recent days. A dry line of air was coming off the Rocky Mountains to the northwest that would collide with unstable tropical moisture pushed up from the Gulf of Mexico—the key ingredients for deadly thunderstorms. Radar projections suggested the worst of it would be concentrated right over central Oklahoma. Sometimes you didn't need the radar to know trouble was brewing. As Smith had left the office early Monday morning, walking out to his car in the dark, he had been hit by a blast of thick, humid air.

Now, inside the building on the second floor, Smith was at his desk analyzing the forecast again. He saw his boss, David Andra, walk by. Andra looked tense and nervous, which was all the data Smith needed to know it was going to be a rough day. He had scheduled a conference call with city officials in the region and updated the Weather Service's Twitter feed once that morning—just after 6:30 A.M.—urging his followers to "get ready" for more severe storms that afternoon. At his desk he looked over data suggesting the worst of the weather would begin to fire up around 1:00 P.M.—hours earlier than usual. He thought of the kids who would be in school at that hour. "Attention school systems, parents and students!!" Smith wrote on Twitter. "We may be dealing with dangerous storms at school dismissal time! Plan ahead!"

He hoped it would be enough, but in the back of his mind he felt a creeping sense of unease.

CHAPTER 4

10:00 A.M., MAY 20

Next to the National Weather Center was a parking lot covered by a giant awning where storm chasers working with the University of Oklahoma and weather agencies kept their trucks, outfitted with mobile radars and other devices. One of the largest of these resembled a king cab pickup on steroids. The bed had been removed, and in the back was a giant mobile Doppler radar that looked a bit like a satellite dish. But it was no ordinary radar.

The RaXpol—short for Rapid X-Pol—is a polarimetric radar eight feet in diameter that sends out pulse waves into the storm. These can measure it not only horizontally but also vertically, giving scientists a more precise read on its size and shape. Firmly hooked into the back of the truck, the RaXpol can rotate at 180 degrees per second—capturing the full atmospheric blueprint of a tornado in seconds. This speed is important because tornadoes change rapidly—so much so that scientists still don't have a full grasp of why some storms produce vortices and others don't, or why some stay on the ground for an hour while others disappear in seconds. They know more than they did twenty years ago, but not enough.

Next to the truck stood the RaXpol's operator, Howard Bluestein, who had spent his entire life trying to solve this riddle. A meteorology professor at OU, Bluestein was widely regarded as one of the weather gods among the scientists. He was one of the best-known storm chasers in the world, a man who was out in the field following tornadoes long before the chase became a form of entertainment or, for some, a sport.

If you had sent out a casting memo for a storm scientist, Bluestein, at sixty-four, would have fit the bill. Standing midheight, with a mat of wiry gray hair, he was known for his distinctive way of dressing while chasing the storms. He almost always wore the same thing: a wrinkled shirt and knee-length khaki shorts with tennis shoes and tall, blindingly white socks. It was the socks that his students and colleagues teased him about. Back in the 1970s they'd gone up only to his ankles, but as he'd gotten older, they had slowly inched up his skinny calves, higher and higher. Part of it was utility: Bluestein was known to sprint through the open, grassy fields of Oklahoma's countryside with his camera to get a good shot of a tornado. It was often too hot to wear jeans, and his tall white socks were like cotton armor protecting his skin from the fire ants, chiggers, and thorny sticker-burr weeds that were often hidden in the deep grass. But that didn't stop the teasing. His students took pictures of him ogling tornadoes. "The tornado, Dr. Bluestein and his socks," one was captioned.

Bluestein didn't mind the ribbing. He had a healthy sense of humor and, for a scientist, was remarkably easygoing. His voice was soft and always seemed to have a tinge of awe when he was talking about the weather. He had an almost constant look of joy on his face, especially if you caught him out in the field watching a storm rise up on the wide expanse of the Oklahoma landscape. It never got old. The sky, he told his students, was nature's finest art museum, with a constantly changing exhibit that could blow you away—not just with its beauty but with its physical power too.

Bluestein had been at OU since 1976, and over the years his gentle voice had developed a subtle drawl. His students were often surprised to hear he was actually from Massachusetts, just outside Boston. Some had the obvious question: How did a Yankee end up here? While Boston wasn't known for severe weather, other than its massive snows in the winter, Bluestein could point to that "one storm" that blew through when he was a kid, the one that changed his life and left him transfixed.

It was June 1953, and he was only four years old at the time. But he could still vividly recall how he'd been outside in the yard playing when the sky had turned a strange, hazy greenish yellow. The wind picked up, and his mother ordered him to come inside. A tornado had been reported in Worcester, about 40 miles to the west—something that was practically unheard of in New England. It was so rare that local television in Boston had interrupted programming to warn of the approaching storm—public tornado warnings did not exist at the time.

The only tornado he'd ever heard of was the one that carried Dorothy and her dog, Toto, away in *The Wizard of Oz*. When he protested, not wanting to go inside, his mother warned him that the storm that was coming would snatch him up into the sky and take him away. Little Howie, as he was known, ran into the house and kept his eyes glued to the window, waiting to see if a twister would come and carry him, like Dorothy, to Oz.

That tornado never made it to Chelsea, the Boston suburb where Bluestein lived, but horrific stories soon circulated of what it had done to Worcester. People spoke of a large, dark cloud of smoke descending on the city with winds no one had ever experienced before. Almost everything in its path was obliterated, including heavy brick buildings that dated back more than a century. The tornado was reported to have marched on for nearly ninety minutes across a span of almost 50 miles, during which time it killed 94 people and injured 1,200. Roughly ten thousand people lost their homes.

The stories of that storm mesmerized the four-year-old, who was far too young to understand the workings of the weather. Forecasting and the science of storms were almost nonexistent back then, though people had been chasing storms for centuries, drawn by their terrifying power. One of America's earliest storm chasers was Benjamin Franklin, who became an accidental meteorologist in 1752 when he sought to prove that lightning was a form of electricity, legend has it, by flying a kite attached to a metal key in the middle of a thunderstorm to test whether it would attract a charge.

But Franklin's fascination wasn't limited to lightning. He is credited with being the first person to have noticed that storms typically move from southwest to northeast—a discovery he made in 1753. Two years later, in 1755, he wrote to a friend to tell him of how he'd been chasing "a small whirlwind" on horseback through the Maryland countryside, watching the funnel as it got bigger and bigger. At one point he lashed at it with a whip to see if it could be broken up, but it seemed impervious to his intervention and darted onward into a forest. When limbs began to rain down upon him from the sky, Franklin became "apprehensive of the danger," he wrote, and stopped, watching as the funnel continued through the trees only to dissipate over a nearby tobacco field.

Franklin didn't call what he saw a "tornado." It isn't in fact clear when that word was first used. The consensus seems to be that it was most likely a play on *tornar,* a Spanish word that means "to turn." Some people called it a twister, and L. Frank Baum wrote that it was a "cyclone" that carried Dorothy and Toto off from Kansas to the great land of Oz, but by then people knew enough about the word "tornado" to fear it. In the late 1800s the U.S. government went so far as to ban the word "tornado" from its internal weather forecasts, distributed mostly within the military, to avoid inciting panic. The ban wasn't lifted until the late 1930s, but even after that the U.S. Army Signal Corps, which was in charge of forecasts at that time, still largely refrained from using the word.

It wasn't until 1952 that the government began publicly issuing tornado watches and warnings—though they were widely derided as inaccurate. While people spoke of major storms that had hit in the past, it was only in the 1950s that official scientific records began to be kept of tornadoes—where they had hit, how many people had died, and the extent of the damage. But the records were inconsistent because there was no standard and generally no understanding of how to truly measure the impact of a tornado.

In 1954 Bluestein's home was hit by a hurricane with winds so strong they tore the tiles off the roof. He and his parents cowered inside, afraid the winds might tear their home completely apart. Between this storm and the tornado that had hit the year before, Bluestein became obsessed with the atmosphere around him, though there was little information in his secondary-school textbooks about the science of weather. It was too obscure.

When the time came to think of college, he enrolled at the Massachusetts Institute of Technology, where he received a doctorate degree in meteorology, focusing his studies on tropical weather and severe storms. In his last year of graduate school in 1976, Bluestein met Edwin Kessler, an MIT graduate who had moved to Oklahoma to head up the National Severe Storms Lab. Kessler suggested that he come to Oklahoma to study the violent weather, but

Bluestein's image of Oklahoma was of a vast dust bowl, something that did not appeal to him whatsoever. Still, he could not resist the lure of the storms, and that summer after graduation, he moved to Norman. Over the years, as he liked to joke, Oklahoma had become something of a paradise to him: a weather junkie in the land of tornadoes.

Starting in the 1970s, thousands of meteorologists moved to Oklahoma to be close to the severe weather. The meteorology school at OU became the largest program in the country—with more than five hundred students enrolled and hundreds more turned away every year simply because there was no room for them. Those who didn't get in sometimes came to Oklahoma anyway, and they studied Mother Nature on their own, packing the roads alongside other meteorologists from all over the country who came to study Oklahoma's legendary storms. A running joke in Oklahoma when I was growing up was that during the spring you couldn't throw a rock without hitting a weather scientist. They were everywhere.

Howard Bluestein hit the open road almost as soon as he arrived. It wasn't long before he experienced his first tornado, and even now he remembers it in specific detail. It was May 20, 1977, when he and a group of students chased a giant tornado that hit the ground in Tipton, a tiny town in the southwest near the Texas border. Driving down a narrow country road, he stopped the car when he saw a silhouette of a vortex crossing the road directly in front of them. Tall and slender like an elephant's trunk, it looked like none of the photographs he'd ever seen. He began to photograph it, the first of many pictures he would take of the thousands of tornadoes he would see in his career.

The excitement of seeing something he had been captivated by for so many years sent adrenaline coursing through his veins, but afterward Bluestein felt guilty. Driving up the road, he found a house missing its roof and scores of power lines that had been ripped apart and thrown to the ground. It was minor damage compared with the things he would see later in life, but he suddenly felt a sickening feeling. How could he have been so excited to see a storm that might have killed someone? It was a tension that everyone who follows storms for a living will at some point experience: You want the storms to be interesting, and when you are chasing one, you have that feeling of anticipation, that excitement and hope that it will develop and produce the tornado you so desperately want to see and study. But that desire often competes with the guilt of knowing how truly terrible storms will ruin people's lives. Over the years, Bluestein had to remind himself and his students, who went through the same emotions, that they were doing research that would contribute to saving people's lives, that they were not complicit in the devastation, though they were its witnesses.

Back in the 1970s almost nothing was known about what was happening inside a tornado. Radar technology offered only so much insight. Bluestein knew that the secret to understanding tornadoes was to somehow get inside them—to measure the winds and gather data on their structure so as to gauge what was happening inside the storms at the moment when they produced a funnel. People had dreamed up ways of doing this before, but none had come to fruition. In the 1970s a scientist offered to drive an armored tank into the path of a tornado, but it was dismissed as a crazy idea—though storm chasers almost thirty years later would eventually do just that. In 1979 Bluestein met Al Bedard and Carl Ramzy, two scientists at the National Oceanic and Atmospheric Administration, and together they came up with the idea of racing ahead of a tornado and deploying a device in its path that would be strong enough to withstand the winds and sophisticated enough to provide actual data about what was going on inside the storm. At a cocktail party in the summer of 1980, the trio, slightly inebriated, came up with the name of their four-hundred-pound, barrel-shaped device: the Totable Tornado Observatory, or TOTO, named after Dorothy's dog in *The Wizard of Oz*.

The following spring Bluestein and his colleagues tried to put TOTO in front of a tornado, but almost every time, as if it knew what they were up to, the tornado shifted course or simply lifted up and disappeared back into the sky. As the men struggled to get the massive machine loaded back into their truck, lighting often struck around them, exposing them to another danger: The device was basically a lightning rod in the middle of storms. In 1982 Bluestein and his team began to take risks they'd never thought they would in a desperate effort to intercept a tornado. Near Altus, Oklahoma, they drove directly into a storm. Their caravan of cars was pelted with gigantic hailstones and shaken by winds that seemed likely to blow them off the road at any moment. They were putting their lives at risk, Bluestein realized, but the allure of scientific discovery was too great to resist. They raced forward, trying to catch the tornado, but suddenly realized they were too close. The twister crossed the road just to their right, about one hundred yards from the front of their truck. This was closer than Bluestein had ever been before. Power lines fell across the road, shattering the windshield of their van. As they watched in horror, the tornado uprooted trees and destroyed a nearby mobile home. It was a close call, but even then they were not able to deploy their machine in time.

Over the years, Bluestein and his researchers would try again, but in the end it was simply too dangerous. A team from the Severe Storms Lab tried for a few more years, and in the spring of 1985 they almost succeeded. But a weak tornado near Ardmore blew the machine over, and it was retired.

TOTO, for all of its failings, eventually made Bluestein and his colleagues famous beyond the science world. The device was the inspiration for the fictional machine "Dorothy" featured in the 1996 movie *Twister*, which made storm chasers like Bluestein (who was a technical consultant on the film) famous. The film prompted a surge in enrollment at OU, where suddenly everyone wanted to be a storm chaser. At the same time, tornadoes became a burgeoning tourist industry in Oklahoma, as guides led visitors from all over the world on storm-chasing expeditions across the state in the springtime.

Bluestein had mixed feelings about this sudden surge of interest. On the one hand, he loved the fact that the public had begun to engage in the important science of storms—which meant more funding for projects to better understand the genesis of tornadoes and to create better warning systems. But he was unnerved by tourists and amateur storm chasers. Suddenly the empty country roads in Oklahoma were as packed as the Massachusetts Turnpike at rush hour—and he suspected many of the weekend chasers didn't appreciate how truly dangerous it could be to put yourself in the path of a tornado.

Bluestein wasn't a daredevil, a fact that sometimes irked his young students, who were hungry to get as close as possible to the storms they chased. He'd had one close call in 1991, when he got within a mile of the tornado and suddenly it turned on him. He was so close he saw the vortex blow a house clean off its foundation right in front of him—sending a bolt of fear through his heart. He survived the storm and came out of it with valuable information, but he vowed never to get that close to a tornado again. He had documented a tornado with winds of more than 280 miles per hour—then categorized as an F5. Nobody had ever seen one with winds that strong before.

Over the years, Bluestein hadn't slowed down in his never-ending pursuit of the storm. Every spring he and his students would travel as much as 10,000 miles, driving their mobile Doppler radar across Oklahoma and the central plains chasing ever-elusive tornadoes. He'd noticed that the storms seemed to be getting bigger and deadlier—though he wasn't sure, since records had been virtually nonexistent until the late 1950s. Who knew what their ancestors had seen? Especially in Oklahoma, which had been a wide-open empty space for hundreds of years until the land run of 1889 put it on the path to statehood. While the Native Americans who lived there had amassed wisdom about how to pacify the demon clouds, as they thought of them, their sacred rituals had never been shared outside their tribes.

In 1999 Bluestein and his team were tracking the epic tornado that wiped out a large swath of Moore when they recorded winds of 302 miles per hour—the fastest wind speed ever recorded near the surface of the earth. Bluestein hadn't recorded another tornado that strong since, but plenty of others were almost equally devastating. He began to notice odd things about the storms—how one year would produce dozens of strong tornadoes, followed by a year when there were almost none. But he couldn't explain why this was. For all the time and money put into studies and equipment, scientists still knew remarkably little about what made tornadoes form.

Like others, he wondered about the effects of global warming. Could an increase in the earth's temperature be responsible for creating ever-deadlier storms, especially in Oklahoma, where the warming of the tropical air coming off the Gulf of Mexico might create more instability when it collided with cooler air coming from Canada? But who was to say that rising temperatures up north, which were contributing to the melting of the ice over the North Pole, might not be weakening the cold blasts from the north? It was a question that Bluestein often debated with his colleagues. The truth was they just didn't know how global warming was impacting the weather in Oklahoma—or whether it was the reason why tornadoes seemed to be getting larger and more inconsistent every season.

All Bluestein could do was press forward. That Sunday night he and his team had had a major breakthrough—right in their own backyard. They had driven their mobile Doppler radar truck with their RaXpol radar close to the tornado that had hit the ground northeast of Norman. It had produced the best data set they had ever gotten on a tornado—a full-scale X-ray of the funnel as it was born, capturing the evolution of the competing updrafts and downdrafts that contributed to the rotation and eventual development of the vortex. Those valuable clues could help unlock the mystery of why some supercell thunderstorms produced tornadoes and others didn't. It could potentially boost meteorologists' ability to predict storms and increase warning times in the future. It was a triumph that made the long days of chasing storms worth it.

It had been a late night, and Bluestein had woken up a little groggy. He checked the forecast and saw that they were in for another wild day of storms. As he prepared to meet up with the graduate students who would accompany him on the chase, he considered where to go. The forecast suggested some of the strongest storms would hit in the central part of the state, south of Oklahoma City, right around Moore. He dreaded the thought of trying to drive his mobile Doppler into the area. He knew the streets would be crowded with local news chasers and amateurs, who drove wildly and paid little attention to the rules of the road. Looking at the forecast, he saw there was a strong potential for storms to the south, and so he made the decision that his team should head south on Interstate 35. If it proved to be fruitless, they could always drive back and position closer to Moore.

CHAPTER 5

THE WONDERFUL WEATHER WIZARD

When I was growing up, it sometimes felt like Gary England was everywhere, an omnipresent, benevolent deity who popped up at the mere mention of a storm. His picture was branded on tornado safety brochures handed out at schools, libraries, and grocery-store checkout lanes and regularly plastered on billboards all over Oklahoma City and its suburbs, looming larger than life over the roads. His grin, so familiar one could almost hear his folksy twang and the happy chuckle that often interrupted forecasts on sunny days, was set against an ominous backdrop of storm clouds and lightning. "Oklahoma's #1 meteorologist," the ads read. "The most trusted name in weather . . . There when it matters most."

To outsiders the billboards must have seemed an odd juxtaposition: the smiling weatherman seemingly giddy in the midst of the apocalypse, like the mythical Wizard of Oz behind the storms. He was such a cult hero in Oklahoma during my childhood that many found it hard to separate him from the storms he covered. To some he simply *was* the weather, the human face and voice of the atmospheric drama they were subjected to every spring.

England didn't particularly like to be associated with terrible storms that killed people and left unspeakable damage in their wake, but he couldn't deny that it was the weather and its mystery that truly animated him. He never felt more alive than when he was trying to outwit Mother Nature and keep people safe. He was almost always plotting and anticipating the next big storm. Being a meteorologist was more than a full-time job: It was his calling, a religion. The weather was his life—and in many ways that was what we had come to expect of those who dared to predict the path of the next big storm.

To be a television meteorologist in Oklahoma, it was not enough to be comfortable on camera or to possess the ability to deliver accurate forecasts. In a part of the country where people feared storms but were also mesmerized and thrilled by them, something more was expected of those entrusted with channeling the wild weather every spring. Our TV weathermen and weatherwomen had to have the smarts and drive of a scientist, the reporting skills of a journalist, and an acutely attuned sense of theater—because for most of us, the storms were a fact of life and a terrible scourge, but they were also a form of entertainment.

When a patch of bad weather blew up, all three major television channels in Oklahoma City would go live with uninterrupted coverage, partly by necessity, as deadly storms put their viewers' lives at risk, but also driven by demand in a state populated by unabashed storm junkies. The wall-to-wall coverage often had the tense feel of a man-versus-nature disaster movie, a life-and-death battle between the weathermen and the storms they covered. It featured a cast of supporting characters who were part daredevil, part hero as they ventured deep into the violent heart of the storm to give viewers a rare glimpse of the monster at work. The head meteorologists anchoring the coverage back at the station were like Luke Skywalker to the storm's Darth Vader, brave warriors on the side of good fighting the forces of evil.

England was revered as the founding father of modern-day storm coverage, but there were younger men nipping at his heels. KFOR's Mike Morgan was his fiercest rival, followed by KOCO's Damon Lane, the fresh-faced upstart weathering his first spring storm season as the head meteorologist at Channel 5. They were all wizards of the weather, shamans of the storm who could conjure an alchemical combination of wisdom and magic. In them one could detect varying degrees of the fire and brimstone of a Holy Roller preacher desperate to save souls from the blazing pits of hell—a character all too familiar to residents of Bible Belt Oklahoma. But there was also the authoritative tone of an unshakable action-film hero there to save the day, because viewers were looking not just for a forecaster but for a hero, one who would stop at nothing to save them from the storm.

To be a weather savior in Oklahoma took a mix of energy, grit, and courage, along with the ability to manage one's emotions in the face of killer storms. Oklahoma's weather gods also had to possess one essential skill that was even harder to attain: the art of knowing the weather so well that they could somehow collect the clues to anticipate its next move. To some of us it seemed almost like magic, though like all good magic it required a great deal of mastery. It was more than just reading radar data. It required an ingrained sense deep within, a gut feeling of what the storm would do.

After four decades and thousands of storms, Gary England was incontestably one of these storm whisperers. More than anyone, he appreciated how far weather forecasting had come, how much technology had changed his profession and added precious minutes to warning times. But as much as he relied on the new radars and technology, he was also a believer in that gut feeling he had about the weather, that suffocating sense he would get that something bad was coming. And as he drove to the KWTV studio that Monday morning, he had an uneasy feeling that this time the worst might happen close to home. A tornado was bad anywhere, but it was a nightmare scenario when it took aim at a city. As he tapped his fingers on the steering wheel and waited for the light to change, eager to get to work and check the radar, England hoped this time his gut was wrong. But it rarely was.

Over the years, he had come to feel a little like a battlefield commander. Most people were aware only of the hours he spent on air every spring warning of approaching storms and then diligently talking through them as they hit, tracking them down to the exact streets where people needed to take shelter or get out of the way. What they didn't see were the hours he spent off air meticulously gaming out every possible strategy for how to cover the storms. He was not a man with many hobbies. Sometimes he played golf, but he wasn't any good at it and he often found himself back home thinking about the weather, obsessing over the station's coverage and considering what it should do differently in the future. His entire life revolved around anticipating that next big storm. And on the days when he knew bad weather was coming, he contemplated the station's coverage much as a general analyzes the theater of war, plotting where to deploy his "ground troops," as he called them. They were his army of storm chasers who raced toward a tornado on the ground and in the sky and got as close as possible—sometimes too close, England thought—to gauge its strength and direction so that he could warn the people in its path.

Radar projections often gave a good idea of where the moist, warm air off the Gulf of Mexico would collide with the dry, cool air sweeping down from Canada. The unstable atmosphere triggered by that volatile mix fueled the most ferocious thunderstorms, but the collision line often extended hundreds of miles across the state. England's job was to determine where to position his chasers, who were outfitted with sophisticated high-definition cameras that streamed live images of what they were seeing in the sky around them back to the station—and ultimately to the world.

In those crucial early moments in the life of a storm, a radar could tell you only so much. It could tell you a tornado *might* be forming but not that it definitely was. While the National Weather Service had posted storm spotters in every county and city in Oklahoma, it was often the live pictures transmitted by storm chasers on one or more of the local television stations that gave the Weather Service the definitive evidence that it was time to declare a tornado warning.

England often pointed to this when critics mocked the station's coverage as over-the-top or belittled it as nothing more than entertainment. While he conceded that some of his viewers were storm fanatics who loved the thrill of the chase—and sometimes his chasers got caught up in the adrenaline—he truly believed deep in his heart that what he and his team were doing was a genuine public service, and more often than not, people agreed. While it was easy to pinpoint where thunderstorms would erupt and which ones had conditions favorable to producing a tornado, no one knew if a funnel would actually hit the ground or where it would happen. All England could do was examine the storm projections and preposition his team based on the forecast and his gut sense of what the weather might do. For all of the radars and technology, tornadoes, in some ways, continued to be as mysterious as they had been when he was a little boy.

Gary England was born in 1939 in a small wooden farmhouse with no electricity in Seiling, Oklahoma, the tiniest of tiny towns near the Texas border, where the seemingly endless short-grass prairie had been ravaged by the extreme drought of the Dust Bowl. His parents were farmers struggling to raise livestock off the dry land. The Great Depression had not made things easy. Cash was so tight that his parents paid the doctor who delivered him in the form of live chickens—a transaction that was not uncommon in those days.

Fewer than two hundred people lived in or around Seiling at the time, spread so far apart that one could go for days without seeing anyone. There was not much for a child to do beyond tending livestock and looking up at the sky. And as much as England liked his pigs, what he really loved was the mystery of the weather. There were wild blizzards that dropped what felt like yards of snow, followed by blistering-hot summers with blinding dust storms that could turn the day as dark as night. But it was the spring that most excited him, when ominous thunderheads would suddenly explode, unleashing terrifying winds, torrential rains, jagged zigzags of lightning, and gigantic clumps of hail. The storms were particularly dangerous on the wide-open landscape of the farm, where there was nowhere to escape if you were caught out in the open fields. On more than one occasion when he was a boy, Gary and his family were forced to run for their lives when a storm blew up.

Back then forecasting simply didn't exist; you had to rely on folk wisdom and superstitions passed down through the generations. If you spotted more furry caterpillars in the fall or your cow's hair was thicker than usual, a bitter winter was coming, his parents told him. Winds from the east and achy bones meant rain was on the way. In storm season people looked for even more peculiar clues, like flies congregating on the screen door. If the birds stopped singing, it was red alert. Later in life England still clung to those signs from nature, indicators that were often as accurate as any offered by technology.

His first memory of a tornado was in April 1947, when a twister made a direct hit on the nearby town of Woodward. Swirling to life 100 miles away in the Texas panhandle, it was said to be nearly 2 miles wide and had been on the ground for almost an hour as it approached the city just before 9:00 P.M. Still, there was no warning, and the tornado leveled a hundred city blocks in Woodward, engulfing what remained in a terrible inferno. In all, at least a hundred people died—it was the deadliest tornado in Oklahoma's history.

Gary was just seven years old at the time, but decades later he still remembered the sky that night before the storm—how the clouds had looked like fuzzy pink egg cartons as the sun set. He learned years later that these were mammatus clouds and those puffs, sinking pouches of air that were usually indicative of a severe thunderstorm. He and his parents had stood outside their home looking at the odd sight, and his father declared in a matter-of-fact voice, "Somewhere tonight, there's going to be a bad tornado." A few hours later, after the sun had gone down, Gary was lying in bed wide awake. A light wind opened his curtains, and through his open window he could see his hound dog, Cookie, nosing around the front yard looking for night critters. Suddenly Cookie went rigid, and a few seconds later he let out a low, mournful howl, a sound Gary had never heard before. It scared him to death. Not long after, he heard the sound of sirens screaming in the distance, coming closer and closer. It went on all night, and he barely slept.

Television did not exist in Oklahoma back in 1947, and news and weather coverage on the radio was almost unheard of. So it wasn't until the next morning, once his father had gone out to investigate, that the family learned about the deadly tornado next door. Later he listened in horror as adults told stories of how its winds were so strong they had literally blown people's clothes off and police had found naked people impaled on telephone poles. He saw pictures of the aftermath, wagons piled with dead bodies and devastation as far as the eye could see. And he heard terrible stories of how kids had been sucked up by the storm and dropped far away, miraculously alive but never to be reunited with their families. The stories scared him. It was the first time he realized that the weather, as fascinating as it was, could be ruthless.

A few summers later Gary and his father were cleaning out one of their livestock pens when they were hit by the fiercest winds he had ever felt in his life. With dirt and debris flying in the air around them, they both dropped to the ground and clawed their way toward a brick chicken coop, where Gary's dad threw his body onto his son and grabbed a support beam buried deep in the ground. It seemed to be their only hope of not being sucked away. Hanging on for dear life, he heard the windows around him breaking and opened his eyes just as the building's tin roof peeled away like the lid of a soup can. Chickens, squawking for dear life, were zooming past his head like "feathered bullets," he later recalled, and at that moment he believed his young life was over. But then, with a flash of lightning and a ground-shaking crash of thunder, the storm was suddenly over—vanishing almost as quickly as it had come. Covered in a mix of mud, bird droppings, and feathers, he sat there shaking and terrified but thrilled by the storm. His father, who was by then no stranger to the random assaults, was not quite so excited. "Good Lord," he said to his son. "Will we ever know when these darn things are going to hit?"

At that point the only warning system one could hope for was a police officer parked on the west side of town on stormy days to keep watch for funnels. If the officer spotted a storm coming, he would radio back to the station or, more often in those days, race back to town and blow the emergency siren himself. After that storm Gary and his family moved closer to town. As he grew up, he'd hear the siren go off seconds before the storms hit. He and his family would race to the storm cellar—crawling down into the dark hole in the ground that also served as storage for the dozens of mason jars his mom canned every year. Sometimes he wasn't sure what was more terrifying—that roar in the distance or the darkness of the cellar, where snakes and black widows with their deadly venom lurked.

England's fascination with storms only grew as he got older. He looked forward to the spring with a mix of fear and anticipation. He was ten or eleven when he finally saw his first tornado, a funnel that magically appeared in the distance when he was riding the school bus home one spring afternoon. It dropped down in a field near the North Canadian River, which ran south of town. It wasn't a big tornado, and it faded away quickly, but he was mesmerized. His dad had taken a job as a delivery driver for a bread company, and Gary occasionally joined him on the long routes around western Oklahoma. The truck didn't have a radio, and his dad passed the time singing old country songs while Gary stared out the window at the sky, looking for signs of that next storm.

Television had arrived in Oklahoma by then, though England

and his family were too poor to own a set. The first time he saw a television was through the front window of his uncle's hardware store. A crowd had gathered around a brown box where he could see a faint picture of people who appeared to be caught in a snowstorm. The reception was poor—Seiling was more than 100 miles away from Oklahoma City, home of the state's only television station at that point—but soon the picture became clearer as tall antennas began to rise on the landscape like metal weeds. He would walk by the hardware store as often as he could, staring into that storefront where the brown box gave him a glimpse of a world that seemed so far away.

By then Gary was old enough to begin to think of what his future might hold. He figured he'd probably be a pig farmer someday—he'd always liked pigs. But one fateful night he walked past the hardware store and saw something he'd never seen before: a man standing in front of a map of Oklahoma that was covered in chalk lines. He couldn't hear what the man was saying, but crude lines on the map appeared to represent weather fronts, cold air and hot air, and they were converging right over Oklahoma. He watched as the man wrote numbers over different regions of the state. In one corner of the map he wrote, in all caps, "RAIN." A day later it did rain, just as the man had predicted—and England was hooked.

Though England didn't learn his identity until later, that man was Harry Volkman, the very first television weatherman in the state of Oklahoma and one of the first broadcast meteorologists in the entire country. A Boston native who was obsessed with the weather before he could even read, Volkman came to Oklahoma when he was discharged from the army after World War II. He enrolled at an aeronautical school in Tulsa, one of the few institutions at the time to offer a degree in meteorology. Forecasting back then was primarily viewed as a function of the military, but Volkman's interest wasn't just scientific. As a child he'd seen his mother petrified by the sudden appearance of thunderstorms, and he dreamed of being able to tell people what was coming so that they could be prepared and could perhaps even appreciate the weather around them. He was a precocious kid who even started his own amateur radio station at one point using his family's roof antenna. In Tulsa he revived those skills and took a job as a disc jockey at a local radio station, where he begged the management to let him do the forecasts too. Finally they relented, and he began to do a nightly weather report.

Even in a place like Oklahoma, where the weather has such an impact on people's lives, many of Volkman's colleagues had no actual knowledge of its most basic science. A colleague who introduced him could barely pronounce his new title. On air the man called him the station's "meaty-e-rologist." In 1949 KOTV, Tulsa's first television station, went on air, and Volkman pitched himself as a forecaster. The station's staff dismissed him, telling him they weren't even sure they would do weather. A few months later, after he'd taken a job working as a janitor and doing other odd jobs at KOTV, Volkman finally got his shot. He went on air with a plastic map of Oklahoma and illustrated his forecast by drawing over it with a grease pencil that could be wiped away after every show.

The U.S. Weather Bureau, which handled forecasting at the time, shared only broad sketches of what it thought the skies would do, and few people outside the military had access to weather radars. Volkman had learned Morse code in the army as part of a team that decoded weather updates sent between units to protect artillery. In Tulsa, and later in Oklahoma City, he used a shortwave radio to tap into those transmissions, listening to coded messages sent to and from nearby military bases with atmospheric observations and forecasts. He used them to craft his own forecasts.

In March 1952 Volkman moved to Oklahoma City and joined WKY-TV—or, as the locals knew it, Channel 4. (Decades later it would change its call letters to KFOR, as it is known today.) By then the Weather Bureau knew he'd been cracking military forecasts—but it didn't stop him. In his first week on the job a potentially deadly outbreak of severe storms erupted, threatening Oklahoma City. With the skies growing ever more ominous, Volkman and his boss, Buddy Sugg, a former navy officer, heard transmissions over the radio that a "tornado alert"—the early version of a "tornado watch"—had been issued by forecasters at nearby Tinker Air Force Base. Officials there had started to take the weather seriously after two tornadoes hit the base within days of each other in 1947, almost wiping out its fleet of B-2 bombers, but though their forecasts were considered among the most accurate in the air force, they were kept secret from the public. Some were leaked to Volkman, who was still monitoring the coded messages, but he was limited in what he could do with the information. The FCC had actually banned radio and television broadcasters from using the words "tornado" or "tornado alert"—concerned that they could cause mass panic. Sugg would have none of it. He felt that to not alert the public was to needlessly put lives at risk. He told Volkman they absolutely had to get the alerts on the air. It was their duty. "We could get arrested," Volkman said. "I'm giving you an order," Sugg replied. "If they want to arrest anyone, let them arrest me."

The station dispatched a reporter to Tinker with a hidden microphone, and on base he recorded audio of the tornado alert, which listed specific counties that were at risk. Back at the station Volkman interrupted programming and, in front of his crude map, warned viewers of the impending storm heading toward Oklahoma City. Though nothing touched the ground that day, it was the first televised tornado watch in history. Government officials were furious—they threatened to arrest him and strip the station of its broadcasting license. But in the end they did nothing because they knew they wouldn't have the support of the public, who sent Volkman thank-you cards and kind notes. After that he kept issuing tornado warnings, including one for a 1954 twister that wiped out part of Meeker, east of Oklahoma City. A few months later, in early 1955, he was hired away by a relatively new rival station, KWTV. It was the opening salvo in a bitter and personal war spanning decades between Channel 9 and Channel 4 for weather supremacy in Oklahoma City.

England knew nothing of Volkman's history or the important role he had played in the development of television meteorology. All he knew was that he was dazzled. The idea that someone could predict the weather blew his young mind. Amused by their son's interest, his parents accommodated him by driving him over to his grandparents' house every Sunday night. They were the first in the family to own a television set, and while the adults talked, Gary would park himself right at the foot of the television, inches away from the screen, listening intently. At the time, the pioneering weatherman was doing forecasts twice a day every day. He had his own Sunday-night program, *Weather Station*, which sometimes had the feel of a variety show. An accomplished vocalist in his church choir, Volkman occasionally sang a sentence or two when proclaiming the forecast, and as he talked about air fronts moving through the state, he would enact them with a big "*Whoooshhh.*" England loved it, and one night he turned to his father and excitedly declared that he wanted to be like Harry Volkman when he grew up. "Well, what is he?" his father replied. "I don't know," England said, "but I want to be one."

While Volkman had started to change the way people thought about forecasting and public awareness, most universities around Oklahoma still didn't offer meteorology degrees when England graduated from high school. Only the military had weather training, so he joined the navy and after a couple of years was able to take classes at its weather school based in New Jersey. It was there that he finally learned why Oklahoma's weather was so volatile—what all those lines on Volkman's crude weather map really meant. Until then he had believed that no one but God really knew what Oklahoma's weather would do—and while in many ways that was still true, he finally understood that there was vital data available that suggested when and where storms would erupt—clues most Oklahomans knew nothing about.

After a stint in the Midway Islands, where he helped guide navy pilots through some of the wildest weather conditions on the planet, including massive tropical storms, England left the navy and went back to Oklahoma, where he got married and began taking classes at the University of Oklahoma. Decades later OU would offer one of the most celebrated meteorology programs in the country, but in the early 1960s it still didn't offer a weather degree. He was forced to major in math, a subject he had barely studied in high school, with a meteorology "option." His adviser was beyond skeptical, telling him he wouldn't make it in meteorology, but "you can try." All he wanted to do was be a TV weatherman. He had no idea how hard it would be to get there.

As he struggled through classes—made more difficult by his dyslexia, which wouldn't be diagnosed until years later—he got a part-time job at the Atmospheric Research Lab on campus. Scientists were only just beginning to study the origins of tornadoes and what made them so deadly, and he was right there on the front lines. But he couldn't give up on the idea of television, and he contacted David Grant, who had replaced Volkman at KWTV. Grant told him to make an audition tape. Suddenly England was terrified. In all his years of dreaming of being on television, he'd never practiced in front of a camera. But he did it, and then later he auditioned in person. When Grant called to offer him a gig doing the weather on the weekends, he astonished his wife by turning it down. He was too terrified of going on television.

Instead he and Mary moved to New Orleans, where he took a job forecasting weather and oceanographic conditions for a private meteorological firm whose primary client was the offshore oil industry. He spent a few years guiding clients through storms, including Hurricane Camille—one of the most destructive hurricanes to ever hit the Louisiana Gulf Coast until Katrina. But all that time he couldn't stop thinking about the storms back in Oklahoma. In 1970, when he saw reports of a tornado that had hit parts of Oklahoma City without warning, he decided to go back, more confident in his abilities and convinced he could make a difference. But when he went home for interviews, none of the Oklahoma City television stations were interested. He had no on-air experience.

Dejected, he went to KTOK, the first radio station in Oklahoma to have its own weather radar. It was an old device, repurposed from a decommissioned airplane, but it was a radar nonetheless. The general manager told him they didn't need a meteorologist. Their talk-show hosts and disc jockeys were more than capable of reading the radar, he said. England refused to give up. As spring approached, he spent almost every morning at the station, sitting in the lobby, where he drank free coffee and waited, convinced that they would need him. It was a gamble, but he had no other prospects. Finally one morning he heard someone running down the hall. Severe storms were erupting to the west of Oklahoma City, right in the middle of the early-morning rush hour. Nobody at the station knew what to do. "Can you read this radar?" the manager asked. When England nodded, the man yelled, "You're hired! Now get back there and tell the audience what is happening with this storm!"

Those early months on the radio were a trying time for England. All the confidence he'd had when he was trying to get the job vanished when he found himself on air. His mouth went dry, his personality faded, and he struggled to do anything and everything. Through the glass of the studio, he could see his colleagues laughing every time he tried to pronounce the strange names of counties around Oklahoma he'd never even heard of: Pontotoc, Pottawatomie, Pushmataha. His office was the dusty attic of the old house west of downtown where KTOK's studios were located, right next to the old radar, which wasn't even strong enough to measure the weather immediately around it. He began to wonder if this would be both the beginning and the end of his illustrious career as a broadcast meteorologist.

Soon a disc jockey named Bob Riggins, the top-rated morning drive-time host in the city, took pity on him. One morning he pulled him aside and told him that being on the radio was about having fun, having a personality. England had no idea what he was talking about. Riggins shoved him in a room and told him to laugh. England produced something that, as he later recalled, sounded like a pervert making an obscene phone call. Riggins was incensed. "Laugh!" he screamed, and England was so startled that he fell backward. He began to laugh at the silliness of the situation. That, Riggins declared, was a real laugh, and he ordered him to practice it every day until he could do it on air so that it sounded natural.

The disc jockey gave England an on-air nickname—"the Wonderful Weather Wizard"—and told him he needed a shtick that could get him through the months when the weather wasn't so bad. A few weeks earlier England had brought in a tiny green lizard that he'd captured at the lake, and some of the secretaries at the station had screamed at the sight of his miniscule new pet. Riggins told him that he thought he should make that lizard part of his weather reports—except it should be something more supernatural. "An 805-pound thunder lizard," he suggested. And thus was born one of the stranger elements of England's weather career—an imaginary giant lizard that changed colors with the weather and was so ugly that cows turned their head in shame. On air England began to casually mention his fictitious lizard at the tail end of his weather reports: "It's partly cloudy skies, and good Lord, that ugly thunder lizard was spotted again near mile marker 107!" To England's surprise, listeners began to call in, reporting their run-ins with a creature that was wholly made up—how they'd seen it scrambling down Interstate 35 in pursuit of a Coors truck or chasing horses in a field off Route 66. They were all in on the joke. It became one of the most popular segments on the radio and eventually part of the lore of Gary England.

It took him awhile, but England finally began to loosen up. While he'd initially tried to dial back his strange sense of humor to sound less like the country boy he was, he now let it all out, peppering his weather reports with the folksy language and homespun colloquialisms of his childhood. There were "good Lords" and "great God almightys" and "gosh darns." "Jiminy Christmas!" he'd shout when he saw something interesting on the radar. Storms were "big uglies," "suckers," and "rascals." "Hide the women and children! Put the mule in the barn!" he'd say on cold days. He was speaking a language that was distinctly Oklahoman, and listeners loved it. Soon he got the call he had been dreaming about. KWTV was interested in hiring him as its chief meteorologist. On October 16, 1972, England delivered his first television forecast, scratching out the weather patterns on a chalkboard map of Oklahoma. It was primitive stuff, considering what was to come, but he was thrilled.

KWTV had hired him because of his popularity on the radio and obvious skill at forecasting the weather. But when Gary England got on air, some at the station were appalled at how untelevision he actually was. He didn't have the slick look or polished demeanor of a broadcaster. Though he dressed the part, in brand-new sport jackets and suits, England still looked and sounded a little like that boy from the farm, with his deep twang, cowboy boots, and quirky sense of humor. Following Riggins's advice, he continued to inject personality into his weather reports. During one Friday-night forecast, he coined his most famous phrase of all, one that he'd use for decades: "Jump back! Throw me down, Loretta! It's Friday night in the big town," he'd yell, sometimes doing a little dance. No one knew who Loretta was—not even England. He'd just made it up. But as charismatic and jokey as he was on calm days, his playful banter vanished in an instant when dangerous weather arrived. He was deadly serious about storms.

Still, some of his managers could not get past how he talked and looked, and a consultant told the station that it should get rid of him as soon as possible. But KWTV's ratings shot through the roof. Viewers loved him, a fact that saved his job on more than one occasion. He used his popularity and role in the station's surging ratings to do what had made him want to be on television in the first place: to give people the kind of warning he'd never had about dangerous storms. He felt it wasn't enough to depend on data from the National Weather Service. If KWTV wanted to be serious about the weather, it would have to approach it as scientists would, and for that it needed a real radar. The news director at the time thought he was nuts, but England went over him and appealed to the station's owner, John Griffin, who had an interest not only in the weather (he was an amateur pilot) but also in keeping the station a step ahead in terms of technology. To everyone's surprise, Griffin signed off on the purchase of a brand-new Enterprise radar—the same kind that government meteorologists were using.

England was thrilled, but he knew the radar on its own wouldn't be enough. And so, ahead of the spring storm season, he began assembling a team of ham-radio operators across the state that he could count on as his eyes and ears. At the same time, to the great skepticism of the news department, he begged the assignment desk to send reporters and cameramen into the field where he thought storms might erupt. When they refused, he bribed some of the staff to work on their days off, promising he'd buy them six-packs of beer. They were his early army of storm chasers, and along with the radar, the collective effort gave England one of his first major breakthroughs at

KWTV. In May 1973 he cut into programming when the radar suggested a tornado was developing near Union City, west of Oklahoma City. His chasers confirmed the funnel, and he showed his viewers a radar image of what was happening—one of the first times a radar image of a tornado, as crude as it was, was shown on television. He realized only after the fact that he'd issued a tornado warning before the National Weather Service, and it marked the beginning of a tumultuous relationship with government meteorologists and others in the business who considered him brash and reckless for not following the traditional rules of forecasting.

In some ways it was in England's blood to push the limits. Oklahoma, after all, had famously been settled by the "Sooners," people who had sneaked onto what was formerly Indian territory to stake their claims on property well before the kickoff of the land run of 1889 that settled the state. People had frowned on them—on their failure to follow the rules. But later they celebrated the Sooners' spirit, claiming the Sooner as an embodiment of Oklahoman ingenuity. Members of the meteorological community didn't like people who broke the rules. They didn't understand England or his vision of how storms should be covered on television and how the public should be warned.

Back then England heard people within the weather community complain that he was an outlaw, but he simply didn't care. Weren't they all in the business of trying to save lives? It only made him want to do more. As weather technology improved, he begged the station to invest more money in his operation—and usually he got it. In 1977 KWTV became the proud owner of a weather-satellite machine that offered the clearest images of the clouds and storm fronts over Oklahoma the public had ever seen. Later that year it became the first station in Oklahoma to have a color radar, an incredible development for viewers, who now could more graphically see the violence of the storms.

That radar had barely been unpacked and installed when England began to dream about an even newer piece of technology. It would be his biggest ask of all—and his riskiest. Years earlier the National Severe Storms Lab had captured a full scan of the Union City tornado with a Doppler radar. Now, England read, the lab was studying whether Doppler radars could be used to add minutes to the warning times before storms hit. Preliminary tests suggested that the Doppler could add at least twenty minutes' advance notice of a storm because of its ability to measure rotation in the clouds beyond where the human eye could see. If the technology were proven, it would be an almost unbelievable step forward. At the time, the top-of-the-line radar typically gave about three or four minutes' warning. Twenty minutes seemed like an eternity by comparison—if it actually worked.

England was thrilled by the concept, but having worked in college with meteorologists whose studies were funded by federal grants, he worried that the government would take forever to unveil its officially sanctioned Doppler. He didn't want to wait. He called Neil Braswell, an engineer at Enterprise Radar, the Alabama firm that had built KWTV's last two radars, and asked him if he could build a Doppler—and, if so, how much it would it cost. There was long pause on the other end of the line. Doppler radar technology was so new that few people had actually built one—much less for a television station. Even the government wasn't entirely sure it would offer the breakthrough in warning times that people wanted. Braswell told England he would get back to him.

England heard nothing for several months, then finally, on a crisp day in the fall of 1978, he got the call. Braswell told him he could build a Doppler for the station, but it would take at least two years. The preliminary price: at least $250,000—more than KWTV had spent on all of the weather equipment England had requested so far. It was a major investment for technology that had not really been tested and might not work, but England had a hunch the Doppler would change forecasting forever. Still, he was nervous. How would he ever persuade the station to go for it? In a series of meetings with Griffin over the following weeks, he made the case—arguing that the radar could save lives in a way no other technology had before. It could change the very nature of weather forecasting, and KWTV had the chance to be on the front lines, to make history.

In their final meeting England nervously sat at the end of a long conference table, wondering if he'd gone too far. He was in the room with Griffin and several other station executives, who thought he was crazy. The news director, one of several he had worked under at this point, made it clear he wanted him out and was not so secretly shopping around for a replacement. In the meeting Griffin suddenly looked up and gave England a stare that made the weatherman wonder if he was about to lose his job. "We have spent large sums of money in your area," Griffin said. "Not once have you misled me on what this television station needed. We're going to buy this Doppler radar." As the meeting ended, England sat there stunned, unable to move as everyone else filed out. *This radar had better work,* he thought.

And it did—though it took longer to build than Braswell had anticipated. Three years later, in May 1981, England became the first person in history to use a Doppler radar to warn the public about a coming storm. Getting there was a bumpy ride. No one had ever used a Doppler in real time before, and when England finally sat down and turned on the radar he had spent years dreaming about, the monitor produced an image of storm clouds over Oklahoma that, to him, looked like a giant mess of scrambled eggs. He had no idea what any of it meant—and no one to ask. He was the first person to use the radar in this way, and he would simply have to learn on his own. He barely had time to decipher the radar's output before the first dangerous storms took aim at Oklahoma City. Again he angered the National Weather Service when he issued a slew of tornado warnings before they did—but now he was working with better technology. As he'd suspected, many Weather Service offices wouldn't get Doppler technology until years later. In fact, the full National Weather Service Doppler network, which it called NEXRAD (for Next-Generation Radar), didn't come online until the early 1990s.

England's use of the Doppler radar was big news both inside and outside Oklahoma. National reporters from the *Washington Post* and *Wall Street Journal* descended on the station, curious about the renegade weatherman who had come to use a Doppler radar to publicly forecast tornadoes before anyone else. "I absolutely love this new equipment," England gushed to the *Post*. "If it had hair, I'd marry it."

But the radar was only one step: Now he planned to take storm coverage to new heights. In 1981, the year he got his Doppler, England persuaded KWTV to send the station's helicopter, *Ranger 9*, out toward a storm in western Oklahoma. Suddenly a tornado dropped to the ground and the station went to live video from the helicopter. It was not only the first time a helicopter had been used to chase a tornado but also the first time live video of a tornado had been captured by a camera mounted on a helicopter. But before anyone knew what was happening, the helicopter was sucked into the inflow of the storm. If viewers at home were getting a closer and closer look at the tornado, it was because the helicopter was being dragged toward the funnel. Suddenly, as England and his colleagues watched, the helicopter appeared to break free of the storm, but as it did, the live video went black. England worried the helicopter might have crashed, but seconds later the pilot radioed in: The crew was shaken up but fine.

Exhilarated, England kept dreaming of different ways to cover the storms and warn the public—and as he did, he continued to break new ground. In March 1982, now more savvy with the Doppler (which the station had christened its Doppler StormScan), England spotted rotation in two separate storms about 60 miles south of Oklahoma City. He cut into programming and issued tornado warnings for both—showing viewers the Doppler radar image of the storms and their circulations. It was another first. Viewers had never before seen live Doppler images of a tornado as it was forming, much less of two. England meticulously tracked their movement, talking until his voice was rough and hoarse, urging viewers, "Take your tornado precautions." One of the tornadoes eventually hit a tiny town called Ada, wiping out fifty-one mobile homes and killing one person. But the death toll could have been much higher. Thanks to his Doppler data, England had warned Ada residents an hour before the storm actually hit that it was potentially headed their way. The station's investment in the Doppler was paying off in ways that England had only dreamed of.

At the same time technology was beginning to change the industry. The computer revolution helped to introduce better on-air graphics and offered access to a slew of new forecast data. Suddenly England had access to real-time weather information and forecasts through the National Weather Service. KWTV invested in two new radars: an updated Doppler that offered even more specific, closer-range images and a machine called the LiveLine 5 that allowed England to create detailed satellite weather maps of the storms over Oklahoma and put them in motion so he could play them on air for viewers. The radar also helped him develop a more detailed five-day forecast—which was highly unusual back then. The days of standing in front of a weather map with chalk seemed like ancient history. Now England stood in front of a green screen, giving him the ability to walk right into an image projecting radar or satellite data so that he could point out where storms were likely to form. He was not just a forecaster; he was a teacher, and suddenly Oklahomans who had always had some awareness of the sky around them became fluent in the scientific terms of weather—learning about mesocyclones and barometric pressures. At last they were given the tools to understand how it actually worked.

By then England was on his way to becoming an Oklahoma legend. He wrote a book, *Those Terrible Twisters,* and traveled the state to share stories with rapt, standing-room-only audiences about the wild weather and how they could protect themselves from it. He marched in parades. He signed autographs at the grocery store. He even rode a bull at a rodeo to promote the station and its weather coverage—not that he needed to. Everybody knew the name "Gary England" by that point. After initially dismissing his brand of forecasting as over-the-top, other stations scrambled to catch up to KWTV in the ratings, both with technology and staff. In the late 1980s Channel 4 got its own Doppler radar—the first color Doppler radar in the United States. And KOCO brought in a big name: Wayne Shattuck, a longtime meteorologist who had worked in Miami and Dallas and had once been rumored to be in the running for the weatherman spot on *Good Morning America*. The local weather wars among the stations were about to begin in earnest.

It seemed to many like a strange choice for a rising meteorologist to choose a television market that had regularly been at the bottom of the top fifty in the country. But given its position right at the heart of the nation's Tornado Alley, Oklahoma began to gain a reputation as a place to be for exciting weather, a market where the news stations were like cutting-edge weather scientists. They were using technology that stations in other, larger cities simply didn't have access to. At the same time, interest in weather was skyrocketing. At the University of Oklahoma, which was finally offering a meteorology degree, enrollment jumped in the late 1980s and early 1990s, and there were many dual majors of broadcast journalism and meteorology. Many people, it seemed, wanted to be Gary England, and when I was in high school and college, I was one of them.

CHAPTER 6

THE WEATHER WARS

It wasn't until 1989 that England found a truly worthy opponent in the local weather wars: Mike Morgan, a native of nearby Tulsa who had been hired by Channel 5 as a deputy to Shattuck two years before. When Shattuck left to take a job in Los Angeles, Morgan was promoted to chief meteorologist at KOCO. He was only twenty-six—and on most days he looked younger than that. He was tall and skinny with thick, dark brown hair. Some women thought he looked a little like the dreamy Jake Ryan from *Sixteen Candles,* and they oohed and aahed over him when he made public appearances, including at the annual state fair—where Morgan was often the popular attraction at the KOCO booth.

But behind his youthful good looks was a true weather geek. Twenty-four years younger than England, Morgan had never known a world where television didn't exist. He had become intrigued by the weather at a time when Oklahoma television was just starting to cover storms in a real way. His father, a real estate broker, was as obsessed with storms as he was, and together they'd jump in the car and chase tornadoes across northeast Oklahoma.

On June 8, 1974, Morgan's father heard that a wild storm was headed their way. It had produced a tornado that hit the National Weather Service's office in Oklahoma City, knocking it out of commission for a bit. He grabbed his son and they jumped in the car and drove right into the heart of the storm as it blew into Tulsa. This was the exact opposite of how people were told to behave around tornadoes, and decades later Morgan regularly told his viewers on air to get out of the path of storms. But on that night the future weatherman and his father parked near Oral Roberts University and watched as the tornado passed them by. Decades later Morgan, who was ten at the time, could still vividly recall how he smushed his face against the cool glass of the car window, watching the cottonwood trees above him sway wildly in the wind and rain. It was too dark to see it, but the tornado had passed almost overhead, and Morgan was hooked. He couldn't imagine doing anything with his life other than chasing that big storm.

And chase it he did. At thirteen he talked his way into an internship at the Tulsa office of the National Weather Service, where he did anything he was asked just to be close to the action. Two years later he met Don Woods, a legendary television meteorologist at Tulsa's KTUL, and though he didn't even have a driver's license, he talked Woods into letting him chase storms and photograph them for the station—usually with his dad. After attending the University of Oklahoma, where he studied meteorology, Morgan landed his first on-air job at KJRH, the NBC affiliate in Tulsa. He was only twenty-two, but even then he was a walking, talking encyclopedia of storms.

Twenty-seven years later, Morgan knew so much about storms that it sometimes seemed as if the information came spilling out: He couldn't quite stop himself from going on and on about them, dropping random tidbits about the width of a storm or how it compared with a tornado here or there. And not just in Oklahoma. He could channel storms all over the country. If there were ever a *Jeopardy!* tournament based solely on tornado trivia, Morgan would have been the grand champion and then some. He seemed to know every detail of every storm. Sometimes, when you met him, it was hard to tell if he was being a book-smart weather obsessive or if he was showing off. Some suspected his endless banter to be rooted in insecurity, a feeling that he had to prove he knew his stuff—because Morgan, even if he sometimes won in the ratings, could never quite emerge from the shadow of the great Gary England. That know-it-all need to display his knowledge was a personality tic that rubbed many people the wrong way—including England, who could barely contain his disdain for his younger rival, a feeling that was abundantly mutual.

Nobody could really say how the bad blood had begun. It was just there, like a severe storm that had exploded out of nowhere. These two men's open hated for each other became a juicy subplot in the regular drama of Oklahoma weather every spring. People compared it to the Red River rivalry—the legendary college football showdown between the OU Sooners and the University of Texas Longhorns. But it was more like a soap opera, where the ever-changing drama of who had besmirched whom was the talk of morning radio. In the early 1990s people flipped back and forth between KWTV, England's station, and KOCO, where Morgan worked, trying to keep up with the various digs the two made at each other—though to catch them you had to listen closely. Both were careful never to actually mention the other's name on air. It was always "the other guys" or "the other station" or, as England once described Morgan, "one *young* television meteorologist at another station." There was never any mystery to anyone in Oklahoma as to whom they were talking about.

One of the earliest skirmishes I remember erupted in 1990, when Gary England unveiled his "First Warning," a tiny graphic map positioned in one corner of the television screen that allowed the station to show in which region a storm watch or warning had been issued without interrupting programming. It was a key invention that was quickly embraced nationwide and is still used today in every city in the country. Almost simultaneously KOCO, under Morgan's direction, unveiled a similar technology called "First Alert," only its version automatically popped up on the screen when the National Weather Service issued a warning or a watch—whereas England's version, KOCO coyly pointed out, had to be manually updated. That the two inventions came out within days of each other immediately prompted heated charges of espionage on both sides. Who had come up with the idea? England ultimately retained the credit. Morgan, who didn't have many defenders, felt he had been unfairly denied a well-earned victory.

When Morgan quit KOCO to work for KFOR in 1993, the weather wars only intensified. The two men battled over who had the best radar and who was the fastest to get out tornado warnings. That year England went after KFOR when one of its storm chasers frantically claimed on air that he had seen a tornado doing major damage in the tiny town of Ryan, Oklahoma. England saw no major storm on the Doppler, and KWTV's chasers, who happened to be parked right near the KFOR staffer, didn't see any damage either. At England's urging, KWTV ran an exposé accusing KFOR of hyping storms for the purpose of ratings, which it deemed "irresponsible."

KFOR fired the storm chaser, but the station and its defenders retaliated by accusing England of racheting up the ratings war by, among other things, dispatching KWTV's helicopter to fly near tornadoes when the value of that kind of coverage was questionable. Ironically, years later all the stations would have storm chasers in helicopters in the air—Oklahoma City is the only city in the country where people regularly take such risks to track storms.

At KOCO, Morgan claimed credit for being the first station in the country to equip its storm chasers with the capability to send still photos of storms over military satellite phones. Early in his tenure at KFOR, he took this one step further, giving his team cameras that transmitted live video of the storms over cell phones. But England refused to give an inch. He bragged that a KWTV anchor had already transmitted video between two Macintosh computers using cellular phone lines. Indeed, he seemed to take delight in even the littlest triumphs over his rival.

In 1995 much of Oklahoma erupted in excitement when it was announced that the film *Twister*, a movie produced by Steven Spielberg about storm chasers, would be filmed in the state. England was tapped as a technical adviser, and he and several other local meteorologists, including Morgan, were cast in bit parts. In the opening scene the film showed archival footage of England from the 1970s declaring a tornado warning, and he and Rick Mitchell, a friendly, easygoing meteorologist who had replaced Morgan at KOCO, were featured later in the film during warning sequences. But Morgan was seen in the film only in passing—briefly glimpsed on a television screen in the opening minutes of the film. Afterward England joked that he had finally claimed the ultimate triumph over Morgan and KFOR: In the movie he had saved Helen Hunt's life.

Even *Twister* couldn't bring an end to the weather wars. At the film's red-carpet premiere in Oklahoma City, which was attended by Helen Hunt and Bill Paxton, Rick Mitchell, who had never met his competitors, watched with a mix of amazement and amusement as England worked the room like a presidential candidate—shaking hands and patting backs. Mitchell got the cold shoulder both from him and from Morgan—though Morgan's wife, Marla, a beautiful and outgoing former rodeo queen, went out of her way to say hello to both of her husband's rivals. England and Morgan were just feet apart at one point, but they didn't speak to each other or to Mitchell, who until then had not fully grasped the intensity of competition in the Oklahoma City weather market.

Generally friendly, without much of a taste for warfare, Mitchell emerged as the calm counterpoint to the weather war between England and Morgan. His drama was mostly with Mother Nature. In 1998 Mitchell was live on air when a tornado took aim at the station. While he remained at the weather desk, a reporter and a cameraman peered out the station's back door, where they saw a funnel cloud furiously rotating over the station. Even as Mitchell warned people to take cover, the reporter looked up at the storm until suddenly he screamed that it was on the ground. Several loud crashes later, the screen went black, but viewers could hear Mitchell's deep baritone, calm and reassuring against the backdrop of people screaming like something out of horror movie. "I have just experienced a tornado. It passed not thirty feet from the station," Mitchell said in a matter-of-fact voice, so calm it sounded as if nothing unusual had happened. "If we're still on, I want to alert everyone:

We're okay." The storm had wrecked the station and left a large dent in the dome covering its Doppler radar—even as it missed KFOR just down the road. After that KOCO saw a bump in the ratings, thanks in part to the no-drama Mitchell.

One of the most fraught battles in the weather wars was over which station had the best radar technology. It was a never-ending arms race that escalated every spring—until 2005, when Morgan finally seemed to win a clear victory by obtaining the equivalent of a nuclear weapon in the war over radars: KFOR built a one-million-watt Doppler radar and erected it just southwest of Moore, right in the path of the May 3, 1999, tornado, where storms seemed to constantly erupt. It was, Morgan bragged, four times stronger than the Doppler radars used by the other television stations in town, giving it a more comprehensive and broader view of weather in the region. The station could now get better reads on storms heading into the state from Texas or Kansas. And KFOR would continue to use its old Doppler as well—making it the only station with two Dopplers at its disposal. Morgan had finally bested KWTV on technology—though England would have none of it.

Despite the fierceness of their rivalry, Morgan and England actually had many things in common. They were both obsessed with the weather and its power—and had been since they were kids. They were both outwardly concerned with warning times and protecting people in the path of the storms. And both found it hard to walk away from their jobs after hours. While Morgan actually did have some hobbies—he liked to build model trains—he was consumed with the coverage and how to make it better. After so many deadly storms, he had a hard time comprehending how some people could choose not to pay attention to the weather or simply ignore warnings. He didn't understand how so many people continued to die. On particularly stormy days Morgan was far more emotional than England. His coverage had an edge, a sky-is-falling sense of drama that the other stations didn't—and though people criticized it, they watched, and KFOR began to win in the ratings.

But Morgan was still in England's shadow—and though he tried to connect with people in a personal way, as England had early in his career, something was off. In 2010 Morgan's wife gave him a tie covered in tiny rhinestones that he began to wear on the worst storm days. KFOR started a Facebook page and a Twitter feed about Morgan's "Bedazzled Severe Weather Tie." Morgan said he wore it in the hope that viewers who caught only a glimpse of him would realize it was a particularly bad-weather day, but it proved to be as incendiary as his coverage. People either loved it or hated it. Though he had helped KFOR be competitive and even win the ratings war, he didn't seem to enjoy himself on air. Even among his colleagues he came off as defensive and testy. He couldn't understand why people railed on him for being dramatic when England, in his view, was far worse. It came down to one crucial difference between the two: While England's folksy manner helped mask his fierce competitive streak, Morgan found it harder to hide his emotions. He couldn't shake the perception that he was a know-it-all, concerned above all with winning the ratings game.

The fierce competition between the two men was in many ways good for viewers. It made storm forecasting in Oklahoma City better than in any other market in the country, and people became more fluent as a result in the science of storms. It was one big reality show that was also a lesson in the weather. Over the years, the stations went to great extremes to stay on top, recruiting talent and poaching the competition.

One of the biggest hires was Jim Gardner, a helicopter pilot originally from Oklahoma who had been working in Los Angeles for decades. He had won an Emmy for his aerial coverage of O. J. Simpson fleeing the police in his white Bronco in 1994. He'd covered earthquakes and mudslides and fires—and had even flown some Hollywood helicopter stunt work on his off time. But nothing compared with the thrill of flying into the storms back in Oklahoma, where Gardner, working for KFOR, seemed to get perilously close to gigantic tornadoes, giving people at home a high-definition view of Mother Nature's fury. On May 3, 1999, Gardner became a household name when he flew for more than an hour tracking one of the strongest tornadoes ever recorded on the face of the earth. But unlike Morgan, who grew distressed at the sight of the storm and the death and damage in its wake, Gardner had nerves of steel and a calm, folksy air that reminded some of Gary England.

It wasn't long before other stations began to try to hire him away. Gardner finally left—defecting to KWTV in 2011. KFOR replaced him with Jon Welsh, an Army National Reserve pilot who had just come back to Oklahoma after flying combat missions in Iraq, finally elevating the weather wars to an actual military level.

But the biggest shake-up was at KOCO. After eighteen years on the air, Rick Mitchell decided to leave Oklahoma City. In July 2012 he was offered a morning weather gig at NBC's affiliate in Dallas with the promise that he would eventually become the station's chief meteorologist. Even though it was a bigger market, Mitchell struggled with the decision. Oklahoma was the big leagues when it came to weather, but in some ways he had hit a wall. Like his competitors, he had dedicated much of his life to trying to protect Oklahomans from the storms, but in doing so he'd made sacrifices of his own. He'd been forced to skip his son's basketball games and his daughter's school events because of his long hours tracking storms. His daughter Zoe, who was just days old when he arrived in Oklahoma City, had just graduated from high school that spring. "I wish you'd been around more," she'd told him as she prepared to head off to college. "You missed a lot of things." It broke Mitchell's heart. He vowed to spend more time with his family. Though Dallas was a bigger city, the job would not be as intense. Dallas stations didn't interrupt programming for hours on end for thunderstorms—though Mitchell knew all it would take was one big tornado to change that. He hoped it wouldn't come.

KOCO promoted one of his deputies, Damon Lane, to succeed him. A native of northern Virginia, just south of Washington, D.C., Lane, who was then thirty-one, had been at the station since 2009, working the morning weather shift and acting as a backup on block-buster storm days. KOCO was only his second job in television. Before that he'd been in Abilene, Texas, where he'd been named the city's favorite television meteorologist for three years in a row. They'd had storms in Texas, but nothing like the ones that hit Oklahoma City. Lane was young, good-looking, and ambitious, but he hadn't always wanted to be on television. He'd grown up fascinated with the weather—an interest his mother, who was a science teacher, encouraged. At first, he thought he'd be an aviation meteorologist—a little like what Gary England had been early in his career—but an internship at a CBS affiliate in Norfolk, Virginia, during his first year of college changed that. Lane was bitten by the television bug, though he still took classes in aviation meteorology just in case landing a job in front of the camera didn't work out.

At KOCO, Lane had been watching and learning from Mitchell, who had become his mentor those last three years, and he'd been watching the other stations too, observing how Gary England and Mike Morgan did their jobs. He pitched himself as someone who could chart that middle ground as Mitchell had—a calm and steady presence who could avoid the drama and could also appeal to new audiences. He had started taking Spanish lessons so that he could give bilingual weather warnings, a not-insignificant attribute in a market that was becoming ever more heavily Hispanic.

At first KOCO had thought of hiring a veteran and had looked to the other stations in town to see if it could lure away someone who had more experience with the high-octane atmosphere of severe weather days. But in the end it saw Lane as someone who could be a future star. Maybe he would attract a younger demographic. Was he ready? He thought he was.

An open question heading into the 2013 storm season was how much longer England would stay on air. KWTV had given him what it called a lifetime contract—though it technically ran through 2016. He was now seventy-three, and while he was still a legend, it was obvious that he no longer felt the same thrill on the job as he once had. It wasn't that the storms excited him less. He still never felt more alive than when he was in the studio trying to protect people from that looming storm. But he didn't like the direction he felt storm coverage was going, how sensationalistic it had become. He felt the storm chasers took too many risks, and on air he often couldn't control himself, lecturing his team to pull back. "You're too close," he would say, sometimes with a hint of exasperation.

In late 2012 KWTV had hired a man it billed as England's

eventual successor: David Payne, Morgan's right-hand man at KFOR, who had made his name as a daredevil storm chaser willing to take more risks than anyone when driving into a storm. If Morgan was dramatic, Payne was even more so, and while he'd signed off on the hire, England didn't much like having one of his rival's protégés in the wings, and he worried about what this decision meant for coverage going forward.

Payne's defection was a major blow to Morgan, but he wasted no time in replacing him, hiring Reed Timmer, a thirty-three-year-old former reality-TV star as the station's marquee storm chaser. The trouble was Timmer barely advertised his connection to KFOR and seemed to spend more time doing his own thing, shooting videos for his Web site and ferrying around other meteorologists, including talent from The Weather Channel. Nonetheless, hiring Timmer gave KFOR access to what was undoubtedly the most famous storm-chasing vehicle in the country: the Dominator, a ten-thousand-pound SUV that Timmer and his storm-chasing team had transformed into a tank. Designed with bulletproof glass and Kevlar and outfitted with the best cameras, the vehicle was built to be driven into tornadoes. Timmer had done so several times for the show *Storm Chasers*, which had aired on the Discovery Channel.

Timmer was an unabashed thrill seeker who often screamed and cursed while driving into the storms. But he also considered himself a scientist. A native of Michigan, he was getting his doctorate in meteorology at OU—a fact Morgan often mentioned on air. The Dominator, which was quickly rebranded as the 4Warn Dominator under Timmer's contract with KFOR, had cannons that could shoot probes into tornadoes to measure winds and other conditions. It was a lot like the fictional "Dorothy" in *Twister*. Nobody really knew what came out of Timmer's research. They only saw his videos of close calls with the storms. Timmer was so popular with the public that few at the station dared to complain publicly, but privately some assailed him as everything that was wrong with weather coverage. There were now thousands of people like him clogging the roads every spring, amateur storm chasers who ignored the risks to get ever closer to the storms.

No one was more unnerved by it all than Gary England—which was perhaps ironic, since he in many ways had started it all. He had been the original renegade, the man who rebelled against the National Weather Service and went to extremes to cover storms in ways that people had never even imagined. But now he worried that the public had come to think of the weather merely as entertainment. He worried that the coverage had desensitized viewers to how truly destructive and deadly the storms could be.

As he pulled into the station that Monday and headed into the studio under an increasingly dark sky, England hoped people would be paying attention that afternoon and that they wouldn't think of this one as a harmless joyride.

At KWTV and its rival stations, the storm chasers were already being dispatched into position. As England walked into his office just off the studio floor, he could hear the whir of Jim Gardner's helicopter powering up from the landing pad out back, preparing to search for the storm. England had deployed his other ground troops, as he called them, hours earlier.

KWTV had seven teams of two chasers—one to drive, the other to operate the camera and satellite equipment. Though they were on the payroll, most of the chasers had day jobs that had nothing to do with the weather, which they put on hold during the spring. They had somehow parlayed their obsession with spotting tornadoes into a paying gig. There was a mechanic, a computer technician, and a retired Oklahoma City cop. Two were husband and wife teams—Val and Amy Castor and Hank and Patty Brown—who had been chasing storms for KWTV for so long they were household names. In both instances, it was the men who got most of the airtime, as they narrated the storms they chased, but England always credited their wives as the brains behind the operation—the ones who mastered all the technology needed to keep their mobile studio up and running while keeping their daredevil husbands somewhat in check.

It was always a gamble where to preposition storm chasers. Though the forecast had suggested the worst storms would be to the south in the direction of Texas, England, acting on a hunch, had kept most of his "StormTrackers," as they were branded on air, closer to Oklahoma City. At KFOR, Mike Morgan sent most of his teams—including Reed Timmer, who was ferrying around a crew from The Weather Channel in his Dominator—south. Helicopter pilot Jon Welsh was hovering around Oklahoma City, keeping an eye out for developments to the west.

At KOCO, Damon Lane and his team were operating at a disadvantage to their rivals. That morning, Lane had waked up to an e-mail from the Federal Aviation Administration saying it was grounding Sky 5, the station's helicopter, for its annual inspection and certification. KOCO had a smaller chase team than the other stations—three teams of two people—and the chopper, their most important tool, was now out of commission for the day. Lane, who already felt like an underdog going up against England and Morgan, was frustrated. Couldn't the FAA have waited until June or a day when the weather was not expected to be so stormy? But he was determined not to stew about things he couldn't change. The FAA had forced his hand. While the forecast still suggested the most volatile storms would erupt to the south, Lane, like England, had a hunch it would be closer to Oklahoma City—maybe right over Moore, his newly adopted hometown, where he lived with his wife, Melissa. Stay close to Oklahoma City, Lane told his troops. It was a gamble, and he hoped it was right.

CHAPTER 7

PLAZA TOWERS ELEMENTARY, MAY 20

The rain began with a handful of big fat drops that cut through the thick, humid air so few and far between it wasn't immediately clear if it was actually raining or just dripping from some invisible gutter that seemed to envelop the entire city of Moore.

As the clock neared 2:00 P.M. at Plaza Towers Elementary on the west side of town, the temperature hovered around eighty degrees—though it felt about ten degrees warmer. The air was so turbid and muggy that standing outside for just a few seconds would make your skin clammy and damp with sweat. May was usually the wettest month of the year in Oklahoma, but even so, the atmosphere was unusually swampy—in sharp contrast to recent days, when the heat had been so dry it had felt like the entire state was caught in the outflow of a blazing-hot furnace.

A loud bang of thunder in the distance rattled Plaza's old windows and then the heavens opened, unleashing a ferocious torrent of precipitation so heavy it was hard to see directly across the street. But just as quickly as the rain had come, it suddenly ceased, as if some unseen hand hovering in the clouds had turned off a spigot. It had been like this for most of the afternoon, as weather fronts began moving through town—some fiercer than others. The sky grew dark, then light again. There was lightning, then a peek of sun, followed by more rain in an unsettling cycle repeated again and again.

Sitting in her office near Plaza's front entrance, her windows facing due north, Amy Simpson, the school's principal, tried to think of it as just another day of thunderstorms. But in the back of her mind she felt a nagging sense of worry. The forecast hadn't improved since she'd left the house that morning—in some ways it had grown more ominous. Alerts kept flashing on her cell phone, punctuated by tense e-mails from the head of Moore Public Schools urging staff citywide to stay alert. Dangerous storms with a strong likelihood of tornadoes, possibly hitting around school dismissal time, the forecast said. That was soon. Classes were scheduled to end at 4:00 P.M.—a little over two hours away. "Keep calm, watch for valid information and pray," one of the e-mails from the head office read. "It is May in Oklahoma. We can do this."

The tone of the message worried Simpson. Was it really going to be that bad? Whatever was to happen, she knew the school was as ready as it could be. Like most schools in Oklahoma—and most homes, surprisingly—Plaza didn't have a storm shelter. So students and teachers had been instructed to go to what were believed to be the safest spots in the building: the interior hallways. It was where kids for generations had been taught to go when the weather turned bad. Under her supervision Plaza's five hundred students and fifty staff members had regularly participated in tornado drills, faithfully practicing their duck-and-cover positions in the school's hallways. Only a few weeks earlier they'd had a drill, a refresher before storm season officially began. The sirens had wailed a few times, but Simpson had never known a tornado to actually hit during school hours—not when she was a kid going to class in Moore and not in her nearly twenty years as an educator in her hometown. As a rumble of thunder shook the building, Simpson hoped that this wouldn't be a first. The idea of a tornado hitting so early in the day seemed so far-fetched that she was more worried about things she thought actually would happen: heavy rains, high winds, and bruising chunks of hail. There were plenty of latchkey kids at Plaza, and there was no way she could send them home in conditions like that, however close they lived. But her mind kept returning to the forecast. Possible tornadoes hitting around dismissal time. Could it really happen?

Simpson wasn't the only one at Plaza Towers who was worried. Virtually everybody in the building had come to school that morning having listened to the ominous forecast, and while they tried to go on with their day, many simply couldn't. They looked outside at the sky and worried. What was coming? Would it hit before school let out? Some of the teachers checked the weather radar on their iPads or pulled up the live streams of the local television stations on their iPhones—discreetly so as not to scare the kids. By then many of the Oklahoma City stations had gone to uninterrupted coverage. Outside in the halls the teachers told their colleagues in hushed voices what they were seeing. Just as predicted, a line of storms was developing toward the west; if they blew up, as the weather forecasters were anticipating, Moore would be right in the bull's-eye of the storm.

Jennifer Doan, a third-grade teacher, had woken up with an almost oppressive feeling that something bad was going to happen. The day before, a tornado had touched the ground not far from her house in Edmond, and with the forecast predicting even more dangerous storms that Monday, she worried about driving home after school in the middle of heavy rain and whatever else the weather would bring. But there was something deeper, something she couldn't quite put her finger on, that was nagging at her. As she had prepared to leave the house that morning just after sunrise, she'd leaned over and kissed her fiancé, Nyle, who was still in bed. "I'm worried," she had told him. "I don't have a good feeling." Still drowsy, he'd told her to call in sick. But she couldn't. It was the last week of school, she'd said, she couldn't just skip work.

Thirty miles away, Erin Baxter, a twenty-seven-year-old kindergarten teacher, was experiencing a similar feeling of dread as she sat in her kitchen in Norman and watched the forecast before heading in to work. She had grown up in south Oklahoma City and, like Simpson, had gone to school in Moore her entire life. She had been in junior high when the May 3, 1999, tornado had hit, and fourteen years later not one storm had passed that hadn't made her think back to that day. The tornado had missed her house by a mile or so, but one of her friends had been seriously injured and she could still remember how scary the sky had been, that feeling that some uncontrollable monster was preying on her helpless city. While she loved a bout of really stormy weather, as most Oklahomans do, she had never forgotten how mean and unsparing a nasty storm could be. On television she heard a forecaster repeat the warning that some of the more dangerous storms could develop in the afternoon, possibly as early as 3:00 P.M. Parents and schools should be alert, he said. As she switched the television off, Baxter closed her eyes and said a little prayer. *Please, God,* she thought. *If there are storms, please let them be a little later.*

At school the teachers put on brave faces for the kids, but Simpson could see they were worried. As she walked the halls, she saw her staff joking and laughing with the students, who were beside themselves knowing summer vacation was only days away. But there was something in their eyes, something in the way they talked. Simpson knew them well enough to know they were on edge. While she was nervous too, she was determined to stay focused and positive. She knew that, as head of school, people looked to her to see how she was reacting and handling things, and she knew she had to keep it together, no matter what happened.

Simpson hadn't had time to obsessively check the radar, which was probably a good thing. She was simply too busy, and she left it up to her office assistant, Penny, who was so vigilant in her task that her colleagues referred to her as Plaza's "radar watcher." If a bad storm was coming, Simpson knew Penny would come running.

For Simpson that Monday was one of the most hectic days of the year, but it was also a day she had been looking forward to for weeks. That morning she had overseen the year-end award ceremonies for the first- and second-grade classes and prepared for others later in the week. Nothing made her job more fulfilling than seeing her students happy and confident in what they had accomplished. She had fretted over every detail of the ceremonies, spending most of Sunday afternoon, her day off, helping the teachers set up the ceremonies and organize the individual awards to honor students who had excelled in subjects like math or spelling. The end-of-the-year awards were a big deal at any school, but Simpson considered them to be especially important at Plaza, a school that had gone through a few tough years.

Built in 1966, Plaza Towers was one of the oldest elementary schools in Moore, opened just four years after Moore officially became a city. Its flat, one-story building was located on SW Eleventh Street, a few blocks east of the city line between Oklahoma City and Moore, right in the center of what had used to be one of the city's most thriving neighborhoods. But over the years, as Moore had expanded, people had moved to newer parts of town, and the neighborhood had gone from being one of the city's more affluent to being one of its poorest. Still, Plaza had been regarded as one of the city's top elementary schools, with a roster of active parents who valued education as much as the teachers did. The students had consistently scored high on state education tests, buoyed by parents who spent their evenings reading with the kids or helping them study.

But when a brand-new elementary school had opened a few miles away in 2010, many of Plaza's most active families had transferred—and several of the teachers had followed. Plaza had gone from being one of the better schools in the district to being one that was considered to be struggling. Some of the parents worked multiple jobs trying to make ends meet, and many of the kids were left to fend for themselves. It had been up to the teachers to fill that absence, encouraging them to read and study in their spare time—even if no one at home was nagging them to do so. Though morale had been low among the staff, the teachers who had stayed behind had thought of themselves as survivors put there by God to help kids who truly needed them.

And slowly Plaza had started to build itself back up—largely thanks to Simpson, an assistant principal who had been promoted to the top job in 2010. She had simply refused to give up on her school or her students, even if the odds sometimes felt stacked against them.

Simpson had not always known she wanted to be an educator. Her father sold NAPA auto parts, and her mother was an administrative assistant at an oil-services company. When she graduated from

Moore High School and went on to the University of Oklahoma, she hadn't decided what she would do with her life. It wasn't until her sophomore year of college that she realized she wanted to be a teacher, though the instinct had always been there. Back in middle school and into high school, Simpson, who was a good student, often found herself silently critiquing her instructors. She watched how they delivered their lesson plans and considered what she would have done differently. She especially cringed at teachers who were unkind and impatient with students who were struggling. Only years later did she realize that this was an early sign of her calling in education.

She never worked anywhere but in Moore. She did her student teaching in her hometown, and when she graduated from OU, she landed a permanent job with the school system, teaching third and sixth grades for almost ten years. She got a master's degree after that and moved into administration, working as an assistant principal at three different elementary schools, including Plaza, over the next five years. Every year Simpson wondered if it was her turn to be promoted to head principal, and when she wasn't, she wondered why she had been overlooked. Her reviews were good, and she had the experience. "You're itching for the big chair," one of the principals she worked for told her, "but you've gotta be careful: You might not want the big chair once you've got it."

But Simpson wanted it, even if it wasn't easy. Standing five foot three, with long blond hair and an easy smile, she was often compared to Grace Kelly by her colleagues at Plaza, who saw a bit of the reserved Hitchcock blonde in her demeanor. She was gentle and soft-spoken and kind, but inside there was a fiery grit, a toughness. She was a fighter, a rock when others would have been inclined to cave. She hadn't fully known how tough she really was until she was promoted to the top job at Plaza. In some ways it was the last job anybody would have wanted: taking over a struggling school. But Simpson refused to give up on Plaza, even if she and her teachers often struggled to get parents to understand how important early education was to their kids and be invested in it. She believed in the importance of personal touch, in making sure people knew they were loved and important. And though she had five hundred students, Simpson knew almost every one of them by name—and their parents too, when she saw them. She saw the award ceremonies not only as a way of celebrating the kids and encouraging them but also as a chance to engage their parents and to show them why education was important.

In her mind the little things mattered. She was a firm believer in routine, and that morning she'd started off the school day as she always did—gathering her students in the cafeteria for their daily "Rise and Shine" assembly, where they said the Pledge of Allegiance and recited Plaza's school creed:

> I am a proud Plaza Tower Panther.
> I am a capable and dependable student,
> Full of possibilities and potential.
> I choose to think before I act, using good judgment.
> I accept the responsibilities for my actions.
> I do not have the right to interfere with the learning or
> well-being of others.
> My destiny is in my hands.
> I am one in a million and proud of it.
> I am a proud Plaza Tower Panther, yeah!

Simpson couldn't help but smile as she listened to her kids in their tiny singsong voices passionately chanting their special creed.

She knew most didn't know what it all meant, what destiny and potential were, but she believed in the power of words and that speaking things made them happen. Her students *were* one in a million. They *were* full of potential. She knew all of their sweet faces and loved them nearly as much as she did her own kids. She knew her teachers felt much as she did. What they wouldn't do for them! Glancing toward the windows, Simpson saw that it had started to rain.

That morning had been a blur of love and hugs. Simpson had dressed up for the awards—wearing a nice dress and a pair of open-toed sandals with kitten heels. She'd cheered and clapped for the first and second graders as enthusiastically if they were her own, and then she'd hugged and joked with the parents who had shown up, making them feel important too. They were all partners, after all, in building up these tiny little humans.

Before lunch Simpson had helped the sixth graders practice for Recognition Night, which was essentially their graduation ceremony before heading off the next fall to junior high. It was scheduled for Tuesday night at the school, and Simpson had weeks ago come up with what she considered to be the perfect song to play as they marched down the aisle to accept their certificates marking yet another step in the journey toward adulthood. She had picked "Baby I'm a Star" by Prince, from the *Purple Rain* soundtrack, a mainstay from her own childhood in Moore. It was fast and upbeat, and as the kids practiced marching down the aisle, they strutted like little peacocks, happy and blissful. Simpson found herself grinning and laughing with them, her eyes a little moist. She hoped that all of their days would be as happy as this. Outside the sun peeked through the clouds. Maybe the storms would hold off, she thought. Maybe it wouldn't be as bad as they were saying.

But at 2:00 P.M., as she sat in her office awaiting the arrival of a candidate who was interviewing for a teaching position set to open in the fall, Simpson looked out at the dark sky and started to worry. Down the hall the kids were starting to get antsy too. In Baxter's kindergarten class they were getting scared and nervous at the sounds of the rumbling thunder. To soothe them the teacher took out paper and crayons and began drawing clouds and the sun as she talked to them about the weather and how it could be stormy at times. And as they worked, she began to notice kids from other classes walking down the hall toward the front office. It kept happening, dozens of kids were walking by.

Around 2:30 P.M. Simpson was wrapping up her interview when she heard a series of ominous beeps—some from cell phones and one from a weather radio near the front desk. There was quick knock at her door and as it opened, her assistant, Penny, stuck her head in. Her eyes were as wide as saucers, and Simpson knew instantly that something was wrong. "There's a lot of parents out here," Penny told her. "Okay, how many?" Simpson said, trying to read the clues on her staffer's face to see what was being left unsaid. "More than usual," Penny replied, alarm in her voice and all over her face.

Simpson quickly wrapped up the interview. It wasn't unusual for parents to pick up their kids early on storm days, but when she emerged into the main lobby of the front office, she walked into chaos. She found a long line of terrified adults—too many to count—looking out the windows and checking their phones as they waited to sign out their children. The way it usually worked was that parents would sign a form, and then their kids would be called or escorted to the office, but Simpson knew instantly it wouldn't work that way today. She had never seen a group of people who looked more anxious or afraid. Fear seemed to be wafting off them, and

Simpson raised her voice and told the parents that they could walk back toward the classrooms and pick up their kids and stop back by the office on the way out to confirm they had their child. It was hardly usual procedure, but there were no strangers in the room. Simpson knew almost all of their names and faces—though she'd never seen them this agitated. Still, she didn't ask what was happening. Between the look on Penny's face and the parents, she knew something bad was coming.

Outside the rain began to pour in sheets, and the wind howled. Giant pieces of hail began to pelt the building—banging off the skylights so hard that Simpson worried the glass might shatter. Then, as it had earlier in the day, the wind briefly let up. It was then Simpson heard a sound she had dreaded—a sound she couldn't believe she was actually hearing. It was 2:40 P.M. and the tornado sirens in Moore started to wail. Around the room her staff began to look panicked and the parents grew even more terrified, running out of the office toward their kids' classrooms.

Without missing a beat, Simpson calmly walked to the school intercom, which hung on the wall closest to her office door. "Get into your places," she ordered. She was calm and firm—just as she knew she needed to be. She barely recognized the sound of her own voice. Something had taken over.

CHAPTER 8

2:45 P.M., MAY 20

It began as nothing more than a wispy little funnel, dancing shyly between the clouds and the ground in the countryside just north of Newcastle, a tiny farming town southwest of Moore. From certain angles it looked like nature's version of a needle on a record player, innocently dropping to the ground before gently lifting right back up, as if guided by some unseen force looking for that one perfect song on a vinyl LP.

This dance has long captivated generations of weather-obsessed Oklahomans: the moment when something so unearthly suddenly swirls to life in the wide-open prairie sky, giving rise to a feeling of childlike wonder but also a sobering sense of dread. While some storms are quick to erupt, others, like this one, seem to draw out the mystery—flirting with the ground but never quite touching, as if deliberately prolonging the tension.

Over the years, in the full bloom of modern-day weather coverage, this scene of true uncertainty—would the storm actually produce a tornado?—had transformed one of the few genuinely suspenseful moments of life in this part of the country into something even more dramatic. Through the lens of television, the mystery had become a breathless, edge-of-your-seat roller-coaster ride. The anxiety—and to some the thrill—of not really knowing what the weather would do was the prime attraction of the increasingly tense reality show of storm season in Oklahoma. People watched not just because they were scared for their lives but also because they couldn't tear their eyes away from the undeniably riveting theater of nature's fury.

That Monday, in a state still jittery from the twisters that had just swept through, was no exception. Shortly before 3:00 P.M., the point in the afternoon when local television would normally be airing the final climactic moments of the daytime soaps, viewers were instead tuned in to a drama of another kind unfolding in the skies south of Oklahoma City, where it now appeared that the storm near Newcastle might drop a tornado at any second.

The unscripted thriller had been anticipated for hours, even days. And though it was developing just as the National Weather Service had warned it might, there was an air of almost stunned disbelief even among those who had put the forecasts together. What they were seeing was the worst-case scenario, a nightmare thunderhead that was growing in size and strength by the second. A storm that, if it kept its current track, was headed right toward Moore.

In a horrifying cosmic unity, many of those tracking the storm—the scientists down in Norman, the Oklahoma City television weathermen at their rival studios, the town officials at Moore's City Hall and many of the people in the storm's path—had the same terrifying sense of déjà vu as they thought back to the deadly tornado that had come along this very same path fourteen years earlier. In so many ways it seemed like May 3, 1999, all over again—except this storm was gathering force hours earlier, when many kids were still in school, and the farmland that had been ravaged back then was now occupied by hundreds of new homes in a booming suburb that had dramatically increased in size. Many more people were at risk.

Twenty-five miles to the north Gary England was on air in the chaos of KWTV's studio, anxiously toggling among the increasingly ominous images beamed back by his team of storm chasers, who were themselves growing more and more panicked at what they were seeing. The radar showed the storm quickly intensifying, with winds upward of 200 miles per hour feeding into the updraft, suggesting a dangerous tornado was imminent.

On air England steeled himself to appear calm and authoritative, believing that he better served the public by remaining focused and telling them clearly where the storm was heading. He wanted to be the steady hand that people for decades had come to rely on in moments of crisis like this. But inside he felt a mix of dread and anxiety over what this storm might do. It wasn't just the fear of experiencing May 3 all over again—though, like others, he couldn't stop thinking back to that terrible day, a memory that always seemed to come up when storms erupted to the west of the city. It was more than that. Looking at the landscape, at all those new buildings in south Oklahoma City and Moore that showed up as place markers on the radar, he worried that this storm could be so much worse because there was simply so much more to destroy. As he glanced at a live image of the storm, zeroing in on the point where the funnel seemed to be flitting down once again, that morbid question that always haunted him in storm season was again dancing in his head: How many people were going to die?

By then the drama playing out west of Moore had gone national. The Weather Channel and twenty-four-hour cable news networks had picked up the live feeds of the Oklahoma City television stations and added their own breathless commentary. England and his counterparts at KFOR and KOCO had at this point been on air for almost two hours—since around 1:00 P.M., well before the first storms erupted near the Texas border. While the sky was hazy from the thick humidity, the sun was still shining in and around Oklahoma City when the stations broke into regular programming. But with the dry line inching its way into the central part of the state from the west and threatening to collide with the thick coat of moisture hanging over Oklahoma City like a fog, the atmosphere was so unstable it was like a ticking time bomb. England now thought the worst could happen at any second and that it would escalate quickly from there.

Within a half hour the bad weather began to roll in, pounding the Oklahoma City area with high winds, heavy rain, and, in some spots, hailstones the size of baseballs. On air the stations alternated between shots of sinister-looking clouds and increasingly vivid Doppler radar imagery of storms that appeared to be exploding like fireworks. The radar, which uses different colors to rate a storm's intensity, produced vivid Technicolor images that looked like something you'd see peering through an old-fashioned kaleidoscope. The weather fronts were going from green to yellow to orange to crimson, a color used only for the most dangerous storms, almost as quickly as the radar could update.

But as bad as these storms were, it was a tiny blip of a cloud that suddenly popped up in the sky a few minutes before 2:00 P.M. about 30 miles southwest of Moore that sent the forecasters into genuine panic. At KFOR Mike Morgan, who had been a nervous wreck all day, was on air wearing his trademark severe-weather sparkly tie—this one in tones of blue and silver—when he first saw the telltale signs of a tornado on the radar just north of a town called Chickasha. It was a speck of a cloud that seemed to "blow up out of the clear blue sky," as he put it. Dashing off camera, Morgan frantically grabbed his iPhone to text his cavalry of storm chasers and redeploy them in that direction. As he did so, he watched the cloud begin to spin like a top. It was something he had rarely seen in all of his decades obsessing about the weather, and his heart began to race.

Down the block at the KOCO studios, Damon Lane was seeing the same thing and feeling a similar sense of alarm. In a period of about twenty minutes, he watched as the cloud, which continued to rotate, quickly erupted into a full-fledged thunderstorm, picking up wind and speed as it headed toward south Oklahoma City and Moore. But then, in the farmland north of Newcastle, the storm suddenly slowed down, even as it began to rotate ever more furiously and grow increasingly dark and ominous in the western sky. It was like a bull that had stopped to build up its strength before charging at its target. And as it did so, that slender funnel began to tease—but not touch—the land below, slyly hinting at what was to come.

Though he maintained his cool on air, Lane was panicked. What was happening was more than just a storm. It was suddenly very personal. Moore was his home, and if the storm moved due east, it would come very close to hitting his house on the eastern side of town. A little while earlier, when it had become clear that the storm might be aiming toward Moore, he had texted his wife Melissa, who was at work at a nonprofit near downtown Oklahoma City, and suggested she head home early to get into the shelter with their two dogs, Skyler and Binx, who were in the backyard and would be helpless against the storm. Just after the tornado sirens began to wail in Moore at 2:40 P.M., she had texted him to say she was on the road, and though Lane knew she had time—it was usually just a fifteen- or twenty-minute drive at most from her office to Moore—he began to worry that she was cutting it too close. Should he tell her to turn around and drive back to safety? But if he did, what would happen to his dogs?

By then every excruciating moment of the storm's terrible buildup was playing out via live camera feeds from an army of chasers on the ground and in the sky who were tracking the incipient tornado as a hunter stalks its prey. As the funnel appeared and disappeared again and again, the event began to take on the tense air of a standoff between the monster in the clouds and the adrenaline-pumped chasers below, who started to sound a little like overexcited sportscasters calling a play-by-play. "Here it comes! Here it comes!" KWTV's David Payne frantically yelled at one point from his position along 149th Street, east of the storm, as the funnel slowly began to descend toward the ground. "Wow, guys, look at the spin! Look at the spin!" he cried, yelling into his phone so intensely that his voice became almost distorted on air. Within seconds the would-be tornado was gone again, swallowed back up into the towering black wall of cloud that, for people watching at home, now took up the entire television screen.

In some ways, what was happening was a moment of triumph for weather coverage, the full display of how far journalism, technology, and science had come in dealing with the deadly storms that had routinely killed people with little warning as recently as twenty years ago. Now, with their streaming video from the field and the pinpoint precision of advanced Doppler radar, Oklahoma's weather media had become an army of first responders, giving people in the storm's path an unprecedented level of advance notice that saved untold numbers of lives.

But for England, who had devoted so much of his life to trying to keep the public safe from storms like this, it was hard to feel anything but concern. In his gut he had known almost from the moment he saw that tiny cloud spinning in the air near Chickasha that it was going to be the storm everyone had been fearing all day. Though he was not an idealist, part of him privately hoped for that rare miracle. Maybe the storm, as bad as it looked, wouldn't fully develop; maybe it would go away as quickly as it had come. He knew it was wishful thinking, but it wasn't unheard of. There had been plenty of instances over the years of the Doppler picking up every ominous sign that a tornado was coming—the strong winds, the intense circulation, and that familiar hook shape that develops on the radar when the rain is carried into the updraft of a rotating storm. But sometimes, in the rarest of cases, a tornado never actually touched the ground. England was always thankful for the reprieve—though viewers didn't often agree. They made their displeasure known in phone calls and angry e-mails, complaining that he'd interrupted their television shows for nothing. What he would give for a few angry e-mails to make this monster go away.

He was brought back from his reverie by a commotion in the studio. "Guys, we have a tornado here," Jim Gardner, the station's helicopter pilot, called out over the radio from his position about a mile south of the storm—though his bird's-eye view made him seem so much closer. It was 2:55 P.M., fifteen minutes after the tornado sirens had gone off in south Oklahoma City and Moore and almost forty-five minutes since the National Weather Service and local TV stations had begun warning people in the storm's path that it could turn deadly. A slender gray vortex had finally emerged from the clouds, and at 2:56 P.M., according to the National Weather Service, it was officially on the ground. As seen from Gardner's helicopter, which was flying at eye level to the storm, the tornado had dropped to the ground so gracefully, so casually, that it almost belied the true horror of the moment. A nightmare storm, getting stronger by the second, was now heading directly for Moore.

As the world watched, it suddenly morphed into a hulking beast devouring everything in its path, which at that moment wasn't much beyond trees and the occasional farm. The twister initially took the form of a towering gray stovepipe. It began to slice through electrical wires as easily as a marathon runner tearing through ribbons at the finish line. And as it did so, bright flashes lit up the funnel at its base, giving it an effect so horrifying it looked like something Hollywood might have dreamed up. But this wasn't computer-generated imagery. Within seconds the tornado had swelled into a raging monster at least half a mile wide and growing, its rotation and winds so violent that it began to drag the entire cloud structure around it to the ground. On air England, who tried to remain calm, began to read off the streets in the path of the storm, and as he did so, a massive explosion of something briefly illuminated the demonic funnel. "My god," England cried out, the horror in his voice palpable, "get below ground if at all possible!"

At the National Weather Service in Norman, about 15 miles to the southeast of the storm, forecasters in the second-floor command center decided to issue the most dire warning possible: a "tornado emergency" for south Oklahoma City and Moore. It was an alert reserved for only the most devastating storms, the ones that are 100 percent guaranteed to hit, when people's lives are determined to be at most risk. To those who didn't know better, the room seemed unusually calm, a stark contrast to the increasingly frantic television coverage that was playing on the giant screens mounted at the front of the room.

But at the workstations those who had been trained to remain cool under pressure were visibly tense. The potentially deadly tornado they had been warning people about all day had exploded to life right in their backyard, not far from their homes and those of friends and family. This was their city under attack. Rick Smith, who had been manning the agency's social-media feed all day, began to send out urgent messages to the public, knowing that even with the saturation coverage and all the warnings, not everybody listened when advised to take cover. "This is as serious as it gets," Smith wrote on the organization's Twitter feed. "Please seek shelter now!"

Heading north on Interstate 44 in Newcastle, just south of the Oklahoma City line, Chance Coldiron, a storm chaser for KOCO, was closer than anyone to the tornado. He was driving almost right beside it, about half a mile away, as it began to tear through the farmland on its way toward Moore. Before his eyes it went from being a towering vortex, rising more than a thousand feet in the air, to a monstrous black cloud of death that seemed to swallow the entire western sky. As Coldiron and his chasing partner, Justin Cox, slowed to allow the twister to cross the highway directly in front of them, they stared in near silence at a storm that was more violent than anything they had ever seen before. It was like Armageddon come alive, a vast, churning maul of death shrouded in swirling debris. As they watched, the tornado blew apart an old section of the Interstate 44 bridge, crossing the North Canadian River, which divided Newcastle and Oklahoma City. Giant uprooted trees were being tossed around like tiny splinters, and they could see roofs from destroyed houses and random scraps of metal that looked no larger than Skittles as they hovered in the air around the tornado. Suddenly Coldiron cried out in shock. "Oh, those are cars! Oh my gosh, those are cars!" he screamed.

At KFOR, Morgan was growing more panicked by the second as he watched the tornado crossing into what was now officially Oklahoma City. The funnel was so shrouded in debris he could barely see it, and it hadn't even hit a heavily populated area yet. Morgan could not imagine how anyone watching the coverage could fail to get how bad the storm was, but he knew from past tornadoes that there were always people who didn't take shelter or waited until it was simply too late. The thought terrified him, but it also made him angry that people could be so careless with their lives. Morgan knew all too well what people said about him, that he was sometimes too dramatic on air, that he scared his viewers unnecessarily. But at this moment, as he looked at the increasingly ferocious storm, he didn't care. And so, with the air of a frustrated fire-and-brimstone preacher trying to save souls from the very brink of hell, he began to plead with his viewers, begging them to realize how serious the storm was, that another unmerciful tornado was coming for Moore and no one was safe. They needed to do whatever it would take to save their lives and those of people they cared about.

While England and Lane had been urging people to get below ground, Morgan cast the situation in even starker terms. It wouldn't be enough, he said, to go to an interior closet or bathroom—long the method of choice for many Oklahomans. Most homes weren't built with basements; the ground was damp and sandy, and basement rooms often leaked, making their upkeep too costly. And even though Moore had been hit several times before, many people didn't have exterior storm shelters or safe rooms, and if they did, some were too scared to use them—worried that debris could trap them inside. Now Morgan pleaded with his viewers to use their underground shelters, telling them it was the only way they could be sure to survive what was coming at them. "If you can't get below ground, get out of its way," Morgan declared, with mounting alarm in his voice. "You never want to say it, but we're going to say it right now: This is May 3 all over again as far as the intensity of this tornado, where it is heading. Something has to change fast, or it's going to be very close to a May 3 event."

Less than ten minutes had passed since the tornado hit the ground. As it began to churn its way through a mostly rural neighborhood south of 149th Street in Oklahoma City, it swelled in size to nearly a mile wide, though it looked much larger. The debris around it was so thick it reminded some of the storms that hit during the Dust Bowl, the horrifying "black blizzards" that crawled along the landscape devouring everything in their path.

Six miles across town, Steve Eddy, Moore's city manager, was on the first floor of City Hall in the emergency command center watching the nightmare unfold on television. Outside the sirens were wailing—a sound that never failed to send chills down his spine, no matter how often he'd heard them growing up. Eddy was known to be unflappable, but as he heard Morgan liken the storm to May 3, his heart sank. Perhaps more than anybody Eddy knew the horror of what that meant. He had been on the front lines of that disaster and remembered vividly how overwhelming, how exceedingly awful it had been. Standing there watching another tornado approach, his mind was busy thinking of everything that would need to be done the second the storm lifted—deploying the police and emergency workers to the hard-hit neighborhoods, making official requests for state and federal support, implementing a disaster plan that was now hauntingly familiar because they'd been through this deadly scenario so many times before.

Eddy knew he didn't have time to dwell on questions he didn't have the answers to, that he needed to remain focused for the people of his city, who had already been through so much. But for a moment he couldn't help himself. Why was this happening to Moore again? What was it that made his city so vulnerable, so unlucky? On television he caught an up-close glimpse of that massive black cloud grinding its way toward the western part of his city, beamed out by one of the storm trackers frantically driving away from it. The storm was now less than 3 miles from the Moore city line and showed no signs of lifting. *Oh shit,* Eddy thought to himself.

CHAPTER 9

3:00 P.M., MAY 20

Anthony Connel left work early to beat the storm, but as he found himself stuck in heavy traffic heading south on Interstate 44, he wondered if he'd made the right decision. At fifty-one Connel was a lifelong Oklahoman. He had long since grown used to the volatile springtime weather, though he'd had more close encounters than he would have liked. Over the years, he and his wife, Virginia, a math teacher at Southmoore High School in Moore, had watched as threatening storms had passed by—including one or two that produced funnel clouds—but it wasn't something he worried much about. The May 3 storm barely missed his home on May Avenue just south of 149th Street, but in the end they had always been spared.

Suddenly, a little under 2 miles from his home, with the May Avenue exit finally in sight, traffic ground to a dead stop. Frustrated and stuck, Connel sat in his truck and listened as the radio broadcast frantic reports about the tornado that had hit the ground near Newcastle, just southwest of his house. He began to wonder if his luck had finally run out. Looking across the wide-open land to the east, he could make out his neighborhood in the distance—a somewhat rural community where you had close neighbors but also enough acreage to raise horses or other livestock. He and his wife had two miniature donkeys named Gizmo and Lil Bit, furry companions they loved as much as one could love a pet. The donkeys lived in his backyard, right behind the garage where he'd spent years painstakingly restoring a cherry red 1970 Plymouth Road Runner, a car for which they didn't even make parts anymore. Except for the occasional weekend spin or car show, it sat in his garage with a giant stuffed Wile E. Coyote (from Looney Tunes) in the backseat, a nod to the car's name. He'd parked the car there to keep it safe from the elements, but now it was at risk, along with everything else he and his wife owned.

Right behind his house was a storm shelter, which he left unlocked during most of the spring in case of days like this. His wife was still at work—he'd called her to tell her he was heading home—but he knew some of his neighbors, who didn't have underground safe spots of their own, were probably already crouched inside. He hoped they would be safe.

Suddenly he saw it in the distance: an angry, swirling monster cloud that was so huge and wide it didn't even look like a regular tornado. It seemed to take up the entire sky as it passed over the highway about a mile ahead of him. It was moving in a slow diagonal to the northeast, and unless it suddenly changed direction, his house was in its bull's-eye. All Connel could do was watch. He felt sick to his stomach as he watched the massive black cloud devour everything in its path—trees, cars, and towering electrical transformers that looked like robots standing high above the prairie. They had once seemed strong enough to withstand anything, but now they flashed in anger as they were bent and ripped apart by the tornado's hellish winds. Connel had never felt so helpless in his life as he did now. He watched the black monster drawing closer and closer to his neighborhood until suddenly he couldn't see his house anymore. It was engulfed by the tornado.

Six miles to the east, along SE Fourth Street in Moore, Robert Romines, the soon-to-be superintendent of Moore Public Schools, had gathered with his colleagues at the administration building to watch the tornado on television. Outside the storm sirens were wailing, but nobody moved an inch. The worst-case scenario that had seemed so unimaginable hours earlier was actually happening: A tornado was on the ground, and more than a dozen of their thirty-two schools were close to or within its projected path. Of these, only two had storm shelters: Westmoore High School and Kelley Elementary, which had taken direct hits from the 1999 tornado and had been rebuilt with concrete safe rooms able to shelter hundreds of people.

Now, at dozens of schools across the district, the children who hadn't been checked out by their parents were crouching and taking cover in interior hallways the way they had practiced so many times before. But nobody had ever dreamed they would actually have to take cover for real—not even Romines, who had practiced the same drills when he was kid growing up in Moore. It was simply unheard of for tornadoes to hit so early in the day. An untold number of the district's 23,000 kids were now at risk and Romines, a teddy bear of a man who wore his heart on his sleeve, was almost physically sick with worry—not just as an educator but also as a parent. His youngest daughter, Avery, was at school at Wayland Bonds Elementary on May Avenue just north of 149th Street, right in the tornado's path, and he knew the school had no shelter.

Suddenly Susie Pierce, Romines's boss, who was just days away from retiring as superintendent, rushed down the hall, worry written all over her face. She had just gotten off the phone with Michelle McNear, the principal at Wayland Bonds, who had told her she could see the storm in the distance. McNear, a Moore native who had known Romines since they were kids, told Pierce to tell him that she was with his daughter. "Tell Romines it's going to be okay," McNear said.

But almost as soon as the words were out of her mouth, the power went out, and McNear could see the tornado, so terrifyingly close entire trees were swirling in the air around it. "It's in our backyard," she told Pierce, her words steady but fear in her voice. It looked like the school was going to take a direct hit. And then the connection went dead.

As Pierce relayed the phone call, fear shot through Romines's heart and he suddenly knew he couldn't just sit there anymore. "I'm sorry," he said, his voice choking, "but I have to go. I have to get over there." He jumped to his feet and ran out of the room; on his heels was Jeff Horn, the school district's operations manager, who told him he would come with him. As the two ran outside to one of the district's official trucks, the sirens were blaring and the wind was picking up. Looking to the west, Romines could see the dark cloud in the distance. *Go away*, he thought, *please just go away*.

Live on KOCO, Damon Lane was trying to remain calm as he looked at a terrifying image of the dark twister as it headed down 149th Street, a road he had driven so many times since he had moved to Oklahoma in 2009. The image he was looking at came from two of the station's best storm chasers—Danielle Dozier and

Chris Lee, a photojournalist who had pursued hundreds of storms over the years for KOCO. Dozier, a meteorologist who had worked with Lane since they were both on air in Abilene, Texas, was, like Lee, a calm presence in the field, but as they sat just east of the storm, Lane could hear the anxiety in their voices. As Dozier and Lee took turns describing what they were seeing and where the storm seemed to be headed, viewers at home could hear the deafening roar of the tornado, which was now so large their live video simply looked like a black screen.

Lane thought of his wife, Melissa, who should have been home by now. He had texted her a few minutes earlier, warning her to take shelter immediately, and she hadn't yet written back. It made him nervous, but he willed himself to remain focused. He had a job to do. On camera Lane began to tick off all the streets in the path of the storm and to call out by name the stores and shops and restaurants along the way, to give viewers a more specific sense of where the storm was going. It was what every television meteorologist in Tornado Alley had learned to do over the years, calling out neighborhood landmarks to drill into people how close the storm really was to them. It was more effective than simply relying on the map. But it only made Lane think of Melissa more. She didn't pay much attention to street names either. When she'd moved to Moore from Dallas the previous fall after they'd gotten married, he'd tried to tell her which streets to take to get from their house to Target, but in the end he'd just had to name the stores along the way: Make a left at the 7-Eleven; turn right after the Sonic; and it was just past the Starbucks on the left.

Now Lane listed all the businesses he could think of along and near 149th Street, which turned into Nineteenth Street as it crossed from Oklahoma City into Moore, just as he had with his wife. Dick's Sporting Goods, Walmart, the Warren Theatres, Home Depot, the

Moore Athletic Club, "A Buffalo Wild Wings on the westhand side there," he said. He could picture that area so vividly in his head. These weren't just names on the map: They were the stores where he shopped, the places he went. "We are not trying to scare you," Lane told his viewers, an edge in his voice, "but this is a very large tornado, and we want you to understand the tone we are using right now as a very serious situation, a life-threatening situation. . . . You need to take our warnings very seriously." As he said this, trying to remain composed, Lane kept thinking of his wife. Where was she? Would she beat the storm?

The tornado traveled almost due east along 149th Street and had no mercy for any structure standing in its path. Many of the homes and farms along the road were literally wiped off their foundations in seconds as it passed. Behind one of the houses, Dan Garland was crammed into a tiny shelter with his wife and eight other neighbors, holding the door shut against the most intense winds he had ever experienced in his life. Suddenly, as he later recounted to the Associated Press, he began to feel the latch twist in his hand. The storm was trying to get in. He and another man quickly braced themselves and grabbed the door together, using their combined weight to hold it shut, praying it would be enough to save their lives. Across the road, fields of tall trees that had withstood the strong winds that regularly swept through the plains were torn and splintered in an instant.

On Gary England's Doppler radar the eye of the twister had gone from crimson to almost black as the tornado's winds began to exceed 200 miles per hour. The debris was so intense it began to show up on the radar, as it was hurled thousands of feet into the air and began to rotate in the upper levels of the storm. The ring of debris—the "debris ball," as meteorologists refer to it—was more than a mile wide and growing. And those not directly in the path of the storm weren't safe either. For at least a mile around it on all sides, straight-line winds exceeding 80 miles per hour were toppling trees and power lines, doing major damage to cars and homes, and nearly blowing off the road people trying to chase the storm.

About a quarter mile to the storm's south, Val Castor and his wife, Amy, two veteran storm chasers for KWTV, kept having to flee their positions as electrical lines were snapped by the tornado's winds. Castor, who had tracked the 1999 tornado and hundreds of others for Channel 9, was stunned at the storm's ferocity. He was known for being a steady hand in the face of terrible weather, but as he phoned in to the station with a report from Pennsylvania Avenue just south of the storm, the alarm in his voice was palpable. What was in front of him was total mayhem, worse than what he had seen the day before. "I see boards. I see roofs of houses. I see tin. Everything is flying through the air. . . . There is just a ton of debris," Castor told England, his voice panicked.

Suddenly Castor went somber and quiet. In the passenger seat Amy zoomed their camera in on the twister as it crossed the road directly in front of them. In the shot everything—trees, signs, homes—disintegrated in mere seconds in the cyclonic winds. "Gary, there's houses in the air here," Castor said, his voice deadly quiet.

At KWTV England let out a huge sigh on air. "I know," he said, the heartache evident in his voice.

CHAPTER 10

3:05 P.M., MAY 20

LaDonna Cobb and her husband, Steve, had raced to Briarwood Elementary to pick up their three daughters—Cydney, eleven, Jordan, nine, and Erin, seven—and take them out of the storm's way. But as the tornado began to wind its way toward Moore, Cobb, an assistant teacher at the school who worked with the prekindergarten classes, suddenly couldn't leave. She couldn't bear to walk away from the four-year-olds she had taught every day for the last eight months, who now sat crouched and trembling along a hallway near their classroom as the storm approached. If only the bad weather were coming through an hour later, the kids would be with their parents and presumably safer. But she couldn't think about that now. She had to confront the situation as it was.

Blond and tan, Cobb was thirty-eight, but she looked at least ten years younger. No one could believe she had three kids, much less an eleven-year-old, and at school some of the little boys had crushes on her, which they confessed only to their mothers. They thought Mrs. Cobb was so pretty. She wasn't even supposed to be at Briarwood that day: She had taken the afternoon off to join her husband to sign the closing papers on their new home about a mile and a half away.

It was an exciting day for them. For the better part of the spring, the family had been crammed into a tiny apartment after their original home, a few blocks down the street from Briarwood, had sold earlier than they'd expected. With most of their belongings in storage, they had borrowed Steve's sister's truck and planned to begin moving stuff into their new home that afternoon, just in time for summer.

Cobb knew storms were in the forecast, but it wasn't until her iPhone began blaring an emergency warning about a tornado approaching Moore that she realized how bad it really was. She and Steve quickly headed to Briarwood, just off 149th Street, a few blocks shy of the Moore city limits, where they found the school in total chaos. Unlike Plaza Towers, which had a classic school building layout, Briarwood was made up of four separate "pods," or buildings of four classrooms apiece, linked by open-air sidewalks. Frantic parents were scrambling everywhere looking for their kids, who were being sheltered in different spots all over the grounds—from bathrooms to interior hallways to closets. As Steve marched off to find their daughters, Cobb stopped by her classroom in the main building. She was pained by the looks of fear on her students' faces as her colleague Stacey Montgomery and her friend Katie Dodd, who had filled in for her that day, took turns rubbing the kids' backs and singing nursery songs to keep them calm. For the most part they were succeeding, but Cobb could tell the kids were frightened. They shouldn't have to be going through something like this, she thought, not at their age.

It wasn't long before Steve reappeared at her side. He was generally easygoing, which was why she had fallen in love with him so long ago. But he looked nervous, which alarmed her. "We need to go," he said, the urgency clear in his voice. But Cobb shook her head. "I can't leave," she told him. She dropped to the ground and began to try to comfort her students alongside her colleagues. She simply could not stand the idea of the children going through the storm without their parents. Cobb knew she would want someone to do the same thing for her kids if they were separated. And so she rubbed their tiny backs and tried to reassure them. "It's going to be okay," Cobb said again and again. In her heart she couldn't believe that the storm was really going to hit. It had to miss them. It just had to. Outside, the storm sirens continued their ominous wail.

A little over a mile to the northeast, Amy Simpson was trying to keep everyone calm as kids and teachers took shelter in the hallways of Plaza Towers Elementary. It wasn't easy. Just as they were at Briarwood, parents were running through the hallways in a panic looking for their kids in hopes of escaping the approaching storm. Outside the wind had whipped up, and sheets of heavy rain and hail began to pound the building. It sounded like a war zone outside, but Simpson was determined to keep the environment inside as calm as possible. It was the only thing she felt she could actually control in a situation that was rapidly turning into a nightmare.

Suddenly a frantic father rushed through the school's front door, flew past Simpson, and slipped on the floor, which was wet from people coming in out of the rain. She reached out and grabbed him by the back of his shirt, saving him from crashing to the ground. "Calm down!" she ordered as she helped steady him. "You can't go down my hall like that. You have to remain calm." The man was livid. "A fucking tornado is coming!" he screamed, cursing her as kids nearby watched and began to cry. "*Calm down*," Simpson repeated, a little more emphatic but mostly unmoved by his emotional outburst. "I'm not going to let you scare my kids."

She began to walk the halls of Plaza's front building, checking on her staff and students as they sat crouched on their knees on the cold concrete floors, with their heads against the interior brick walls. It was their usual tornado position. As she patrolled, Simpson could hear the storm picking up intensity outside, and it scared her. But she forced herself to remain focused and strong. The kids were young, but they were smart, and they were incredibly intuitive. She knew if they sensed her fear they would be even more terrified than they already were. She couldn't let that happen. She had to be strong, strong enough for everyone—even her teachers, who were being so very brave but were, she knew, panicked inside. She thought of Karen Marinelli, one of her first-grade teachers, who had witnessed the power of tornadoes firsthand. In her first year as a teacher Marinelli's classroom at Kelley Elementary had been obliterated by the 1999 tornado. And now here she was in another storm's path. Simpson could only imagine what she must be feeling.

She didn't have time to stop and think about the monster that was putting all of them at risk. She tried not to think of what it could take from her, how she might not see her husband, the love of her life, or her beloved kids ever again. She didn't have time to think of herself. She didn't have time to think, period. She could only act, and her goal at the moment was to keep as many people as possible at Plaza calm and safe—or as safe as they could be in a nearly fifty-year-old school building built in era when tornadoes were generally much gentler and less frequent than they were now. While some of the classes at Briarwood, which had opened in 1985, were taking shelter in classrooms where the only window was in the door leading to the hallway, almost every room at Plaza had several windows, which made them too dangerous. But the hallways weren't ideal either. Many were lined with glass skylights—an aesthetically appealing design that allowed natural light to flow in. As hail began to pound the glass above, Simpson worried they might come crashing down at any moment, making an already bad situation even worse.

Still, her teachers were doing what they could to keep their students calm, and she loved them for it. As she walked the halls, she could hear tiny voices chanting their ABCs. In the hallway closest at the front of the building, Erin Baxter was leading her prekindergarten class in a rendition of "Twinkle, Twinkle, Little Star." Other teachers were trying to get their students' minds off the storm raging outside by asking them to talk about how they planned to spend their summer vacation, which was just days away. All they had to do was make it through this terrible moment.

As she approached one corridor, Simpson heard the voice of Gary England, as a teacher had pulled up KWTV's streaming coverage of the storm on her iPhone. "If you are not below ground, you will not survive this," she heard someone tell England. Her heart sank, and she rushed down the hall and ordered the teacher to turn it off. "The kids don't need to hear that," she snapped, in a tone she rarely used with anyone, even her own kids when they were acting up. She felt bad, but she didn't want her students feeling more helpless and scared than they already did in the face of a monster storm from which the hallways of this old school were their only shelter.

At Briarwood, Steve Cobb tried again to convince his wife that they needed to leave, but again she refused to budge. Up and down the hallways scared teachers were beginning to improvise ways to protect their students. They handed kids the heaviest books they could find that weren't already packed up for the end of school year. "Cover your heads," the teachers ordered. They piled backpacks and mats and extra blankets on top of the kids to cushion them in case of debris. One teacher raided her closet and found the sweaters she used on cold days and bundled up her kids, who began to sweat in the increasingly humid hallways. Like the lights, the school's air-conditioning system was going on and off as the power flickered from the already-intense winds outside. Leesa Kniffen and Suzanne Haley, first-grade teachers, began pushing desks against the interior wall of Kniffen's classroom and ordered students to brace themselves underneath, in the hope that the desks would act as buffers between the students and any debris should the building come down. All the while parents continued to rush into the school yelling for their kids.

In the sky about a mile to the south, KWTV's Jim Gardner continued to hover in his helicopter, watching the storm move east. The tornado was so wrapped up in rain and debris, he could barely make out the funnel. It just looked like a massive black wall on the ground heading toward Moore. As he panned to the east, Gardner caught a glimpse of something that made his stomach drop: a long line of car headlights snaking down Santa Fe Avenue that appeared to be several miles long. The traffic jam was worse than any he'd ever seen in Oklahoma, and instantly he suspected they were cars driven by parents rushing to get to their kids. But these people were in serious danger. They were sitting right in the path of the storm, a mile or less from the front edge of the tornado. He frantically called out to England and the crew in the studio to get on air, knowing there was a chance that many of those people might be listening to KWTV, which was being simulcast on the radio. "It's a logjam, Gary!" Gardner cried. "Those people need to get out of there!" As Gardner panned over to show how close the tornado was, England began acting almost like a traffic reporter, calling out the coordinates of where the storm was and redirecting drivers down different streets. "Get the heck out of there! Go north!" England ordered. For some it was too late to get out of the path of the storm, and he advised them to start looking for a large, sturdy building where they could take cover. "Do not get caught in your car like this!" England said.

For some in Moore, school buildings seemed to be the safest spots, and as Baxter sat with her kids at Plaza Towers, she saw people from the neighborhood begin to run in and take shelter alongside them, believing it might be safer than their own homes, which were about as old the school. She saw husbands and wives, people young and old. One man even came in with his dog, which looked friendly but spooked.

Down the hall, on the east side of the school, Janice Brim, a sixth-grade teacher, got a text from her husband, Mark, who was watching the storm from near their home at 119th Street and May Avenue in south Oklahoma City—about 3 miles northwest of Plaza Towers. He had grabbed their dog and driven west when it looked like the tornado might come his way, but now, heading back east, he watched as the storm passed about 2 miles directly south of him. Even from this distance he could see the twister's fury, how it was ripping apart everything in its path. And it appeared to be headed straight for his wife and her school. He was a builder, and he knew Plaza Towers. Sheltering in the hallway wasn't going to be enough. "You have to take deeper shelter," he said, calling her to emphasize the urgency.

By then Brim had five students left. The rest of her class had been checked out early by their parents. She considered her options.

Near her classroom was a printer closet—a tiny space no bigger than five feet by five feet. But the closet, which was right next to the bathrooms, looked sturdy, so she piled her students in. They barely fit, and once inside they covered themselves with backpacks. Other teachers nearby followed her lead, shoving their students into the bathrooms.

As the wind howled outside, Brim and her students began to sing to ease the tension—mostly old church praise songs like Psalm 91. "I will not be afraid of the terror by night, nor the arrow that flies in the day," they sang. "He will cover me with his feathers, and under his wings I will hide." Brim knew how scared her kids were. They were physically shaking, and their voices trembled in a way that just killed her. Why was this happening to kids who had barely had a chance to live their lives? Brim tried not to cry. Unlike the other students at Plaza, her kids were old enough to understand what was happening, old enough to feel the fear that comes with knowing.

As they paused to think of another song to sing, one of the boys turned to Brim. And even in the darkened closet, with just a sliver of light coming through the door, she could see his eyes wide with terror. "Mrs. Brim, promise me we aren't going to die?" he said. Brim did everything she could not to burst into tears as she paused to consider her answer. She couldn't lie to them, not now. "I can't promise you that," she finally said, her voice thick. "But I can tell you that God is a lot stronger than this tornado."

CHAPTER 11

3:10 P.M., MAY 20

With the tornado bearing down on Moore from the west, Alyson Costilla was driving as fast as she could to get out of its way. As she headed south, she could see the ominous clouds to her right in the distance. She wanted to stop and stare, but she kept driving. It was what her mother, Terri Long, had ordered her to do. "Drive as far to the south as you can," she'd said. And there had been something in her mother's voice that made it clear she'd better listen.

Less than an hour earlier Alyson had been on her way to her last class of the day at Southmoore High School, just off Nineteenth Street in Moore. She was five days away from graduating, and though she still had to get through her final classes and exams, she was already caught up in that euphoric state of mind that slowly overtakes high-school seniors so tantalizingly close to the finish line. There had been days of signing yearbooks and taking photos and tearful hugs among friends who swore to remain close forever even as they knew deep down they would probably drift apart.

Alyson was already thinking of her life beyond high school. She had been accepted at Oklahoma State University in Stillwater, an hour north of Moore, where she planned to study sports medicine.

Her mother was already a rabid OSU fan, but together they bought new burnt-orange T-shirts emblazoned with Pistol Pete, the school's cowboy mascot, and proudly wore them to celebrate her admission. Though she wouldn't actually move to campus until August, she and her mother had already been plotting all the things they'd buy for her dorm room. Sometimes her mom seemed more excited than she was.

Alyson had always heard girls talk about their close relationships with their mothers, but Terri, who would celebrate her fiftieth birthday in exactly a week, really was her best friend. There was no one in the world she was closer to. They spent hours together talking and shopping and hanging out at school events, where Terri often volunteered. When Alyson's cheerleading squad competed at the national championships in Dallas, Terri was there with the other cheer moms. Her mother had even camped out with her to see the *Twilight* movie a few years earlier. The day before, she and her mom had spent hours at Penn Square Mall looking for the perfect dress for her to wear to her graduation that coming Saturday. It took all day to find a dress, but Terri didn't seem to mind. It was precious time spent with her daughter, who would soon be gone, on her own.

Terri Long was occasionally misty-eyed at the thought of sending her youngest baby out into the world. Her two older kids, Terry Don and Jenna, were well out of the nest now and had children of their own—adorable toddlers who referred to their grandmother as "Mimi." But she could barely control her excitement about Alyson's graduation. She'd sent out invitations to the family weeks before, and when her daughter had come home with her royal blue cap and gown, she'd immediately made her try them on. As her daughter had modeled for her, she had been beside herself with joy. "I'm so proud of you," she'd said, her eyes wet with tears.

To her family and friends Terri Long was a rock, a calming force who had raised her kids to be strong, even when it was hard to be. She had an adventurous spirit. She loved Harley-Davidsons—so much that her username for everything was "Crazy4Harleys2." And she often quoted Janis Joplin, telling her kids, "Don't compromise yourself. You're all you've got." But that day she was visibly nervous, which wasn't like her.

A registrar at the Federal Aviation Administration, she was at her office near the Oklahoma City airport when she first saw reports of bad weather developing to the south. It was the usual routine in Moore, where she'd lived for half of her life, but this storm looked more treacherous than the bad front that had moved through the previous day. Concerned, she called the administration office at Southmoore and asked that her daughter be released early. Then she phoned Alyson and told her to go their home on SW Fourteenth, a few blocks west of Plaza Towers Elementary. She was leaving work early and would meet her there, she said. She promised to be home soon.

With the clouds growing more ominous by the second, her coworkers had urged her to wait out the storm at work, arguing that it was too dangerous to drive into Moore. But even as the emergency sirens began to wail, she wouldn't stay put. She needed to get to her daughter, and out the door she ran. Just after she began her 14-mile commute home, the tornado dropped from the clouds and began its march toward Moore. Listening to the weather reports in the car, Long knew she probably wouldn't beat the storm, and she called Alyson and told her to get out of the house and head south.

Now, driving in the heavy rain toward Norman, it was Alyson's turn to worry. According to the radio, the tornado was cutting down 149th Street, the route her mother sometimes took to get home from work. She tried calling her mom again and again but couldn't get through. She began to panic. Finally, after another attempt, her mother answered, but Alyson could barely understand what she was saying. It sounded like she was saying she was driving down Interstate 44 toward home. But that made no sense to Alyson because that would place her mother directly in the path of the storm, and she wouldn't take a risk like that. But before she could ask her to explain, the call abruptly cut out.

At KOCO Damon Lane briefly stepped off camera and again he texted his wife, Melissa. It had been nearly half an hour since she'd told him she was leaving work, and she still hadn't responded to his last message. On radar the tornado was on 149th Street in Oklahoma City. But as it tracked toward Moore, it appeared to be moving a little bit to the northeast, putting it on a path that would take it right to his house, a few blocks south of Fourth Street on the east side of town. His heart began to beat even faster. Could this really be happening?

When Lane had moved to Moore four years ago, right after taking the job at Channel 5, he had known better than anyone the city's history with treacherous weather. He had even studied previous Moore storms, including the 1999 tornado, in meteorology classes at the University of North Carolina. But even now, watching live images of a monster twister taking dead aim at his home, there was a part of him that could not really believe on a personal level what was actually happening. He had always known intellectually that weather was ruthless and anybody was at risk. But now, with his wife, his dogs, and his home seemingly in the path of a killer tornado, Lane suddenly understood in a sick-to-your-stomach, heart-wrenching way how savage and arbitrary this beast really was.

He had never really considered what it might be like to be on air following a storm that was putting his own family at deadly risk. It wasn't something they taught you at school. But now here he was, and it was happening. It felt at times like an out-of-body experience. But the adrenaline kept him going, and even as he began to list streets and businesses increasingly close to his home, Lane knew he had a responsibility to the tens of thousands of other people who lived in Moore or had family there and were going through the same nightmare he was. He messaged his wife again. "Are u in the shelter?" he wrote. Located in the garage, the underground cubby was brand new, a surprise wedding gift Lane hoped his family would never have to use.

In the sky south of Moore, KFOR helicopter pilot Jon Welsh was monitoring a tornado that was now wrapped in so much rain and debris it looked like a dark fog of death slowly drifting toward Moore, illuminated only by massive power flashes as it blocked out the afternoon sun. And as he flew, listening to both air traffic control and producers back at the studio, Welsh was frantically texting his wife. Like Lane, he lived in Moore—almost in the same spot, except he was on the north side of Fourth Street and Lane on the south, near Bryant Avenue. When the tornado had hit the ground, Welsh had grabbed his cell phone, which still worked at this altitude, and called his wife, Alison, who was out running errands with their youngest daughter, Maddie. "Is it really that bad?" she'd asked him when he told her the storm was headed toward Moore. She told her husband she was going to go pick up their oldest daughter, Morgan, from school and then head home. But he sensed she didn't understand how serious the storm was. "You have to get to the shelter *now*," he'd emphatically told her, as he watched the vortex rapidly expand in size. "I *am not* kidding."

Welsh didn't hear from his wife after that. He assumed but didn't know for sure that she'd made it home. Now, as the storm prepared to cross into Moore from Oklahoma City, she wasn't responding to text messages, which wasn't like her. It made him nervous. While Lane could see on the radar that his house was in danger, Welsh could physically see from the helicopter that his house was in the bull's-eye of the storm, and it scared him to death.

As he stood ready to go back on air with Mike Morgan, Welsh took several deep breaths and tried to remain calm, tapping into the military training that had helped him keep his head when he was flying combat missions over war-torn Baghdad. That had been scary, but it was nothing like this. His heart ached as he thought of his young family in the path of a tornado that was heartlessly ripping apart everything in its wake. Describing for KFOR's audience what he was seeing, Welsh realized his wife might be listening. "It's going towards the Moore, Warren Theatre area," Welsh said in a voice that did not betray the panic he was feeling. And then, just as calmly, he stated his worst nightmare in a tone that could be described as nothing less than matter-of-fact. "It's going right basically towards my house," he said.

At Plaza Towers Amy Simpson was still walking the halls, checking on her students and teachers. The wind was howling outside, and she could hear the old building creak around her in response to the pressure of the storm. At that point the power started to go on and off, scaring the kids, who were beginning to cry. The teachers did their best to console them, but even as they put on brave faces and tried to distract their students with songs and stories and anything else that would keep their minds off the storm raging outside, Simpson knew her staff was scared too. They all were. She suddenly thought of all the time she'd spent crouched in the hallway in her tornado position as a kid growing up in Moore. It was a memory she had always associated with fun, getting out of class to hang out in the hallway, where the lights had been shut off to mimic the real scenario of the storm. She'd always had snacks and her favorite stuffed animal. One year she'd even had a tiny flashlight. Even recently, as she'd practiced the drill as a teacher and now as principal, it had never entered her mind to feel any fear: They'd never been in any real danger. How she wished this were just another drill.

Suddenly she felt her iPhone vibrate. It was a text message from her husband, Lindy, who had picked up their kids from school and was at their house a couple of miles to the southeast of Plaza. Scarlet and Roarke were already in a neighbor's underground storm shelter, but Lindy was nervously pacing the driveway outside, listening to the weather broadcasts and braving the heavy rain and hail to look at the storm toward the west. He feared the worst, and he did not mince words with his wife. "It's going to hit you," he wrote. Panic shot through Simpson's heart, but she willed herself to remain calm, knowing that it was her responsibility to the students and her staff to keep it together even in the face of a nightmare storm that threatened to kill them all.

Rushing back to her office, she passed a side door and saw the back building several yards away where Plaza's second- and third-grade classes were held. She paused. Simpson knew many of the kids had been checked out early because she'd seen them dash through the hallway with their mom or dad. But she didn't know how many kids were left, and she began to worry. She wanted to go to them, to check on them, to make sure they were safe and so that she would know who was there. But as she walked to the door, she could see the sky raining down huge chunks of hail, and she thought of her husband's message warning her that the storm was coming for them. At this point she didn't know how far the tornado was from the school. She couldn't see it. And she worried she wouldn't have time to make it back to the intercom in her office, where she wanted to be to pass along the final warning when the storm was about to hit. So she turned and kept walking, her pace a little quicker than before, praying that the back building would be safe.

When she reached the front of the school, Simpson saw kids lined up with their parents, who were still rushing last minute to get out of the storm's way. As hail and heavy rain continued to pelt the ground outside, one little girl began to cry and told her she didn't want to go because she was too scared. Simpson was scared too, but she didn't dare show it. In her head she reminded herself to be strong. "No, ma'am," she told the little girl, as she fluffed up her backpack around her. "You have to go with your mom and dad." But as she nudged her to the door, Simpson had a second thought and stopped. She grabbed a heavy hardcover textbook off a shelf nearby and told the little girl to use it to cover her head. Simpson began to do the same with other kids as they left the school, doing anything she could to protect their fragile little bodies from the unmerciful storm outside. Soon the shelf was bare.

For a moment Simpson found herself thinking of her own kids, wishing she'd hugged them a little tighter that morning before school. She would see them again. She didn't dare let herself think otherwise. *We're going to make it through this*, she told herself. She walked back into the hallway, wondering if she had time to make one more lap to check on the students. Outside there seemed to be a lull in the storm, and she could hear the gentle little voices of her kindergartners singing nursery rhymes. They sounded like tiny angels straight from heaven.

A mother and father rushed past Simpson with their kid. She paused, watching them as they raced out the front entrance and ran toward the parking lot. Silently she prayed they would be safe. But suddenly she saw them glance west and stop dead in their tracks. Their faces wrenched in fear, they grabbed their child and quickly ran back toward the school. Simpson's stomach dropped as she felt panic seize her body. At that very moment she knew the nightmare was real: The tornado was on their doorstep. She didn't even wait to hear what the parents would say before turning and rushing back into her office. Around her the lights began to flicker again, and she prayed the power would stay on long enough for her to get on the intercom one last time. She lifted the receiver, and in a voice that was so calm she couldn't believe it was coming from her body, she said the words that she had dreaded since the moment she had heard the storm sirens wail almost a half hour before.

"It's here," she said, and in the distance she could hear the tornado's roar.

CHAPTER 12

3:15 P.M., MAY 20

Lando Hite was inside one of the barns at Celestial Acres, a horse-training facility on the grounds of the 160-acre Orr Family Farm just off 149th Street and Western Avenue, when he noticed the horses were starting to act a little spooked. Outside the wind was picking up, but Hite, a twenty-four-year-old Oklahoma native, didn't think much of it. There had been bad weather the day before and the day before that. It was a typical spring day in Oklahoma and he was used to the afternoon storms, even if the horses weren't.

Tall and skinny with a gentle drawl, Hite was a self-described cowboy, or at least that's what he said when people asked him what he did for a living. He slept on a bunk inside a tiny tack room at the farm, where he worked as a caretaker and exercise rider for more than a dozen Thoroughbred racehorses. As they often were at this time of year, the stables were almost full—packed with some sixty-five other Thoroughbreds and quarter horses in town to compete in the spring races at Remington Park, on the north side of Oklahoma City.

There were no meets that Monday, and Hite spent the day as he usually did, grooming and riding the horses around Celestial Acres' training track. It sat alongside the agriculture theme park operated by the Orr family, which featured pony rides and a petting zoo full of chickens, pigs, rabbits, goats, and sheep. The farm was a popular place in May, often crawling with kids on their end-of-the-school-year field trips, but it was quiet on this Monday as a result of the ominous skies. Soon enough the heavens opened up, pounding the barns with heavy rain, large hail, and blistering winds as loud claps of thunder shook the ground like tiny earthquakes.

Hite stayed inside with the horses until he noticed that the storm had suddenly let up. Walking out into the yard to enjoy the reprieve, he immediately sensed that something was off. It was strangely quiet. There were no birds chirping, no sound of traffic, just an eerie stillness. That's when he glanced toward the west and saw it in the distance: an angry black vortex on the ground no more than a mile away heading down 149th Street straight for him. He had never seen a tornado before, only on television or in the movies. He stood frozen for a second wondering what to do, until he was hit by a straight-on wind gust that almost blew him to the ground.

Hearing a horse neighing behind him, he booked it back to the stables and began freeing all the animals he could, running from building to building as he herded them from their stalls toward the open pasture behind the farm. He hoped that allowing the horses to run free might give them a better chance of surviving the monster tornado than they would have penned up in buildings that already seemed to be swaying in the terrible winds. By now the funnel was bearing down on the farm like a freight train, and it suddenly seemed he was living out a scene from *Twister.* Branches and pieces of boards began to fly past him like deadly stakes, and as the tornado got closer, he saw entire roofs of houses floating in the sky almost in slow motion, seemingly as weightless as feathers. As the horses ran frantically in the nearby field, Hite began to wonder if this was it for him. He had no idea where to take shelter. Everybody on the farm seemed to have vanished. It was just him and the horses.

With the tornado now just a few hundred yards away, Hite saw what looked to be a horse suddenly lifted in the air in the distance. He did the only thing he thought might save his life: He raced back to one of the barns, ran inside, and dove into a horse stall. He barely had time to cover his head before the storm was upon him, a roaring, swirling devil that consumed the building around him in seconds. Hite had never heard anything so loud in his life, and as he clutched a beam, he felt his ears popping as the storm began to suck at his body, tearing off his shoes and his shirt. The building collapsed in a heap of boards and mangled aluminum, and he felt himself beginning to tumble over and over, as if he were in a blender full of wood. It seemed to last forever. Suddenly he felt himself falling, buried by debris that seemed determined to drive him deeper and deeper into the muddy, wet ground. It was as if the storm were intent on literally digging his grave. There was no way he was going to survive this, just no way, he thought, as he felt his body being drilled deeper into the earth. And then, suddenly, it stopped.

A few blocks away at Briarwood Elementary, LaDonna Cobb saw her husband, Steve, rush through the side door leading into the interior hallway where she and her pre-K class were taking shelter in the main building. He had been outside looking at the storm. She was certain he was going to try once again to persuade her to leave with their daughters, who were taking shelter with their classmates, and flee the tornado, and the word "no" was forming on the tip of her tongue when she suddenly froze at the sight of his face. He wore a look she had never seen before in the more than fifteen years they had been together, something that was beyond fear. "Get out here now," Steve ordered, in a tone that made her stomach drop.

Cobb nervously followed him out the door, and together they walked quickly down the sidewalk toward the side of the building. Outside there seemed to be a brief reprieve from the heavy rain and hail. For a moment Cobb wondered if her prayers had been answered and the storm was going to miss them. But then she peered around the corner of the building, and there it was: a towering black funnel so close and so huge it seemed to eat up the entire western sky. It was at least half a mile away, but even so she could see entire trees and houses swirling in the air around it. A building in the distance took a direct hit, and she saw it explode into splinters. She gasped, and her heart seemed to stop. It was too late to run. Briarwood was going to take a direct hit.

In a panic, Cobb and her husband turned and raced toward the first door they found, banging to be let in. It happened to be the outdoor entrance to their daughter Erin's first-grade classroom, and inside the kids were gathered along an interior wall, crouched on their knees with their heads bowed to the floor. When the teacher let them in, Cobb rushed toward her youngest, dropped to the ground, and used her slender body to cover her and as many of her classmates as she could, gathering them underneath her in a tight embrace. She was determined to be a human shield between their tiny bodies and the horrible, ruthless storm that was coming for them. There was nothing to protect her, nothing to bear the weight of something crashing on her body as the storm hit, but she didn't care. Like so many of her colleagues at Briarwood, all she could think about were the kids, their young lives barely started and now in such great danger. As the power suddenly went out, leaving them in the dark, the kids beneath her began to cry and shake in fear. "It's going to be okay," she said in a shaky voice, not really sure if she was telling the truth.

Outside, Shelly McMillin, the forty-eight-year-old Moore native who was Briarwood's principal, was standing on the west side of the campus watching the tornado grow bigger and bigger as it aimed for the school. All she could think of was May 3, a storm she had survived by jumping into a bathtub at her house and pulling a mattress over her head. The television meteorologists had warned people in the path of that tornado that they could not survive unless they were underground. But McMillin had beaten the odds. She had been above ground on May 3 and had lived, even as her home and her neighborhood were blown away around her.

Now, facing down a tornado that looked every bit as menacing as the one she had encountered fourteen years earlier, McMillin could only think of that miracle. If she'd lived through the most dangerous tornado on record, maybe she and her students and teachers, who had no choice but to ride out the storm in the school, had more of a chance than Mike Morgan and the other guys on television were suggesting. As the storm drew closer, her mind shut off to any scenario other than making it through. *We can do this. We've got to do this,* McMillin thought, a mantra she began to repeat again and again in her head. It was as if someone had physically flipped a switch that shut out the fear and doubt and put her into survival mode. Still, as she ducked back into the building and raced to her office, she began to pray aloud. "Please, God, let it lift," she pleaded to the heavens above. "Please let it lift."

In the adjacent buildings teachers and parents were keeping watch through windows and side doors. They could see the sky had turned pitch-black. Startled by how eerily quiet it was, Amy Chase, a sixth-grade teacher, walked back to her classroom to look out a window that faced west. She shrieked as she saw giant chunks of debris flying in the air over the field adjacent to the school and ran as fast as she could back to the hallway. "It's coming! It's coming!" she screamed as she ran down the corridor, rushing to get back to her students. She began frantically yelling at the kids to put their backpacks over their heads, but she worried it wouldn't be enough to protect them from what was coming, especially for the kindergartners who were crouched near her class. Their little bodies were so vulnerable. Growing more hysterical by the minute, Chase noticed a group of parents near the front-office windows and begged them to use their bodies to protect the kids. At first they just looked at her as if they didn't comprehend what she was saying. "Lay on the babies!" Chase cried. "It's coming!"

Suddenly the unmistakable roar of the tornado began to sound in the distance, growing ever closer as students began to scream in horror. Next door, in the building where the fourth- and fifth-grade classes were held, teachers caught a glimpse of the ominous funnel through the back window and began herding students into reinforced restrooms and closets. Like Chase, they were concerned that the hallways wouldn't be safe enough. On a nearby wall the clock read 3:16 P.M.

Seconds later something huge hit the roof of the school—cars and farm equipment that had been picked up by the funnel along the way now literally dropped out of the sky like bombs, causing parts of the roof to crack and cave under the pressure. "Hold on, hold on!" Cobb screamed as the building suddenly shook like a bomb. It was the sound of a twelve-thousand-gallon water tank, the size of a tiny submarine and weighing more than ten tons when it was empty, being thrown on top of a third-grade classroom in the next building. As the tank landed, it instantly bent the steel girders holding up the roof almost to floor level inside the classroom below. The entire school seemed to shake on impact. Just inches away, a teacher and her students were taking cover. The tank, and another just like it, had been ripped up like torn pieces of paper from their reinforced-cement bases at the Orr Family Farm and carried more than half a mile by the tornado before falling out of the sky. The other tank landed on a house a few blocks east of Briarwood, crushing it to bits.

Back in the hallway where Cobb's pre-K class was taking shelter, the door that led out onto the sidewalk suddenly flew open. Outside was a swirling cyclone of wind and debris with a soundtrack of destruction so loud it drowned out the screams of the teachers, kids, and parents, whose faces were now contorted in absolute terror. Stacey Montgomery, the petite but sturdy teacher, crawled to the door and, struggling against the force of the winds, fought to pull it closed. She wedged her body into a corner and gripped the knob with all the strength she possessed to keep the door shut, her hands shaking and turning white with the pressure.

As the eye of the storm grew near, the wind began to suck at the door, pulling her almost horizontally in the air as parents, who were forcing their kids' heads to the ground, watched in horror. Suddenly the door began to lurch outward, dramatically inhaled hinge by hinge by the tornado. As the door vanished, it almost took Montgomery with it, but somehow she clung to something in the hallway and fought her way back down the hall toward the kids. She felt her shoes sucked off one by one, but she kept going, refusing to let the storm take her. Finally back with the kids, she crawled on top of her students and clung to the floor and nearby wall for dear life, screaming at the top of her lungs for God to save their lives and take the storm away.

As the storm approached Briarwood, it officially became one of the strongest tornadoes captured on record. It was more than a mile wide and its winds were well in excess of 210 miles per hour—this made it an EF5 tornado on the Enhanced Fujita scale, the highest rating a storm can get. The school's roof began to peel away under the pressure of the winds, and as the storm passed directly over the school, the lightning in the clouds above created an almost strobe-like effect inside in the hallways, closets, nooks, and bathrooms where a few hundred students, teachers, and parents were desperately hoping to stay alive. "It's almost over!" Robin Dziedzic, a fifth-grade teacher, yelled to her students as they rode out the storm in a tiny bathroom. But still the storm raged on, and to some it began to feel as though it would never end.

Squished in a closet in her office with several other administrative staff, McMillin found herself keeping a mental tally of the storm's progress based on what she had gone through in 1999. She had already heard the grinding of its approach, followed by the loud crash of debris hitting the school. As her ears began to pop, signaling that the tornado was passing almost overhead, she found a strange solace in being able to physically feel the pressure of the storm on her body. *I'm still alive,* she thought, even as she began to hear the unbearable noise of the building being torn apart all around her.

In the first-grade classroom where Cobb had hunkered down with her husband and daughter, most of the roof was now gone and she could feel her body being sucked into the air. She clawed at the wall in an effort to gain traction against the storm while at the same struggling to keep her body firmly on top of the children beneath her. If she had to fight to stay grounded against the pull of the tornado, Cobb knew that if the wind were to get to the kids the twister would inhale their tiny frames in an instant. She couldn't let that happen. "It's going to be okay! It's going to be okay!" she screamed, repeating herself as she grabbed at the wall with one hand, trying to brace herself, and shielded the kids, who were now crying out in terror, with the other. She could hear a boy underneath her calling out in anguish for his mother, and her heart ached. Suddenly, before she even realized what was happening, the wall Cobb was trying so hard to cling to collapsed on top of her, a pile of heavy cinder blocks that knocked her sharply in the head and buried her. Everything went black.

CHAPTER 13

3:17 P.M., MAY 20

Even from 2 miles away Glenn Lewis could hear that unmistakable roar, a cross between the sound of a freight train and that of a jet engine. He'd heard it before, watching other tornadoes prey on Moore in the nearly two decades since he was first elected mayor. And every time he had hoped he'd never hear that awful sound again. But he had. Four times now he'd helped rebuild his hometown. Four times too many.

Lewis had seen things he had never imagined when he ran for mayor that he would ever see: stunned people crawling out of the rubble of their homes with their bodies impaled by jagged pieces of lumber like giant splinters and other gruesome injuries that looked like what you might expect to find on the front lines of a bloody civil war. These weren't supposed to be things you saw here on the quiet, suburban streets of Moore, the epitome of small-town America. As he watched yet another tornado grind its way toward the heart of his city, he couldn't help but stare in disbelief. Was this really happening to Moore again?

May 3 still haunted the mayor, as it did most people in town who had lived through it. It wasn't that he went out of his way to think about it. A jeweler by trade who was only supposed to be at City Hall part time but often worked well beyond that, Lewis looked like an adult Big Boy statue come to life, with a round, sweet face that was often lit up with a jovial smile. He was easygoing by nature, known to embrace the bright side of bad situations. That's how he'd been raised, and even in tough moments he always tried to ease the tension with his deadpan sense of humor. "I ran to clean up Moore, but I didn't know I'd have to do it piece by piece," he had joked after the '99 tornado—a line he'd use again in different variations over the next fourteen years after other bouts of bad weather.

He was of the opinion that all you could do to get through the tears was try to laugh, pick yourself up, and move on. It was his gentle nature, his ability to be the rock that people could rely on in the most trying of times, that accounted for his having been reelected eight times unopposed since he first became mayor in 1994. Lewis loved Moore and would do anything for its people, and everybody in town knew it.

Moore had rebuilt after May 3, better than before, just as it had after every single other storm that had hit in the years since. But while the city had moved on, the storm had left invisible scars. By now Lewis was something of an expert on how to deal with the aftermath of a tornado, thanks to the kind of on-the-job training that no public servant anywhere in the world would ever want. When he went to mayoral conferences in other parts of the country—alone, since he didn't actually have a formal staff, not even a secretary—people always approached him with a look of respect tinged with pity. It bugged him, though he was too nice to say anything. "How do you do it?" the East Coasters often asked, studying him with the curiosity they'd show a martian. "How can you live there?" Lewis would shrug and smile. "We actually have pretty great weather most of the time," he'd say. They always laughed, even if they looked at him as though he were a bit crazy.

One bright side to all of this—and Lewis actively looked for it—was that he knew Moore would be ready when the next storm came. And deep down, as much as he wished otherwise, he had always known it would. Now here it was, a giant twister that was bigger than anything he'd ever seen—even the milewide '99 tornado. And as he stood outside the back door of his jewelry store just south of Nineteenth Street along Interstate 35, it appeared to be coming right at him. Hadn't Moore already been through enough? Was his city the unluckiest town in America?

All day he had been looped in on conference calls and e-mails between Steve Eddy, his old high-school friend, and other city employees, and all day, as he often did in the spring, he had hoped that Moore would be spared. Even when the emergency warnings went out alerting everyone that a storm was blowing up to the west of town, he'd prayed that somehow it might go away.

Though the city had risen again after the May 3 twister, memories of that day lingered, emotional scars that had never really healed. Lewis never forgot what it was like to drive through neighborhoods once so vibrant with life that looked as though they'd been leveled by an atomic bomb. Overnight Moore's population had dropped precipitously when thousands of people had been forced to relocate, their homes and their entire lives blown away in an instant. Parts of the city resembled a ghost town. The streets didn't look like streets anymore. It was just rubble as far as the eye could see, and when that was gone, it looked like the surface of the moon—empty and barren. No trees, no houses. Just dust and rocks and empty concrete slabs where homes used to be. It was the worst thing you could ever witness as a mayor, much less as a town son who loved his city too deeply to ever consider moving away. While more than half the people who had been hit came back and rebuilt in Moore, Lewis dreaded the idea of ever seeing anything like that again in his hometown.

He could still recall as though it were yesterday the odor of natural gas and cut wood and soil mixed with rain that had wafted through the air as the sun set on the most terrible day he had ever known. It had been the smell of every twister since, both large and small, that disturbing perfume of devastation. But on this Monday, as he watched the storm approach from the west, its greenish black clouds spreading across the sky like an ugly bruise, Lewis began to detect that awful aroma in the air around him. It was as if he could actually smell the tornado coming. But maybe it was all in his head. He didn't know.

A few feet away, from inside the store, he could hear the sound of the television, which his staff had cranked up to full volume. One of the TV weathermen was imploring people in the path of the storm to immediately take cover. His employees had already heeded the call and were crowded into the store's giant vault, which doubled as a safe room, squeezed in alongside their stock of intricate diamond engagement rings—"Oklahoma's largest selection of engagement and bridal rings," the shop's ads bragged. But Lewis couldn't bring himself to go inside. He couldn't take his eyes off the dark clouds to the west. Even as he began to be pelted by hail and the wind whipped up, blowing the rain sideways, he stood there almost dumbstruck watching the approaching storm. He wished it were just a bad dream, that he would wake up and it would be gone. But as the ground began to vibrate around him from the roar and the motion of the twister, he knew it was all too real.

Lewis's cell phone suddenly rang. It was his twenty-nine-year-old daughter, Laura, who had moved away long ago to Washington, D.C., where she worked as an intelligence analyst for the federal government. "Dad," she told him in a firm voice, "you are about to get hit by a tornado. You need to go inside the vault." Lewis couldn't suppress a laugh, even at this horrible moment. How did she know he was standing outside? "What are you guys doing, watching me?" he teased her. But she wasn't in the mood to joke. "Dad, you need to take cover now," she scolded. "It's headed right for you."

Lewis hung up the phone, telling his daughter he loved her and promising her he would go to the vault, but as he inched toward the door, he still couldn't stop staring at the massive twister, so close now that he could see giant chunks of debris flying in the air around it. From KOCO on the television inside he could hear the concerned voice of Damon Lane, a customer who'd come into the store more than a year ago to buy a diamond engagement ring for his future wife. Now the meteorologist was calling out Lewis's store by name on television, warning that it was in the path of the storm. "Lewis Jewelers," Lane declared in a stern voice. "You need to be in your tornado shelter immediately."

If that wasn't a sign, Lewis wasn't sure what was. So he inched toward the back door, stealing one last glance at the storm. It seemed to be more violent than it had been just a few seconds before, tearing away at whole neighborhoods to the west like a rabid dog. And as he took that last look, Lewis heard the storm sirens that had been blaring suddenly go silent. He panicked and quickly called the city's emergency operations office, which controlled the sirens. "You need to get those sirens back on," he said, his quiet drawl so well known at City Hall that he didn't even bother to identify himself. "The tornado is right here." The woman on the other end of the line was quiet for a second. "They are on," she told him.

Lewis paused and tried to make sense of how that could possibly be. And then horror swept over him as he realized what had happened: The tornado had destroyed the sirens. It was already in Moore. It was all really happening. He quickly hung up and ran to the vault as the storm drew ever closer.

At KOCO Damon Lane still hadn't heard from his wife, Melissa, and though he was fighting to remain calm on air, he was beginning to feel more and more panicked. Suddenly, a few feet away, his phone lit up with a message, and Lane quickly tossed the broadcast over to one of his storm chasers in the field while he dashed off camera. To his relief, the message was from Melissa, telling him she'd made it home and was in the shelter. Traffic had been backed up for miles heading south into Moore, in part because of the raging storm ahead of the tornado. She'd only reached the city a few minutes earlier. And as she'd exited Interstate 35 to head east down Fourth Street, she could see the tornado in her rearview mirror looming ominously over the city.

Melissa, a former morning news anchor who'd moved from Dallas to be with her new husband, was well practiced at the art of remaining calm in times of crisis. It was Television 101. But on that Monday she couldn't control the fear that raced through her body at the sight of the tornado. She slammed her foot on the car's accelerator, speeding to get away from the storm, knowing she had only a few minutes at most to get home. Pulling into the driveway, she had barely had time to click open the electric door to the garage before the power went out. Now, as she told Lane by text message, she was in the shelter, but with only one of their dogs. Skylar, their eighty-pound husky, had bitten her when she tried to get him down the stairs of the underground cubby, so she'd locked him inside their pantry instead.

Lane's heart sank. Judging just by the radar, the tornado grinding through Moore was the most dangerous storm he'd seen since he'd started working in television. He was horrified by the ominous live pictures that were coming in of the storm as his chasers raced to the east to stay ahead of it. Even over their scratchy cell-phone connections he could hear the roar of the storm—and they were at least half a mile to a mile ahead of it. He couldn't even begin to imagine what it was like to be in the epicenter of that horrible swirling devil. It wasn't just conjecture when he warned people in the path of the storm to get below ground. Lane increasingly didn't see how anyone in the path of the storm could survive it—much less his dog, who was like a child to him. As the radar updated again, the tornado had moved ever so slightly to the north, putting it on track to go right over his home. Typing as fast as he could so he could jump back on camera, Lane begged his wife to try one more time to save their dog. "He's going to die," he wrote, warning her that the storm was coming but she still had time. "Put on gloves," Lane pleaded. "Please save Skylar! I don't want him to die."

Over Channel 5's airwaves, storm chaser Chance Coldiron was streaming live video of the tornado. It was a dark and ominous wall of debris as it approached his position at Santa Fe Avenue and SW Fourth Street in Moore. He was just northeast of Briarwood Elementary and only a few blocks away from Plaza Towers. "There's a neighborhood addition here about to take a direct hit," Coldiron called out, unable to disguise the alarm in his voice. Lane felt sick. He walked back on camera and stood before the green screen that projected the image of the storm on the Doppler radar. It was now rotating over Moore like a massive hurricane. And as he opened his mouth to speak, his voice was different from before. There was an edge that hadn't been there minutes earlier, an audible tinge of anxiety that Lane had tried to keep in check but that had snuck out. *Keep it together, Lane,* he told himself. *Keep it together.*

Back in Moore, Robert Romines was caught in a heavy, driving rain as he raced south and then west to get around the massive storm. He was still trying to get to his daughter's school at 149th Street and May, which he feared had been hit by the tornado. His calls and texts to the staff at Wayland Bonds Elementary weren't going through, and none of his colleagues had been able to reach them either. He prayed it was just the storm interrupting the cellular airwaves and not something worse. *Oh God, why is this happening?* Romines thought. *How can this be happening?*

By now the truck he was driving was being dinged by huge chunks of hail, but Romines could barely hear it over the heavy beating of his own heart. The rain and wind were so fierce he could barely see out the windshield. He had the steering wheel in a death grip, grabbing it so tight his knuckles were white. He knew he was probably driving like a maniac, weaving around cars and taking side roads to dodge traffic and find a way around the storm, but he didn't care. Nothing was going to stop him from getting to that school. In the passenger seat his colleague Jeff Horn tried again to call Michelle McNear, the principal at Wayland Bonds. All circuits were busy. Romines began to feel as if he couldn't breathe.

Romines wasn't unfamiliar with driving in storms. It was such a normal occurrence it probably should have been a part of the driving test in Oklahoma, but he had a few more skills than most in the art of navigating the weather. In fact, Romines was a proud weather junkie, and ever since he was a kid he had lived for the springtime in Oklahoma, when the biggest storms of the year would roll through. He had been storm chasing before storm chasing was cool, practically since the moment he'd gotten his license at the age of sixteen. Back then his parents had admonished him to stay away from storms, warning him that the weather could turn on you in an instant. And in the most convincing voice possible, he'd promised he would. But then, under the pretense of heading to a friend's house, he'd secretly drive out west and watch the storms rise up and explode along the vast, open farmland. It was something he continued to do well into adulthood. "Be right back," he'd tell his wife, Traci, and off he'd go. She never seemed to mind. It was who he was.

As for others who had grown up in Tornado Alley, storms had an allure for him that he couldn't quite explain, an attraction that couldn't be put into words. It wasn't something he'd ever had to articulate. People here instinctively understood the appeal of stormy weather because most of them felt that way too. It was as if it were somehow ingrained in the collective DNA of an entire region to love thunderstorms and want to be near them.

Romines found something undeniably beautiful about the way the clouds drew up toward the heavens and turned the day as black as night, the way streaks of lightning shot across the sky and zipped toward the ground in unpredictable ways. He was drawn to the ominous clap of thunder, to that odd mix of fear and anticipation that it stirred up deep within him as he wondered what was to come. He found the smell of a coming thunderstorm intoxicating, that luxurious aroma of rain right before it began to fall. It was his favorite smell in the world.

Every so often he'd seen a funnel cloud emerge, slinking to the ground like a tempestuous belly dancer on a mission to seduce and destroy the land below. He couldn't look away. He was drawn to it like a snake to a charmer—though he knew full well that the vortex had the ability to strike and kill and that he, as a mere mortal, would be powerless against it. In 1999 he'd been out of town at an education conference when news broke that Moore had been hit. He'd spent hours trying to reach his wife and family in a city where the lines of communication had been wiped out. He'd been luckier than most that day. Hours later he learned that his family was okay, but as he'd watched other storms form and dissipate since then, he'd thought of that terrible, sick feeling on May 3 as he wondered about the fate of the people he loved. Still he couldn't bring himself to look away. Tornadoes fascinated him.

Now, as he cut a jagged path toward the west side of town, speeding past cars whose drivers had stopped to gawk at the storm, Romines briefly wondered if he wasn't being punished somehow for how much he loved wild weather. How could he have found beauty in something that was so destructive?

On the radio he heard the voice of Gary England, the man who had guided him through so many storms before. He could hear the alarm in England's voice. The storm wasn't letting up. It was only getting stronger. It was now on 149th Street approaching Santa Fe Avenue, England said. Romines's heart sank. That was where Briarwood Elementary was. And to the east of that was Plaza Towers, led by Amy Simpson, whom he'd known since childhood. "This is a critical situation," England continued, the unease in his voice echoing ominously through the car. "Take your tornado precautions. . . . Get below ground, if you can." But Romines knew the kids couldn't. In those old buildings there was nowhere to go but the hallways, closets, and bathrooms. He prayed they would be enough.

As Romines turned west, the rain suddenly let up and he could see the funnel. It was the biggest, scariest thing he'd ever seen, a mile wide or more as it hovered over the entire mass of land between SW Fourth and Nineteenth Streets ahead of him. He slowed the truck as he and Horn waited to see which way the storm would go to avoid being hit. As they did, his phone let out a ding. It was a text message from the counselor at Wayland Bonds. The school had narrowly escaped a direct hit, and Avery and everyone else were okay. Romines felt relief, but it was fleeting. Looking at where the storm was, he was certain Briarwood had been hit, and Plaza Towers either had been or was about to be. As they watched, the storm seemed to slow down, taking its time to destroy everything in its path.

Romines inched the car a little farther to the west, as the storm appeared to be heading north of them. As it got closer to Interstate 35, he could see cars being tossed around inside the funnel, picked up like tiny Hot Wheels, the toy cars he had played with as a boy. He couldn't believe what he was seeing. At that moment Romines knew he would never love tornadoes again.

CHAPTER 14

3:18 P.M., MAY 20

They crowded into the bathtub just as they had practiced only days before, but as the house began to creak and the ground began to shudder, Laurinda Vargyas wondered if it would be enough. Outside the pounding rain and hail had stopped, but she could hear the ghastly roar of the storm. It sounded like a freight train, just as she had always heard people describe it. Vargyas had no idea what to expect. This was her first tornado—the one she had hoped would never come.

The thirty-year-old mother of four was from Kern County, California, a place where so many Oklahomans had gone to escape the terrible disaster of the Dust Bowl eighty years before. But like many Californians in recent years, she and her husband, Phillip, had done a reverse migration. When he'd retired from the navy in 2010, they had left Ridgecrest, California, for Oklahoma City, where there were more jobs and a better quality of life. Oklahoma's wild weather had come up as they discussed their future. Could they really live in a place that was so dangerously stormy? But Phil was from Houston—a city regularly pounded by tropical storms that blew in off the Gulf of Mexico—and in California they faced other risks: wildfires and drought and the threat of earthquakes. The Indian Wells Valley, where they lived while Phil worked at the nearby naval base at China Lake, was considered long overdue for "the big one." A natural disaster, it seemed, could happen anywhere.

In the end the occasional threat of a tornado was trumped by pure economics. It was simply cheaper to live in Oklahoma, and it hadn't been hit as hard by the recession as many states. There was a hopefulness, a sense that things were getting better, that you didn't find in central California. Phil quickly found a job as an IT manager in Oklahoma City, and the family moved. He made just enough so that they could rent a nice house and Laurinda could stay at home with the kids. They weren't rich by any means, and some months were tougher than others, but they had a good life. They lived in a comfortable home on 147th Street, just over the Moore city line in a good neighborhood full of families and kids. They were a block away from Briarwood Elementary, where their oldest children—Damon, eleven, and Aria, eight—went to school. Their daughter Karrina, just a few weeks shy of turning five, went to prekindergarten classes there in the morning while Laurinda stayed home with their newest addition, Sydnee, an angelic baby girl who had been born the previous October.

Sydnee was their "Okie," as Phil called her, because she was born in Oklahoma. A squirming, laughing little bug of a child, she was the delight of the family—"the happiest baby alive," according to everyone who met her. Even Karrina, who Phil and Laurinda had worried might be a little jealous, adored her little sister and treated her like her own little doll. They dressed in matching pink and purple—the same hues as Karrina's beloved Minnie Mouse bedroom set. They looked like tiny princesses, adorned in rainbows and hearts and bright patterns that accentuated their sweet faces. Like

Damon and Aria, they had the bright smiles and angelic laughter that made all the sacrifices a parent has to make for their kids worthwhile. Phil and Laurinda doted on their children and would stop at nothing to protect them.

The Vargyases had been diligent in practicing what to do in case of a tornado, just as they had done fire drills to make sure everyone knew their role. Maybe it was his military background, but Phil strongly believed, and his wife agreed, that it was important to prepare for the worst-case scenarios. So when the storm sirens began to blare, Laurinda grabbed Sydnee and Karrina and hustled toward the bathroom, as they had done in the drills. It was the safest spot in the house, since they didn't have a storm shelter. She and her mother, LaVisa, who had moved from California to Oklahoma in January to be closer to her daughter and grandkids, used their bodies to shield the little ones. And as they sat in the tub waiting for the worst, Laurinda worried about the fate of her older kids, who were at Briarwood Elementary down the street.

Karrina was scared, too young to understand a tornado but old enough to know that what was happening wasn't good. Laurinda and her mother did their best to comfort her, rubbing her back and telling her it was going to be okay. Laurinda didn't like to see her like this, her sweet little girl who spent hours in the backyard dancing and twirling without a care in the world. The previous fall, just before Sydnee had been born, she and Phil had taken Karrina to see a Disney on Ice show at the annual state fair. And there, as her favorite Disney princesses glided across the ice in front of her, Karrina had turned to her parents and excitedly told them she was going to be a figure skater when she grew up. Her parents didn't have the money to pay for lessons, but they would someday, Phil had promised. Now all Laurinda wanted was a chance to see her daughter on the ice. It had to happen. Life couldn't be so cruel as to take that promise away.

Suddenly, with a thunderous howl, the tornado was upon them. As Laurinda and her mother clutched the tiny little girls and each other, the house began to shake and split apart around them, peeling away piece by piece in the terrible winds. Even over the deafening roar, Laurinda could hear and feel the cracking of wood and glass as her body began to be pummeled with bricks and boards and everything else the storm could throw at her. She squeezed her daughters closer, holding them as tightly as she could, praying the storm would go away. But suddenly, before her mind could even process what was happening, Laurinda was sucked into the air and her two little girls ripped from her grasp. She felt herself airborne, tumbling again and again forward and backward and sideways as her body was beaten and slammed by whatever was in the air around her. She was banged in the head, and something was ripping at her skin, and for a moment it felt like her body might explode from the sudden pressure of the storm. Then, just as suddenly as she had been picked up, the storm ruthlessly spit her out, and she landed with a massive thud on the ground in the middle of a neighborhood that she didn't recognize. Opening her eyes, she saw only piles of rocks and sticks as far as the eye could see. It was as though she had been transported through some horrifying portal from her quiet neighborhood into a war zone.

Dazed and bleeding profusely from deep cuts on her head and body, Laurinda tried to sit up against a wall of wind that almost threatened to take her again. The tornado still seemed to be lingering right over her, a massive funnel of cloud and debris that stretched high into the heavens. The air was thick with the remains of the houses that had once stood around her; insulation and boards and other unidentifiable objects pummeled her as she tried to stand up. She began to look around her, scouring the landscape for any sign of her two girls. Over her right shoulder she saw the mangled body of her mother, battered and bloody, her scalp almost ripped off. She looked like she was dead, but as Laurinda crawled to her, she saw that she was still breathing ever so faintly and trying to talk.

Laurinda struggled to her feet against the winds. Things continued to fly at her as the storm seemed determined to take her down. She grabbed a blanket she found on the ground and covered her mother, hoping she could survive until help came. And then she turned and frantically began looking for her daughters. They had to be nearby. Her mind was muddled, and she sensed she was in shock. She could feel the warm ooze of blood from somewhere, but she was numb to the pain. Where were her girls? Where had the storm taken them?

That's when she saw Sydnee in the distance, her tiny seven-month old baby, her little body usually squirming like a happy worm, now lying painfully still on the concrete driveway of a neighbor's house a few yards away. Laurinda ran to her, dodging lumber and insulation that continued to fly in the air, and as she got closer, she realized her daughter, her baby whose life had barely begun, was dead. Laurinda fell her to knees as she picked up Sydnee's lifeless little body and held her close.

Sydnee had only just started to enunciate words, her sweet gurgles and squeals forming little bursts of "Mamas" and "Dadas." Her first word was "Bubba," for her brother Damon, who had spent hours cradling her, the protective older brother of a pack of young sisters. To the west Laurinda could see that Briarwood was nothing but rubble. Were he and Aria gone too? Where was Karrina? Her mind could not seem to focus. It all seemed so unreal. What had happened?

She held her baby to her chest, rocking her as people slowly began to emerge from the debris and survey the apocalyptic landscape around them. There was a strong smell of natural gas punctuated by the odor of disturbed earth and rain. But Laurinda was aware of none of this. All she could focus on was her still little baby who had crawled for the first time only the day before, right in their living room, which was now gone, along with everything else they had.

They had been watching the storm coverage the night before—she and Phil and her mom and the kids. Tornadoes had erupted to the east, toward Shawnee, and that's when Sydnee had begun to coo and shuffle her little body around on the floor. Everybody had stopped to watch, to take in this precious moment that happens only once in a child's life, and Phil, his face beaming with the same joy he'd felt in watching his other kids take their first steps, had suddenly laughed. Sydnee was definitely their Okie, he'd said with a chuckle. Only an Oklahoma baby would crawl for the first time when there where tornadoes on the ground nearby.

Now, not even a day later, a tornado had come and cruelly taken Sydnee away. As the deadly funnel continued to grind its way east, all Laurinda could do was sit in the driveway as it began to rain and hold her lifeless little girl and wonder what had happened to her other kids.

CHAPTER 15

3:19 P.M., MAY 20

As the twister prepared to cross from Oklahoma City into Moore, it suddenly slowed to an excruciating crawl, just as it had right before it had charged east from Newcastle some twenty minutes earlier. But this time, instead of mostly empty farmland, the storm hovered over the neighborhood east of Briarwood Elementary, the most densely populated area on its track so far. It seemed to want to take its time as it violently devoured everything within a mile radius, lingering as it chewed up houses and cars and trees and spit them out, only to suck them up and put them through the grinder once again. As it inched forward, it left the landscape behind it virtually unrecognizable.

Though it had decreased in speed, going from about 40 miles per hour to about 15 or 20, the tornado became stronger than ever, as if eating away at the life of a city was somehow fueling its brutality. By now its winds and rotation were so demonic that entire lawns were vacuumed away in seconds. The ground underneath was scoured so clean of loose dirt that the vortex began to leave deep scars that resembled crop circles indented in the earth.

Every tree within reach of its fierce winds was shorn of its leaves and limbs—and in some cases its bark. Giant, leafy oak trees that had withstood storms for years were quickly carved down to jagged little stumps. Entire homes were swept from their slabs in seconds, the debris chopped and chewed into fragments.

Even with all the attention paid to them in recent years, tornadoes were still a mysterious phenomenon—and this one was no different. As it neared Santa Fe Avenue, houses on some blocks were inhaled and then redeposited in neat, uniform rows like loose hay swept up in a farm field ready to be harvested into bales. It was as if the storm suddenly felt the need to be polite and to organize its mess. Scientists were at a loss to explain why or how it did this. Nobody got close enough to see firsthand because it was simply too dangerous.

But they knew enough to know that windrowing, as it was referred to, happened only when tornadoes were at their most fierce, with winds of at least 200 miles per hour. According to the radar, the winds inside this storm were now hitting around 210 miles per hour as it pounded the neighborhood around Briarwood, though they were probably far stronger. Given its distance, the Doppler radar could only calculate the winds at the top of the storm, and in the rare instances when scientists had been able to get close enough to a vortex to measure its exact wind speed, they had often found the gusts closer to the ground to be much stronger and more violent.

Nobody could get close enough to really know precisely how bad the winds were. Like many of the teams of professional chasers, most of the scientists who fan out to study the storms that regularly erupt during the Oklahoma springtime had headed south, believing the likelihood of tornadoes was stronger in that direction. Now some of these, like Howard Bluestein and his team of OU students, were racing back north, and even though they weren't close enough to get a comprehensive read, the tornado heading toward Moore was so strong they were able to pull some limited ground data on it even from more than 60 miles away.

But those in the immediate path of the tornado didn't need an exact wind reading to understand how bad it was. They could hear it in the way the structure around them creaked ominously and feel how the ground trembled as the storm approached. And then, just as quickly, it was hell on earth as they were caught up in a whirling gyre that latched on to its victims and refused to let go.

At a house on Broadway Circle, a block from where Moore officially began, Shannon Quick was huddled in a dark closet with her mother-in-law, Joy; her two young boys, Jackson, eight, and Tanner, thirteen; and their plump bull terrier, Luke, when the tornado approached. As was true for many in the neighborhood, a storm shelter was an indulgence the family hadn't been able to afford, and when it was too late to escape, they had taken cover in the only place they could—an interior closet. There was no reason to believe it wouldn't protect them now.

Shannon and her family were only hours away from leaving on vacation. They were going to Virginia, and she had checked out her boys early from school to pack. But now they were in the path of a tornado, and as the winds engulfed them, the house began to crumble like a cracker crushed in the ball of someone's fist. In the closet the walls began to disintegrate around them—one wall went and then the other. The boys had been wearing their plastic Little League helmets—placed on their heads by their worried mother, who was heeding Gary England's advice to gird the kids for battle against the storm. Suddenly the helmets were sucked from their heads, leaving them defenseless against the debris around them. And then, just as suddenly, they were all sucked up, catapulted through the air by the tornado for what seemed like an eternity before being viciously hurled back to the ground.

An hour or so earlier, Shannon had been checking items off her to-do list before leaving town. Now she was sprawled on the ground near what used to be her house bleeding to death, the midsection of her body sliced fully open by something that had impaled her as she was tossed around by the tornado. Nearby Jackson lay almost motionless, his tiny body pulverized by the storm. The skin of his right buttock had been torn away; his pelvis was crushed and one of his legs broken. He was losing blood fast. Luke, his beloved dog, moaned and whimpered nearby, injured so badly he would have to be put to sleep.

Shannon's older son, Tanner, who had somehow escaped with only cuts and bruises, roused his grandmother, who was unconscious on the ground nearby. Joy, who was sixty-one, was seriously injured too. "Ma! Ma!" he cried, shaking her a bit. The boys had called her "Ma" since they were small, when they hadn't been able to pronounce the word "Grandma." She had a giant hole in her right arm where blood was gushing out, and one of her heels was crushed and broken. But seeing the panicked look on her grandson's face, she found the strength to rise in spite of the pain and push herself up off the ground. She ran to her daughter-in-law, who kept repeating her boys' names in a voice so faint Joy could barely hear her over the roar of the storm. "Tanner, Jackson, Tanner, Jackson," she slowly whispered again and again, struggling to speak. The forty-year-old coughed and her voice began to gurgle as blood filled her lungs. "They are okay. They are okay," Joy told her, trying to comfort her and keep her calm. "Just lie still." Nearby Tanner sobbed as he looked at his mother, so badly injured. No child was supposed to see his parent like this.

Joy stood up and frantically screamed for help. But there was nobody. They were in the middle of a wasteland, and the tornado was still so close that debris was floating in the air around them. She began to pray, calling out to God to keep her daughter-in-law alive until someone could help them. It didn't seem right that Shannon, who lived to take care of her kids, wouldn't see them grow up. It couldn't be that she was being ripped out of their lives like this, in such a horrid, despicable way. A man, a paramedic, finally ran up, and Shannon grabbed his pant leg as he talked to her, trying to keep her alert until they could get her out of there. But her hand slowly went limp. She died right there on the ground, her face wet from the rain that began to fall in thick droplets from the sky.

The tornado was now such a monster that KFOR's Jon Welsh, sitting a mile to the south and several thousand feet in the air, could hear the roar of the storm over the sound of his headset, which was designed to protect him from the high-frequency pitch of the engine of his helicopter. The storm was even louder than the helicopter, something that had never happened before.

His wife had finally texted him to let him know she was in the shelter with their kids. Welsh was relieved, but his relief was only momentary. Before his eyes the storm was getting bigger and bigger. He knew he had to keep a mental distance from what was happening in order to maintain control—just as he had when he was operating in war zones overseas. But the tornado was so massive as it took aim at the most heavily populated parts of Moore that he could barely believe it. In his heart he knew that people were dying, and it made him feel sick. "This thing is not letting up," he told Mike Morgan.

On the KFOR radar the center of the tornado was now a huge black hole, representing the storm's apocalyptic winds and massive quantity of debris. Between that and the ominous pictures from Welsh and his other chasers, Morgan kept thinking of May 3—not just because of the path of the storm but also because he still worried there were people who weren't listening to the warnings. It wasn't just the tornado's savage winds that killed but also people's reaction to the storm, or their inaction. So many people had died needlessly by waiting too long to take shelter or by not bothering to take cover at all. The thought of that happening again was driving Morgan crazy. Why wouldn't they just listen and get out of there?

While Gary England tried his best to conceal his trauma from the public, Morgan freely admitted to people that he thought he might have a little PTSD from all the bad weather he'd seen and the stress of worrying about viewers in the path of the storm. Though he and England could barely conceal their distaste for each other, they shared that lingering concern about whether they were doing everything they possibly could to save lives. England, who obsessively struggled to keep cool on air, addressed the torture more privately; Morgan had a more frantic air about him, which he now struggled to keep in check.

By now Morgan had played all the cards in his deck in an effort to convince people in Moore of how much danger they were in. He had likened the storm to the May 3 tornado—and even those who hadn't been around knew what that meant. He'd urged people again and again to get underground or "get out of the way"—warning them that an interior closet or bathroom wouldn't be sufficient to protect them from the tornado's intense winds. What more could he do?

His voice had an anxious edge to it, and as the storm crossed Santa Fe Avenue and officially entered the city of Moore, he began to sound almost frustrated as he pleaded with viewers who might be in its trajectory to understand how dire the situation was. Those in the path of the storm should be evacuated by now based on the station's warnings, Morgan declared, a hint of irritation in his voice. And then he began to sound like an upset parent lecturing a child who had misbehaved, repeating himself as he desperately tried to convince people that they were running out of time. "You cannot delay. You can't think. You can't delay. You've got to act!" Morgan said in a voice that verged on panic. "You've got to act! You can't think or delay. You've got to act. And act. And act to save your life and your loved ones' lives. You've got to act!"

For many it was already too late. As the tornado entered the housing addition adjacent to Plaza Towers, entire blocks of homes were wiped out almost instantly by the storm's horrific winds. Some residents had fled to the small number of storm shelters in their backyards, but others took cover in their homes, praying their tiny closets and bathrooms would be enough. For some they weren't. On a single block along SW Fourteenth Street at Ginger Avenue, six people in neighboring homes died as the tornado picked off their houses one by one.

Toward the middle of the block, inside a quaint little blue and white ranch-style home, Gina Stromski, a fifty-one-year-old retiree, was crouched in a closet with her beloved dog, Wylie, riding out the storm. A widow who was such a rabid OU football fan she had an entire room of her house dedicated to Sooner memorabilia, she was on the phone with her brother-in-law as the tornado closed in. "Maybe it will turn," she said hopefully—and then the phone went dead. Next door Cindy Plumley, a forty-nine-year-old nurse, was riding out the storm in her bathroom with her daughter and two grandkids when the house collapsed on top of them, killing her instantly. Earlier that afternoon she had been planning a getaway to mark her fiftieth birthday the following month. She had wanted to take the kids to Disneyland.

Down the street two homes were completely swept off their foundations by the storm. Inside one was Randy Smith, a quiet thirty-nine-year-old electrician who was planning to attend his son Dylan's graduation from Southmoore High School that Saturday. His family had tried to reach him again and again ahead of the storm, but he hadn't picked up his phone. A video-game junkie, he often wore headphones when he played, and afterward his father, Terry, wondered if he'd been too engrossed to notice that the weather outside had turned.

A few doors down Tawauna Robinson and her fiancé, Leslie Johnson, had taken shelter inside a closet at a home they shared with her twenty-five-year-old son Lamarr. Tawauna, a vivacious woman who loved life even on bad days, had only recently moved to Moore from St. Louis to be closer to her son. They loved to dance, and together she and Lamarr would have impromptu dance parties in his tiny rental house, just as they had when he was a toddler back in Missouri. On that Monday Lamarr, who was out of town, could hear the fear in his mother's voice when she called to tell him about the storm. A woman of strong faith, Tawauna was praying the Lord would protect her and Pee Wee, as Johnson was known among his closest friends. No matter what, God had been good to her.

A few hours later her body was found near her fiancé's in the twisted rubble of their home.

Across the street from Gina Stromski's house, Rick Jones, a fifty-four-year-old postal worker, had taken cover in a tiny closet inside the beige and white house where he'd ridden out the 1999 tornado. Jones was a simple man who lived a largely solitary life. He wasn't married and he worked nights sorting mail. A few months before the storm he bought a black Corvette, the flashiest thing he had ever owned. After the storm a stranger who had rushed to Moore to help rescue victims found Jones's body in the closet, where the house had collapsed upon him. A Bible was at his knees. His beloved Corvette was down the block, mangled beyond recognition.

A street away, on Penn Lane, Jerrie Bhonde was sitting inside the shower with her husband, Hemant, as the tornado approached. They didn't have a storm shelter, but even if they had, her husband was so frail he probably wouldn't have been able to make it down the steps. A former worker at the local General Motors plant, Hemant suffered from osteoporosis so severe that he could barely leave the house. Jerrie, his wife of forty years, had retired to care for her husband, who had immigrated to Oklahoma from India decades ago. They spent their entire days together laughing and talking. He often sat at the window looking out at Plaza Towers Elementary across the field from their house. He loved to watch the kids play and frolic—even if he could barely move.

In the bathroom the ground began to shake as the tornado approached, and Jerrie clutched her husband's hand tightly, telling him how much she loved him. Suddenly it was upon them, and the walls around them disintegrated in seconds. The couple began to be sucked into the air by the monster twister, but Jerrie refused to let go. The storm would not take her beloved. Yet the force soon became too much and she felt her grip begin to slip. She barely had time to look at his face one last time before her husband disappeared into the sky.

CHAPTER 16

3:20 P.M., MAY 20

Outside the nearly forty-year-old walls of Plaza Towers Elementary it had grown eerily still. The rain had ceased, the hail had stopped, and even the blustery winds that had been screaming through the school's creaky old windows seemed to have momentarily died down. To anyone who didn't know better, it might have seemed that the storm had miraculously lifted, that the horrible nightmare suddenly was over. Yet it's the silence that people who live in Tornado Alley have learned to fear the most, that ominous pause before the worst usually comes.

The teachers inside Plaza Towers knew it likely wasn't over, but as they crouched down in the dark hallways alongside or on top of their tiny students, some couldn't help but hope that maybe, just maybe, their desperate pleas to God had been answered. That somehow that terrible tornado coming for them had lifted right back up into the sky, sparing their students, their school, and their city. *Lord, lift it, please lift it,* Emily Eischen, a thirty-three-year-old second-grade teacher, silently prayed as she knelt in the hallway of the school's back building.

But in the distance she could hear a dull roar, and as the storm crept closer and closer, the sound grew louder and even more grotesque. The noise was unlike anything she had ever heard before, so horrifying it seemed to come straight from the lowest depths of hell. It was a ghastly combination of the whooshing, high-pitched sound of a whining jet engine and the rattling, metallic rumble of a howling freight train speeding out of control. As it grew near, one could hear snapping wood and the ear-piercing screech of bending steel. It was the gnashing, violent soundtrack of an increasingly demonic monster that pulverized everything in its path, sparing almost nothing on the landscape as it made its way toward Plaza Towers and the heart of Moore.

Inside the school the tornado's roar grew impossibly loud, so deafening that it felt to many as if their ears were about to explode. The building began to shake and the ground rumbled beneath them, and as the storm seemed to be right on top of them, the teachers braced themselves for the hit, anticipating it like the car wreck you see coming too late to prevent. Time seemed to stand still. Instead of hitting the building, the twister only howled painfully louder. The storm had slowed to a crawl—torturously prolonging the terror of the teachers, who clutched their students closer, unsure of what to do.

Near the front of the building Amy Simpson was crammed into a tiny one-person bathroom inside her office, listening to the tornado as it grew near. She was squeezed in with four other women—Penny, her office assistant; a secretary; the school's guidance counselor; and the music teacher. The space was barely four feet wide and there was not an inch of room to spare. Simpson was on the ground, her body wrapped around the slim pedestal of the sink. Her secretary was sitting on the toilet behind her, her knees digging sharply into Simpson's back as she grabbed the top of the sink for reinforcement. The others were jammed in tight on the floor around them. They had covered their heads with cushions taken from their office chairs—though Simpson wondered how much help they would really be.

The electricity had gone out and the bathroom was pitch-black, illuminated only by a thin sliver of light that peeked around the sides of the closed door. But that soon faded as the sky outside grew even darker than it had been before, the daylight now blocked out completely by the ominous wall of a storm that was just blocks away. Simpson had never been so close to a tornado before. Somehow she'd missed all the other storms that had hit Moore over the years. Simpson loved the weather, but she had never once forgotten how dangerous it could be.

Her mother had survived a direct hit from the 1955 tornado that had leveled much of tiny Blackwell, Oklahoma, near the Kansas border. Later categorized as an F5 tornado, the storm had killed twenty people, injured two hundred, and destroyed nearly four hundred buildings, wiping them clear to the ground. Simpson's mother had been only five at the time, but she was still haunted by the vivid memories of that day. Rescuers had dug her out of the rubble of the family home, her tiny body passed from stranger to stranger down a line of people frantically searching for survivors. She had been separated from her family for more than a day. Her parents had thought she was dead, and she had thought she had lost her family forever. It was trauma she'd never really gotten over.

The story had scared Simpson to death when she was a child, but only now did she truly understand how horrifying it was to be in a path of a storm. The sound alone was terrifying. But it was the smell that she noticed the most as the air became rich with the overpowering odor of freshly tilled earth, mowed grass, and lumber. It was a confirmation, as if she needed it, that the tornado was doing major damage as it ravaged its way toward her. She thought of the kids crouched in the hallways, the only shelter they had. She prayed the building would be strong enough to withstand what was coming. Miracles could happen. Her mother was a living, breathing example of one—a tiny child who had survived a deadly tornado.

What was happening seemed so unreal, so alien, as if she were floating outside her body watching someone else's life. She could not comprehend how the day had turned out like this, the final Monday before school let out for the year, a day that was supposed to be a celebration of the kids and how much they had accomplished, with summer vacation just days away. They had been so close to the end of the day, when most of the kids would have been safe with their parents. Why had the tornado formed so early? Unanswerable questions raced through her head, and she could barely wrap her mind around any of them. The storm was coming, and she had to be ready for whatever would happen now. It was her job, her duty. She was the principal, responsible for everybody in the building, the kids and her staff. She wished she could unleash some protective bubble around them to keep them safe, but there was nothing more she could do. She felt completely helpless.

In the dark Simpson felt the other women trembling in fear around her, scared for their lives. Kristin Atchley, the school's counselor, was hanging on to one side of the toilet for dear life and began to cite the Lord's Prayer out loud. "Our father who art in heaven, hallowed be thy name. Thy kingdom come, thy will be done," she said in a shaky voice. Atchley suddenly paused. "I don't want to die," she said as she began to weep. By now the others were quietly crying too, listening to the storm approach and wondering if they would live to see the world outside the bathroom walls.

Simpson was terrified too, but she was determined not to allow the fear to overtake her. She pushed it all to the back of her mind, willing herself to be strong and focused for everyone around her. She was strangely calm, as if some other force had taken over to keep her from really thinking about how much she had to lose. As the tornado inched closer, she leaned her forehead on the cool white porcelain of the sink, which began to vibrate from the energy of the monster grinding its way toward her. All she could do was wait and pray that her school could survive this and be ready for what would come next.

Along the east corridor of the school, where the fourth-, fifth-, and sixth-grade classes were held, Justin Ayers, a twenty-nine-year-old fifth-grade teacher, had been nervously pacing back and forth between the students sheltering inside and the back door at the end of the hallway that led to a concrete courtyard outside. He kept walking out and peering off toward the west looking for the tornado. By then it was hard to see. At more than a mile wide, it was wrapped in so much rain and debris it simply looked like a massive black veil of darkness as it stretched across what seemed to be the entire sky west of the school. Somewhere in the cloud was the killer tornado, but even though they could hear it, the people directly in front of it couldn't see it until it was right on top of them.

Suddenly it was there, a few hundred yards away. Ayers saw a house just on the other side of the school's library suddenly explode in the air as the funnel blasted into it like an unstoppable tank. His heart began to race. Seeing how that house had been so suddenly pulverized, he realized almost instantly that the hallways inside the school would not be enough to protect them from what was coming. He raced as fast as he could back into the building, where he screamed at the top of his lungs at the teachers and students crouched against the walls to get into the bathrooms. "It's coming! It's coming," he yelled, so loud that he could be heard all the way to the front hallway of the building, where first graders, kindergartners, and pre-K classes were huddled.

Paula Fleener, a fourth-grade teacher, jumped to her feet and ran to a bathroom, whose stalls were already crammed with students from another class. Fleener, who at fifty-nine was one of the oldest teachers on staff, grabbed a trash can and hurled it down the hall, quickly making room for her students on the floor near the sinks. She ordered them to crouch and squeeze together with their backpacks over their heads. She then threw her body on top of them, grabbing as many of them as she could underneath her and holding them tight. She thought only of their safety. "I want my mama!" one of her students began to sob as the horrifying roar of the tornado was punctuated by the terrible screech of twisting metal and breaking glass as it began to inhale the neighborhood around them. "I won't let you go," Fleener told the boy, squeezing him and her other students even tighter beneath her.

A few feet away her colleague Rhonda Crosswhite, who taught sixth grade, had thrown her body on top of her students inside one of the stalls. She could feel them shaking underneath her. One girl was crying hysterically, her body heaving with sobs. Another boy lifted his head up to look at Crosswhite, his face gripped with fear. "I love you," he told her, tears running down his face. "Please don't die with me. I don't want to die." Short and blond, Crosswhite, who was forty-four, was a bulldog of a woman, a strong, unfailingly positive mother of three teenage daughters whose voice was so boisterous and loud that she often joked that she had been born with a built-in microphone. She spent her time outside the classroom as a "cheer mom," a special breed of mother who devoted hours to ferrying her youngest daughter, Abby, and her cheerleading squad all over the state for competitions.

But as the tornado neared, it was Crosswhite who became the cheerleader inside that cramped stall, bucking up her students and refusing to give an inch to a ruthless storm that seemed to have no mercy on any of its victims. "I am *not* going to die today," Crosswhite declared matter-of-factly, her booming voice louder than the roar of the storm. "I have other things to do in my life, and I'm not going to die, and you're not going to die. . . . We're going to be fine. I'm protecting you. We're not going to die today." Crosswhite refused to even consider the possibility that the storm would kill them, as if the power of positive thinking would make it go away. Still, she began to pray out loud so her students could hear her, calling on God to protect them, to keep them safe from the destructive tornado.

On the other side of the wall, Janice Brim and her sixth graders were still singing church praise songs that called on God for protection as they sat squeezed in the tiny printer closet. And as the roar of the twister grew louder and louder, Brim and the students raised their voices louder, singing almost at the top of their lungs, as if they were trying to shout the storm away. Brim grabbed the knob of the door to hold it shut, since the lock was broken. She braced her feet in one of the corners of the closet and prepared to hold on tight, hoping she would have enough strength to keep the storm out.

In the back building Jennifer Doan clutched her third graders as close to her as she could. If she could have fit them all under her to protect them, she would have but, small and diminutive with the slightly swollen belly of a woman two months pregnant, she simply couldn't. On her left was Xavier Delgado. On her right was Porter Trammell and next to him was Nicolas McCabe—nine-year-olds who had been so gleeful earlier in the day celebrating their final week of school before summer vacation. Now they were terrified and sobbing, their tiny bodies shaking in fear. "I don't want to die," one of the boys, his voice quivering, told her. Doan, her heart suddenly in her throat, tried her very best not to cry. "It's going to be okay. It's going to be okay," she said again and again, stretching her arms as far as possible to rub the boys' backs and comfort them.

A few feet away Cheryl Littlejohn, another third-grade teacher, was watching for the tornado from one of the classrooms that faced the west. She suddenly saw the funnel begin to tear at the playground equipment just yards away. Littlejohn ran back into the hallway, screaming for the teachers and kids to get down. Up and down the hallway the children cried and screamed as the tornado began to pummel the building, hurling massive pieces of debris against the roof and walls as if they were under attack. The ground began to rumble like an earthquake, and there was the sound of glass shattering as the windows exploded inside the classrooms from the force of the winds. Within seconds the air became thick with dust and insulation as the storm rattled everything loose. It quickly became hard to breathe.

Second-grade teacher Shelly Calvert, her arms stretched around six kids, peeked up just as the back door at the southern end of the hallway was torn open. She watched in terror as the tornado peeled it away hinge by hinge. A choking cloud of dust and debris swept through the hall as the teachers and kids began to feel their bodies being lifted and sucked by the storm—the unseen hand of a monster dragging them helplessly toward the outside.

As she fought to maintain traction against the storm, Calvert felt for a little girl to her right who had been just beyond her fingertips, so tiny and light she worried the storm might suck her away. Feeling nothing, she peeked up and saw that she was gone. As panic raced through her body, she lifted her head up fully, her body now pummeled by debris, looking for the girl. Feeling something at her back, she turned and saw her, motionless on the ground behind her. She quickly grabbed her, shaking her and yelling her name, and for a second the girl didn't move and Calvert worried she might be dead. But then she suddenly came to, coughing and crying. Calvert threw her on top of the kids in front of her and leaned down again as the debris flying through the hallway grew bigger and the winds grew fiercer than anything she had ever imagined. *This is it,* she thought. There was no way they could survive this. Images of her husband and kids and granddaughter flashed through her mind. She prayed she would see them again, but as she and the kids began to be battered by rocks and books and anything else the storm could pick up and hurl at them, she began to lose hope. Above them the roof began to disintegrate, pulled apart by the winds of the massive tornado.

Down the hall Doan was hanging on to her kids for dear life. It was all happening so fast, but for a few brief moments it seemed as though it were in slow motion, like a scene from a horror film, with books and papers and pieces of the rapidly crumbling school swirling and suspended in midair. Before she could even grasp what was happening, the walls had caved in, causing everything to go black. The kids who had been within her grasp suddenly seemed to be gone, their warm touch replaced by cold, jagged pieces of concrete and steel.

In the front hallway Karen Marinelli and her colleagues had heard Ayers's cries warning that the storm was approaching, and they had squeezed their small students even tighter. Marinelli had reached as far as she could around the kids, so far she was touching the teacher next to her. Marinelli had resisted voicing her fears, but as she grabbed her colleague's hand she couldn't hold it in any longer. "I'm scared," she said as she heard the west side of the building begin to creak and crack as the storm devoured it piece by piece. Suddenly the skylights above their heads exploded, spraying glass all over the hallway.

A few feet away Linda Patterson, a pre-K teacher, and her aide, Kaye Johnson, threw their bodies on top of their students as the ceiling began to rain down on them. They were crouched next to Erin Baxter's class, and in an attempt to keep the kids calm Patterson and Johnson were singing the alphabet song. "A, B, C, D, E, F, G . . ." the teachers sang in unison, raising their voices in an effort to be heard over the storm. Underneath her Patterson heard the tiny, muffled voice of one of her students. "I can't breathe," the child said, pushing against her. But Patterson was not about to move. She felt a whoosh of wind at her back as the roof began to peel away. Just as quickly she was being pelted by rocks, cracked plaster, and everything else the storm had gathered up in its maw. The sound was now deafening.

A few feet away Baxter clutched her students closer as she wondered if the building would collapse on top of them. She didn't dare look up, but she felt things whizzing past her head—boards and ceiling tiles. Her ears suddenly began to pop, and she could hear sounds only in a muted, muffled way, as if she were caught underneath a giant glass jar. Her mind flashed back to the May 3 tornado, when one of her friends had been seriously injured by debris flying through the air. She began to pray out loud for God to keep her students safe and for the storm to go away. "It's going to be okay! It's going to be okay!" she yelled. "I love you!" She had no idea if her kids could hear her, but she knew for now they were still alive. She could feel them moving beneath her, but she didn't know how much longer they could survive like this. The tornado seemed to be parked right on top of them.

A little farther down the hall, Jennifer Simonds, a twenty-six-year-old kindergarten teacher, couldn't believe what was happening. A native of Naperville, Illinois, Simonds had been through a few thunderstorms since she'd moved to Oklahoma a few years before, but nothing like this. It was like *The Wizard of Oz* mashed up with a horror movie. She felt her body being pummeled and sucked at by the tornado's winds. It seemed like one big gust of air, and she and her kids would be gone. Only a few minutes earlier she hadn't even really believed the tornado would hit them. This had to be just a precaution. Why would something so terrible happen to a school? But then she had heard the glass shattering in another part of the building. She quickly stood up and grabbed backpacks off hooks nearby and threw them on top of the six students she had left. "This is going to hurt," she said, and she dove on top of them, using her body as a shield. Within seconds the heavy concrete cinder blocks of the wall started to crack apart, and she felt them falling one by one on top of her. Simonds began to worry that she was crushing the kids. Like other teachers, she worried more about their safety than her own. They were so young, just five or six. Their lives had barely begun. She was young too, but at least she'd lived a little bit of a life. She began to cry out loud to God, "Take me! Take me! Not my babies!" She repeated it again and again, as the storm lingered above.

Nearby Marinelli felt something unbearably heavy hit the small of her back, and her pelvis and legs were pushed to the ground, almost flat. Her upper body remained tightly wrapped around the three boys from her class, who began to squirm as the world seemed to be collapsing around them. At that moment Marinelli was sure they were going to die. "What's going on? What's happening?!" one of the boys cried out. Marinelli tried to respond, but she could barely breathe. Whatever it was that had fallen on them felt like it had cut off part of her flow of oxygen, and her voice came out as a labored whisper. "It's okay. It's okay," she repeated. "It's going to be over soon." Pain was shooting through her body, and she wondered how much longer she would be able to last.

In the hallway of the back building where the second- and third-grade classes were, Eischen felt her body being sucked up into the air. She clawed at the wall, trying to pull herself back down, worried that the winds lapping at them like a thirsty dog would take one of her kids. She screamed again to God: "Lift it, Lord! Please lift it!"

On the east side of the building near the fourth-, fifth-, and sixth-grade classrooms, Janice Brim was using every bit of strength she possessed to keep the door to the closet where she and her students were sheltering closed. They were still singing the words to Psalm 91, shouting them now to be heard above the storm. "I will say of the Lord: He is my refuge and fortress," they yelled. By now they had sung the hymn a dozen or so times, and as the tornado began to tear through the school, slowly and agonizingly, they sang it even more fervently. Brim could hear the fear in her kids' voices, but some strange calm had fallen over her. She was prepared to go if the Lord wanted to take her, but she prayed that the storm would spare the kids. In her hand the doorknob began to twist. She struggled to hang on even as it twisted her wrist, spraining it. She ducked her head as the roof above them peeled away, but still she hung on to that door, refusing to let go. "His faithfulness, your sure defense," she sang.

Back at the front of the building Simpson was still grasping the pedestal sink for dear life. The storm seemed as if it had been over them forever, as if it had purposely stopped for maximum impact. It didn't seem to be moving. She and the three other women were crammed so tightly into that bathroom that there was barely an inch of distance between them, but somehow debris was filling in that space—rocks and dust and parts of the ceiling. Waiting for the tornado to hit had been excruciating, and for some reason Simpson had found herself narrating out loud what she believed to be happening outside the bathroom door, like a play-by-play announcer. "It's hitting the library," she'd said matter-of-factly when she heard it tear into the west side of the building. She thought it would move through quickly—that's what most tornadoes did. But it just sat there, and Simpson began to slowly bang her forehead against the porcelain sink, almost like a personal countdown. "It's almost over. It's almost over. It's almost over," she said again and again. Outside the door it sounded like the building was imploding. Crash after crash. She ached to get out of the bathroom and to the kids. She knew from the terrifying sounds that her school had been ripped apart, though she didn't have any idea how badly. But it wouldn't go away.

Simpson had tried to be so calm, to keep it together for her colleagues who were screaming in terror. Suddenly she couldn't control it anymore. "In God's name, go away!" she shouted. "Leave! Go away!" She repeated her cry again and again, maybe eight times, and suddenly she felt a rush of chilly air hit her. The roof above her had been ripped off, and as she peered up she saw right into the heart of the monster storm as it swirled above the school. It felt unreal, almost like a movie. She watched as pieces of boards, insulation, and other debris swirled hundreds of feet in the air above.

Something inexplicable came over her—some presence that took the fear away. It suddenly stopped being bad for her. She had to get out of that bathroom. The kids needed her. Her staff needed her. Plaza needed her. And as Simpson looked up again, she suddenly saw a patch of blue sky. It was finally over.

CHAPTER 17

3:23 P.M., MAY 20

A few blocks east of Plaza Towers, Julie Molotsky had just reached her house on Kings Manor Drive when she saw the tornado in the distance. She had picked up her two grandsons—Jacob, six, and Caden, two—from school and day care. Her daughter, Heather, had called her from work less than a half hour earlier, worried about reports of a tornado on the ground. Her son-in-law, Travis, was a Moore police officer, and he couldn't pick up the kids because he'd been called into work in anticipation of a storm emergency.

Molotsky didn't have a storm shelter, but one of her neighbors did, and she was sure they'd let her and the boys crowd in. The family had hit a rough patch recently, and she had helped out with money and food. She wasn't a rich woman, but she believed in helping others. That's just what you did. It was how she'd been raised.

A tiny creek and park divided her neighborhood from the housing addition that surrounded Plaza Towers, and as she looked west she was horrified to see massive pieces of debris sailing in the air. The tornado was so wide at that point, it seemed to swallow the entire sky. She could see nothing but the storm. She ran in fear to her neighbor's backyard with her grandsons and began beating on the door, which was locked and sealed from the inside. Through a tiny vent she heard her neighbor's voice, someone she'd helped out so often. They wouldn't open the door. The storm was too close, and they didn't have enough room. Molotsky was stunned. She beat on the door again. "Please!" she begged, the tornado now perilously close. There was no response.

Running out of time, Molotsky grabbed her grandsons and ran toward the back fence. She was almost certain that another neighbor, one she didn't know as well, had a shelter. With tree limbs and other debris now sailing past her head, the forty-seven-year-old grandmother kicked down a wooden stockade fence and was relieved to see that there was shelter a few houses away. She grabbed the boys and ran as fast as she could. Beating on the door, she prayed it would open, and it did, just as the twister began devouring homes a few doors down the street.

A few blocks north Terri Long had pulled into a 7-Eleven store at the corner of SW Fourth Street and Telephone Road. She called her daughter Alyson and told her where she was. She was taking shelter with the store's employees and a young mother and her four-month-old baby, who had tried to outrace the storm but couldn't. Long didn't sound worried, and the call was brief. She told her daughter she loved her and hung up. It was the last time Alyson Costilla ever spoke to her mother. The tornado had been heading due east, but it lurched a few blocks to the north as it approached Interstate 35 and made a direct hit on the convenience store, killing Long; twenty-nine-year-old Megan Futrell; and Futrell's four-month-old son, Case.

Futrell, a special-education teacher at Highland West Junior High who was known for her beaming smile and thick mane of curly blond hair, had left school early to run and pick up her son from day care ahead of the storm. Her husband, Cody, had raced to pick up their older son, Kanon, from school. They had planned to meet back home, but Megan never made it. She pulled over when a hailstorm made it impossible for her to see out of her car's front window and decided to ride out the tornado inside the 7-Eleven. Rescuers who ran to the store after the storm had passed were combing through the debris when the saw the tiny foot of a baby. He was dead, cradled tight in the arms of his mother, who was also gone. The sight was so terrible that many of the rescuers, police officers and several civilians, were too distraught to go on.

The tornado continued east, heedless of the carnage in its wake. It made a direct hit on the Moore Medical Center, picking up dozens of mangled cars from nearby parking lots and throwing them in jagged piles near the building's front door. Amazingly, no one died there, and there were no major injuries. Right next door the Warren Theatre, the most recognizable landmark in Moore, also took a direct hit, but aside from having its awning torn apart and some roof damage, it too withstood the tornado's 200-mile-per-hour winds.

At KOCO, Damon Lane was now certain that his home was going to take a direct hit from the storm. On air Chance Coldiron, one of his storm chasers, was showing live video of the tornado, black and menacing as it prepared to cross Interstate 35. The hospital had taken a direct hit, he said, and the storm seemed to be reorganizing, moving a little toward the northeast. Lane quickly texted his wife, Melissa, who was in their underground shelter with their two dogs, having managed to drag down Skylar. "The tornado is going to pass right over," he warned.

In south Oklahoma City near 149th and May, not far from where the tornado had begun, Anthony Connel had finally reached his house—or what was left of it. As he had feared, it was completely leveled—as were most of the homes on his block. Everything was gone, including his two donkeys and his restored cherry red Road Runner parked in the garage. He hadn't heard from his wife, who was still at school at Southmoore—which was close to the path of the tornado. As it began to rain, Connel started going through the debris, trying to salvage what belongings he could. He found some guns and several of the vintage shaving kits that he collected.

Right in the middle of the debris Connel discovered his old solid-oak rocking chair. There wasn't a scratch on it. He pulled it out and took it down the driveway, where he instructed his seventy-seven-year-old neighbor, Gene Tripp, to sit down. Connel watched him and thought about how unfair life could be. Tripp's wife, Billye, had died just a few weeks before. They'd been married for fifty-six years and loved each other until the end like young teenagers. Tripp had barely been able to deal with her death, and now he'd lost everything—all of their belongings and their home. The only thing he really cared about in the house, Tripp told Connel, was her wedding ring, which had been on a shelf in their bedroom when the storm hit. Now it was probably lost forever. As they spoke, a photographer from the local newspaper happened on the scene and took Tripp's picture, which ultimately became an enduring image of the storm—an old man serenely sitting in a rocking chair in a landscape of endless destruction.

Down the road Lando Hite had dug himself out of a pit of debris at the Celestial Acres horse facility on the grounds of the Orr Family Farm. His shirt and shoes had been ripped off by the winds, and his pants would have been too, had it not been for his giant belt buckle. He was covered head to toe in mud, and he wiped the dirt out of his eyes so that he could see. What greeted him was total apocalypse. Almost every building in sight had been leveled, and there were horses, dozens of them, lying dead on the ground. Some had been thrown on top of buildings; others were tangled in power lines that has been ripped apart and tied into knots by the ferocious winds. Those that weren't dead were barely alive—stunned and bloodied by the horrific storm. Some had been impaled by boards and tree limbs. A mother and her filly, battered and bruised, stood huddled together, barely moving. It was the most horrible thing Hite had ever seen. And while he was grateful to be alive, he felt sick. All those innocent horses, majestic animals he had cared for and spent more time with than any other human being. All he could do was stand there stunned. Why had this happened?

LaDonna Cobb had no idea how long she had been unconscious. She awoke in what remained of a first-grade classroom at Briarwood Elementary, half buried under a heavy cinder-block wall with jagged bits of steel rebar poking through the cracks. She heard the voices of children beneath her screaming, including her youngest daughter, Erin. "Mom! Mom! Wake up!" she was yelling. Cobb felt dazed, and her head and face were pounding. She felt blood trickling down the back of her neck. What had happened to her?

She could barely open her eyes. One seemed to be swollen shut. But as she forced her eyes open, she could see Erin beneath her. Her daughter looked like a ghost, almost translucent. Cobb suddenly thought she was dead, having some sort of out-of-body experience where she was looking at the world she had left behind. But then she felt a shooting pain in her head and a feeling that she was about to suffocate. She was very much alive. The wall was crushing her. Her body was bearing all of its weight, hundreds of pounds. She was the only thing keeping it from falling on top of the kids, and she suddenly realized she wouldn't be able to bear the weight much longer. She began yelling, which was hard because she could barely catch her breath. "Crushed!" she managed to yell. "I'm being crushed!" She had no idea what was beyond the wall, if anyone was there to help her or the kids. She had no idea what the tornado had done, what it had left behind.

Suddenly she felt movement. Someone was trying to lift the wall, and after a few seconds it budged. It was her husband, Steve. Using all of his strength, he picked it up enough so that she and the kids could scramble out from underneath it. Her head felt cloudy and hazy, but suddenly things came into terrifying focus. The classroom around her was obliterated. The roof was gone; the walls had collapsed; the windows were blown out. As she struggled to her feet, she could see out into the open pathways that linked the separate classroom pods. It looked like the building had been picked up and crushed like a soda can. Everything was ripped apart or had collapsed. It was total devastation. Her heart raced with terror. She was sure that kids and teachers were dead. How could anyone have survived something like this? What had happened to their other two girls? Were they alive?

Cobb looked at her husband, who was battered and bloody. Her face was pounding, and she reached up and brushed her fingertips over its left side. It was numb and tender to the touch. She knew it was swollen by the way she could feel the rapid pounding of her heart in her face. She didn't know it, but her cheekbone was broken. She was covered in blood, which continued to ooze down her neck from a wound somewhere.

As they climbed out of the classroom, Steve, LaDonna, and Erin stumbled across a literal wasteland. There was destruction in every direction. It smelled like gas and electricity and wet earth. The cars in the parking lot had been sucked away, crushed, and thrown into a nearby field. All of the houses to the east of the school had been completely leveled, reduced to piles of boards and bricks. On the roof of one of the classrooms was a giant tank, the size of a gas truck without the wheels. How had it gotten there? Emotions were running high. There were people stumbling around in shock. Parents were running up to the school from the neighborhood, frantically looking for their kids. And those who emerged from the rubble of the school were received with a mix of tears and stunned disbelief. It was like a bad dream.

A teacher ran up. She was carrying Jordan, the Cobbs' middle daughter, whose leg had been injured by falling bricks. As Steve grabbed her and cradled her, Jordan looked over his shoulder and saw how badly injured her mother was. She began to wail. "My mom! Somebody help my mom! She's going to die!" Jordan screamed. As they walked around searching for their oldest daughter, Cydney, LaDonna tried to soothe her. "I'm okay. I'm okay," she told her. "I'm hurt, but I'll be all right. I'm alive. We're all alive." By then Cydney had emerged unscathed from the flattened school, having ridden out the storm in a bathroom. It was a miracle, Cobb thought. They had all made it. Her girls were crying and scared but fine. Looking back at the wreck of the building, she hoped there would be other miracles.

And there were. One by one over the next few minutes, students and teachers slowly emerged from the rubble of Briarwood. Some were injured, but the majority weren't. They scaled walls and climbed through broken windows to escape the destruction of their classrooms. Near the demolished front office, Shelly McMillin, the principal, saw the faces of her staff, some dirtied and bloodied, as they led their kids out of the building into what had been the parking lot. Scared but relieved, her staff one by one told her that their students were badly shaken but mostly unscathed. There were some injuries, including a teacher whose leg had been impaled on the leg of a chair. But everybody so far seemed to be okay. McMillin could barely believe it, and she silently began to thank God. She looked at her school and wondered how anyone could have made it out alive, but one by one they did. She prayed that the miracles would continue.

Before heading back into the building to look for students, McMillin pulled out her cell phone to call Robert Romines, her friend and the soon-to-be superintendent of Moore Public Schools, but he was suddenly there. Romines and Horn had finally made it, weaving their truck down roads that were nearly impassable, covered with downed telephone poles and trees and other debris. He had run the last few blocks in a panic, and as he walked up to McMillin, he looked at the school and then to her, a stunned, questioning look on his face. It was his worst nightmare come true. Looking at the building, he was certain people were dead, and as they ran inside, his cell phone, which had stopped working, briefly came back to life. It was a text message from Avery, his youngest daughter, whose school had come within blocks of being hit by the tornado. "Daddy, I'm scared," she wrote. Romines, who had willed himself to keep it together, felt tears begin to run down his face as he quickly tapped out a message. "It's going to be okay," he wrote. "Daddy's okay. Mama's okay." But the truth was he didn't know his wife's fate. She worked at an elementary school on the east side of town, and though he believed the storm had stayed to the south of her location, he didn't know for sure, and he'd been unable to reach her.

By then, KWTV was broadcasting the first images of the storm damage, shaky images of destroyed homes and roads covered in debris near Briarwood. Looking at it, Gary England felt sick, but he tried to remain focused. The tornado was still on the ground about 2 miles to the northeast near Interstate 35. But it was so rain wrapped and shrouded in debris that no one could see it. All the live video coming in just showed a giant fog on the ground. The power flashes around the storm—usually a telltale sign that it was on the ground—had slowed down, but that didn't necessarily mean it had lifted. It could have been that the fierce winds ahead of the storm had taken the lines out. No one knew. But on the radar the storm appeared to be weakening a bit, and England hoped against hope that the tornado was done. Just in case, he began to call out streets and locations heading east and northeast in Moore and beyond—including towns that had been hit by a tornado less than twenty-four hours before. They were again in the path of danger.

Suddenly Michael Armstrong, one of the younger meteorologists on staff, yelled, "There's the tornado." But his voice wasn't excited or frantic and full of adrenaline, as it had been nearly a half hour earlier when the tornado was just developing. Instead he sounded disappointed. On air there was a loud collective sigh from England and the others in the studio, followed by several seconds of silence as they looked at live video from Jim Gardner's helicopter. Out of the fog it had emerged, a giant wedge, still larger than life, and it appeared to be regaining strength. Near the bottom the cylinder was being lit anew by massive power flashes. The monster storm was not giving up. "Oh man," England sighed.

As it crossed the highway, the tornado became more volatile. It began to wobble back and forth on its line of destruction, heading northeast, then zigging a few blocks to the south, then north again, before heading due east. A few blocks to the north, along Broadway Avenue, Steve Eddy and his counterparts were in the emergency operations center in the basement of City Hall watching the feeds of the local television stations and listening intently to the city's police and fire radio. An army of emergency workers and other city employees had started to deploy to the west side of town. A police officer who had followed the tornado in his cruiser had radioed in that several neighborhoods, possibly including schools, had taken a direct hit. Eddy was unflappable, but he couldn't help but feel sad for his city and scared for its residents. Why had this happened again?

He quickly brushed the thought aside and tried to focus on the job ahead. He knew from the television images alone that the city had taken a major hit and that his job at City Hall was just beginning. Suddenly, outside the window, Eddy saw debris beginning to rain from the sky: boards and tree limbs and shattered remnants of residents' lives. It looked like they were inside a snow globe of construction materials that was slowly being shaken up. It was the first time that anyone at City Hall realized they were in danger, but while he had sent some of his nonessential employees toward the bathrooms to take cover, Eddy and his colleagues didn't move. They had a job to do, and even if their own lives were at risk, so was the rest of their city. They couldn't lose a minute.

A few blocks to the south, off Broadway and SW Fourth, the tornado was grinding through a residential neighborhood where Barbara Garcia, a seventy-four-year-old grandmother, was taking shelter inside a tiny bathroom in the house where she'd lived for forty-five years. She didn't have a storm cellar, and she went to the only place of safety she knew, the place Oklahomans had been told for decades was a suitable shelter—until the May 3 tornado had changed everything. But she had no choice. It was the bathroom or nothing, and she put the seat down on the toilet and sat there clutching Bowser, her tiny black schnauzer, who was her most beloved companion.

A few minutes later she heard the storm approach. There was a horrifying howl of wind and the sound of snapping boards, and before she knew it, it was on her. The tiny bathroom blew to bits, and sitting on the stool she felt herself spinning and tumbling around. She lost her grip on Bowser, and after a few more minutes of being shaken and stirred around, she came to a dead stop. She was buried in debris but very much alive. But she didn't see her dog. As she climbed out of her house with the help of neighbors, Garcia stared back at her demolished home. All of her belongings were destroyed, splayed out under the ugly sky. But none of that mattered. All she wanted was her dog. Bowser had to be in there somewhere.

Down Interstate 35, Glenn Lewis, Moore's mayor, had emerged from the vault at his jewelry store and run outside. Debris was still raining from the sky, but the buildings within his sight line appeared to be standing. He knew this was not the case a mile to the north and west, where he'd watched the storm eat away at residential neighborhoods before he'd been forced to take shelter himself. Lewis knew he had to get over there, and even as he could still see the tornado hovering in the distance, now grinding through the east side of Moore, he took off running across the parking lot. Two blocks away was Moore's main fire station and dispatch center, and he ran up just as a deputy he knew was about to roll out of the parking lot to the scene. He asked if he could hitch a ride.

As they drove together up Telephone Road toward Nineteenth Street, Lewis could see massive chunks of debris blocking the road about a mile ahead, near the Warren Theatre—pieces of houses and utility poles and wrecked cars in the middle of the road. It reminded him of the other storms that had hit Moore. The sad thing about tornadoes, he had come to realize now that he'd been through four of them—or rather, five, he suddenly realized—was that the devastation looked remarkably the same.

Turning west on Nineteenth Street, Lewis was relieved to see that most of the retail stores along the road, including Target and the new shopping centers, were largely unscathed. But glancing to the north, he could see a neighborhood that looked like it had been bombed. He began to have a sick feeling in the pit of his stomach. In the driver's seat the fire deputy instructed him to lift his feet off the truck's floorboard and to cross his arms over his chest. He wasn't wearing rubber-soled shoes, and the officer was about to start driving over downed electric wires that lay strewn over the road. Lewis did as instructed, and he heard a charged buzz as the vehicle surged forward and made a right turn on Eagle Drive.

It was destruction as far as the eye could see. Homes were wiped clean of their slabs, trees despoiled of their branches and limbs. The grass, he noticed, had been sucked out of the ground. People were climbing out of the wreckage of their homes and stumbling around stunned, and there was that familiar smell in the air—one he recognized from previous tornadoes—a mix of gas and lumber and wet earth. He hated that smell. Lewis felt horrible, but he knew his city would get through it. They'd been through it so many times before. He thought of his desk at City Hall, where there was already a signed declaration of emergency, standing by just in case. All someone had to do was date it.

As prepared as he was for disaster, Lewis felt the air sucked out of his chest as they came around the bend. Ahead he saw what looked to be the remains of an elementary school, crushed and torn apart. Its playground equipment was mangled beyond recognition. People around the neighborhood had climbed out of the rubble of their own homes and were rushing toward the demolished building holding crowbars and other equipment. As they drew alongside the remains of the school, Lewis jumped out of the car and began running. There were still papers flying in the air, as if the whole building had only just exploded. He saw report cards and construction paper with rudimentary drawings. At his feet a sheet of wide-lined handwriting paper fell, the kind used in kindergarten when kids are first learning to write. On it a child had carefully drawn his ABCs, and there was a red star at the top and, in red pen, a hand-drawn smiley face. Lewis suddenly felt sick to his stomach.

Near the front of the building he could just barely make out the words on the red and black sign, which had been twisted and mangled by the tornado. "Plaza Towers Elementary," it read.

CHAPTER 18

3:27 P.M., MAY 20

Amy Simpson stared up at the blue sky above her head, where the roof of her tiny office bathroom used to be. It was such a strange sight after what they'd just been though—a deep blue sky peeking through scattered clouds. She could see only a tiny square of it, but it seemed so calm and perfect compared with the furious mayhem she'd seen overhead only a few minutes before. It was almost like a mirage. In the distance she could still faintly hear the roar of the tornado, but the school no longer seemed to be in danger. Simpson had no idea what was on the other side of that bathroom door, but she knew she needed to get out there and fast. The kids at Plaza Towers needed her.

To get out would not be easy. An air duct had fallen into the bathroom, and a pipe had collapsed across the doorway. Insulation and rocks were piled in what little space there was between her and the four other women sardined into her miniscule bathroom. The door opened inward, and the women would have to contort themselves around the debris to allow Simpson to step out. All five were covered in dirt and muck, but miraculously they were fine. Still, her colleagues were terrified. They were screaming and crying, overcome by what had just happened. But Simpson was strangely calm, as if someone had flipped a switch and put her on autopilot, temporarily taking away all her emotions and her fears. There was no time for tears. She had to be strong for her students and her staff. She was in charge. No one else could do this job for her, and she wouldn't have dared to ask. It was not in her to depend on someone else. It was not how she had been raised.

She slowly stood up and began moving debris so that she could try to get out of the room. The women around her continued to cry and shake as they shuffled around so that she could get the door open. When she finally did, Simpson took one step out and found herself at eye level with the bumper of an overturned car that had been picked up and thrown into the front office. It was sitting on Penny's desk like a stapler or some other benign office tool. Simpson had almost no reaction except to wonder how she might maneuver around it. She studied it for a second, considering her options.

Behind her Simpson could hear her colleagues weeping. "I can't do this," one said in a choked voice. "I can't get out. I can't do this." Simpson knew they weren't stuck physically but that they weren't ready to face the full scope of destruction, which even she hadn't fully gauged yet. Still staring at the bumper of the car, she turned her head ever so slightly and called to the women behind her in a voice so casual it sounded as if she were making random small talk. "Okay," she told them matter-of-factly. "When you come out, there's a car here." One of the women screamed, but Simpson didn't miss a beat. Her voice had no touch of panic or shock. It was just her talking to her staff, as if everything were absolutely normal. "When you come out, you can step on Toree's desk," she continued, referring to the school secretary, whose work space had been wiped clean by the storm. She had no instructions for what to do next. She couldn't see what was beyond the car.

Simpson climbed up on her secretary's desk. The roof of the school was gone, and many of the walls were missing. Looking out, she saw a world she didn't recognize. The neighborhood was completely obliterated. In every direction was massive destruction unlike anything she had ever seen in her life. Houses were demolished. Trees had been reduced to jagged stumps. Even the grass was gone. In the parking lot cars had been picked up and tossed around, flattened like pancakes. She could see her Chevy Tahoe in the north parking lot, its windows blown out and smashed beyond repair. Simpson couldn't believe what she was seeing, but she had no time to try to comprehend it. She didn't even have time to react. She needed to get down and find her way out of the front office and survey the rest of the school.

It was at this point she realized for the first time how poorly dressed she was for a tornado. Her open-toed sandals with their tiny heels were slick and dangerous as she began to climb over the mountain of debris that had accumulated in her office. There were boards and bricks and pieces of chewed-up furniture and everything else mashed up together in a giant pile that was several feet high. She reached the top but was uncertain how to get down without injuring herself.

As she stood there assessing her exit strategy, her cell phone suddenly rang. It was her mother, who was frantic. Simpson realized only later that God himself had probably patched her through, given her mother's history with tornadoes and how haunted she still was from the twister she had survived as a child. She had been watching the tornado on television and was terrified that her daughter had been killed. Now she at least knew she was alive, but there was no time for joy. Simpson was all business. She didn't have time to be anyone's daughter—not at that moment. She had a job to do. "The entire school and neighborhood is gone," she told her mother. "Call 9-1-1." It was one of the few moments that betrayed the actual shock she was in. Scores of rescue workers from all over the region were racing toward Plaza Towers, and in her right mind, Simpson would have known that. But in that moment, she felt like she was completely on her own. As she hung up on her mother, Simpson dialed her husband, Lindy, an off-duty Edmond firefighter who was at their house a little over a mile away. Surprisingly, the call went through, and he answered on the first ring. "The school's gone," she said in a dull voice. "Come and get me right now."

Putting her phone away, Simpson looked around her and saw people racing from their damaged homes toward the school. She knew she could not get off the pile without help, and she began waving her arms, hoping to get someone's attention. Suddenly it all felt like a movie, one of those scenes she'd seen countless times featuring a damsel in distress frantically waving her arms and calling out for help. It all seemed so unreal. It was a bad movie, a nightmare that didn't seem true. A man she didn't recognize dashed over, grabbed her, and helped her down to the ground. He ran away before she could even thank him.

Walking toward what used to be the school's front hallway, she saw dazed and crying kids climbing out of the rubble, and she rushed to help them. There, to her horror, she turned and saw an overturned SUV in the middle of the hallway and beneath it Linda Patterson, a pre-K teacher who was alive but in obvious pain. On the other side of the car, out of Simpson's line of sight, was Jennifer Simonds, one of the kindergarten teachers. Several men rushed past her and gingerly lifted up the car to free the women. As she watched, Simpson was stunned to see kids scramble out from beneath the teachers—a little roughed up but generally okay. The teachers had literally taken on the weight of a car to save the students.

Simpson quickly moved toward the wrecked front of the building and began to direct kids out of the rubble and toward the school's parking lot—putting as much distance as possible between them and the rubble, which seemed at risk of further collapse.

Suddenly the tornado sirens began to wail again. She glanced to the west in fear. She could see rain coming, but she had no idea what else lurked in the clouds. The sirens were wailing to alert residents on the east side of Moore that the tornado was still on the ground, but Simpson did not know that. She frantically surveyed the landscape, wondering where people could take cover.

Erin Baxter, the kindergarten teacher, emerged and together she and Simpson began trying to wrangle the young prekindergarten and kindergarten students, who were crying and scared and chattering to one another. But she found she could barely talk loud enough to get the kids' attention. "*Hey!*" she heard a voice yell from behind her. She turned to see her husband, Lindy. He had been at the school for several minutes helping to evacuate fourth, fifth, and sixth graders from the east side of the building. It was the first time Simpson had seen him, but she had no time to react. As the sirens continued to wail, she quickly directed kids and teachers to the only place she thought would offer shelter—an empty creek bed that ran along the west side of the school property. But when they reached it, they discovered the creek, about five feet deep and usually dry as a bone, was full of rushing water. Her teachers began to look panicked, but Simpson blocked out the worry, quickly trying to think of another place to go. Suddenly the sirens stopped.

Rushing back to the ruins of the school, Simpson was outwardly calm, but her mind was racing, thinking of everything she needed to do. Her responsibility was to get her kids out of this terrible scene and back to their parents. But who knew what had happened beyond these few blocks? Were their parents even alive? Her mind was in overdrive. There was so much to do, so much to comprehend. She just had to keep going.

Behind her Simpson heard a voice. "Amy," her husband said gently. She turned and there he stood, the love of her life, the father of her children. They had been together fourteen years, married for almost thirteen—though it felt as if they'd known each other forever. While she was three years older, she and Lindy had danced around each other's lives for years before they'd ever met. They'd both grown up in Moore and had many of the same friends, who had tried to set them up again and again, but they both refused. It wasn't until a chance meeting at a football game that they had realized they were soul mates. They'd married ten months later and had barely spent a day apart since then. There was no one who knew her better, no one she was more comfortable around, no one she trusted more. After the tornado had passed, he had already been in his truck racing toward the school when she called. Hearing the anguish in her voice, he'd pressed the gas pedal, ignoring the speed limit and figuring the cops had more to worry about than traffic violations. He had raced through intersections where the traffic lights were out. The debris-covered roads had become an obstacle course, and he had raced his truck up on sidewalks and through front yards, dodging poles and uprooted trees. He even took out a mailbox—anything to get to her. Now he pulled her into a hug and held her tight. But as he took a step back to study her face, his blue eyes marked with concern for his wife, Simpson found she could barely speak. "I haven't seen my second or third graders," she said, the words croaking out of her throat. "Where are they?" Lindy asked. "Go to that tree," she said, pointing to a jagged piece of bark stripped of its leaves and limbs. "And turn east."

A few miles east of Plaza, the tornado was still on the ground, dancing back and forth along Fourth Street. It began to veer unpredictably from the north side of the street to the south. On the ground storm chasers watched as the tornado appeared to grow small and then widened again as it moved toward the east, but on radar the winds never weakened, and it continued to demolish everything in its path. It slammed into a residential neighborhood, where it killed two more people: William Sass, sixty-three, who had no known family in the area, and Jeany Neely, a thirty-eight-year-old nurse and single mom who was killed while sheltering in the family closet with her oldest son, Jacob, who survived.

A few blocks away the tornado was headed straight for Highland East Junior High when suddenly it inched a little to the south—missing the main school building but completely wiping out the gym, which had been evacuated not long before. A few more blocks to the east it made a direct hit on the administration building of Moore Public Schools, where Romines worked. The building, a former hospital, was destroyed, but miraculously, the dozens of staff members inside all survived.

On television KOCO's Damon Lane was trying to remain calm, but it was getting harder and harder. The station's radar could drill down to the very block to see where the storm was headed, and he was convinced his house, where his wife was in the shelter, was about to be wiped out. Standing in front of the radar map, he again began to tick through all the neighborhoods in danger—Heatherwood, Rock Creek, and the Creeks at Wimberley, where he lived. He tossed the program over to Chris Lee, a storm chaser who was a quarter mile ahead of the storm, which showed no signs of letting up. Lane wasn't on camera, but his microphone was still on when he exchanged looks with the meteorologists on staff and said flatly, "It's going to hit my house."

CHAPTER 19

3:30 P.M., MAY 20

Time moves slowly when you think you are about to die. Seconds become minutes; minutes become like hours. A single moment, once so fleeting, suddenly feels like an eternity.

Buried under the rubble of what used to be the hallway outside her third-grade classroom at Plaza Towers Elementary, Jennifer Doan found every passing minute more agonizing than the last. She couldn't move, and she could barely breathe. All she wanted to do was wipe her face free of the dust and debris that covered her eyes and mouth, but with the exception of being able to wiggle her left arm a tiny bit, she was completely incapacitated, pinned underneath what seemed to be a mountain of rocks and steel in absolute darkness.

The pressure of the debris on her body seemed to grow ever more excruciating, but every time she tried to move, a sharp jolt of pain shot through her body. It was the worst pain she had ever felt in her life, but it was what was happening in her head that was the real torture, the dark thoughts that she couldn't escape. Was this how she was going to die? Was this how her life was really going to end? It was all she could think about.

Doan couldn't move, but her mind was painfully active, thinking of everything that she didn't want to lose. She pictured her two young girls, ages six and three. She thought of the baby that she carried inside her, a tiny being whose life had not even had a chance to begin. She had been so happy, recently engaged to her longtime boyfriend, Nyle. She loved her job and her students. Everything finally seemed to be coming together after a rough few years that had included a divorce from the father of her two girls. Now, under the rubble, Doan worried it was all lost: Her baby. Her family. Her students. Her life. All possibly taken away in an instant by a ruthless monster that she'd had no chance of even fighting against.

To Doan the tornado seemed to have been over Plaza Towers forever—though in reality it was only a few minutes, if that. In the whirl of it all the students closest to her—Xavier Delgado, Porter Trammell, and Nicolas McCabe—had been torn away from her grasp. Once the storm had passed, Doan could hear the muffled screams and cries of students who, like her, were buried in debris, and she tried to call to them. But as she waited and wondered if someone would come to rescue her and her class, the cries slowly faded out, replaced by something even more terrifying: total silence. The physical pain she felt was suddenly surpassed by almost suffocating mental anguish: Had she just listened to her kids die? Suddenly she felt something move near her. It was Porter, pinned to her right, who was squirming and trying to free himself. He began to scream. "I think Nicolas is dead," he said, referring to his classmate next to him. Doan struggled to breathe.

With every bit of feeling within her, she wanted to rise up and throw off the mountain of debris that had buried her and find her students and get them out. She wanted to claw at the rocks until her fingers bled and to find the bright young smiles that had reminded her every day of why she had become a teacher. She wanted to find the kids whose lives had barely begun, take them in her arms, wipe their tears, and tell them that it would be okay and that they were safe and that this was just one very bad day. But she couldn't move, and she increasingly couldn't breathe. She felt totally helpless. And the longer she waited, the more worried she became—about her kids and about herself and about the city surrounding her.

What had happened outside this concrete tomb she was encased in? Was anyone coming? Was this where her life was going to end? Why had this happened to Moore again?

A few feet away Emily Eischen, the second-grade teacher, had slowly risen to her feet, staring in a daze at what was left of the back building. The roof above their heads was gone, and the ceiling had been replaced with a tangle of cords, wires, and jagged metal that hung precariously above them. She stood in a mess of debris, some so deep it came up to the children's waists. There was broken glass and bricks and books and pieces of classroom furniture that had been torn apart by the storm. She and her students were wet from the rain and covered in mud and pieces of the building, but aside from a few scratches they all seemed okay. Their nerves were jittery. Only a few minutes earlier the storm sirens had started to wail again, scaring the kids and striking fear in the hearts of the teachers, who wondered if they could survive a second strike. But to their relief, the sirens suddenly went off. Outside it was eerily quiet, but silence had never sounded so good.

Only moments earlier Eischen had made her peace with God. She was ready to go if that was what the Lord wanted. But he had spared her and the kids. She looked up saw a little girl, one of her students, with her eyes closed and her hands clasped in prayer.

Eischen's eyes flooded with tears. She hadn't been the only one relying on her faith, and suddenly all she could think about was life. She wanted to get out and live her life to the fullest, to never, ever waste a minute.

A few feet away second-grade teacher Shelly Calvert had leaped to her feet, hugging and kissing her kids. "We made it!" she shouted. "We're okay!" She had been certain they were going to die as she had watched the tornado tear into the building. Both she and Eischen began looking for a way to get out. To their left the building had collapsed, blocking an exit that would have led them to the front of the school. Almost simultaneously they looked to the right, where the back door leading to the playground had been. Suddenly they realized for the first time that a heavy cinder-block wall had collapsed inward, right where the third graders had been. Calvert began shouting for Doan and her students. There was no sound, no movement.

Just seconds earlier Eischen and Calvert had been so joyous, so grateful to be alive, but now they felt terrified and helpless. They feared what had happened to their colleagues and the other kids, but they tried to remain calm. They needed to get their own students to safety. They needed to find a way out.

CHAPTER 20

3:35 P.M., MAY 20

At this point the tornado began to do strange things. Over the last hour Gary England had watched its horrifying transformation from a tiny wisp of a cloud into a terrifying stovepipe of a monster that loomed larger than life over Moore. He had seen so many tornadoes over the course of his career, but he knew he wouldn't ever forget this one. As it moved into east Moore, the twister almost seemed to taunt him—daring him to think it might be over before carelessly flaunting its strength. Over the course of several miles it subsided, then grew big again. As it headed toward Draper Lake, it once again appeared to be weakening just before suddenly swelling back into a larger-than-life stovepipe fed by debris swirling hundreds of feet in the air. At the same time it picked up speed, suggesting it wasn't finished tormenting central Oklahoma.

The storm's updraft was so strong that it acted like a vacuum, sucking evidence of its destruction high up into the clouds, farther than the human eye could see. Panicked calls were streaming in to the local television stations and the National Weather Service. In Midwest City, a little over 10 miles northeast of Moore, the northern edge of the storm system had started to rain down massive chunks of hail, some as big as baseballs. But the callers reported something unusual: Mixed in with the hail were papers, pictures, books, and shoes. They worried that a tornado had somehow dropped undetected upon them, but what they were seeing was debris from Moore that had been sucked up by the twister and circulated around in that mysterious upper atmosphere of the storm that scientists still know so little about. The air above the tornado had been so unstable and violent when it hit Moore that the debris had bounced around in the clouds until it was abruptly spit out miles away, far from the actual destruction.

Back in Moore an adjacent section of the storm began to rotate—threatening to produce a second funnel almost right next to the one that was already on the ground. One tornado was a nightmare, but two? England stared with dread at the images beaming back from Jim Gardner's helicopter. He began to tick off the cities farther east in the path of the storm, including Bethel Acres and Shawnee. If it didn't lift, the tornado was going to come very close to hitting the same areas that had been devastated by Sunday night's storm. England thought of the people there, who were likely trying to recover what belongings they could from their destroyed homes. Now a second, even stronger tornado was bearing down on them. Where would they go? What would they do? Would they even have ample warning? It seemed like an especially cruel move.

Down the road at KOCO Damon Lane had meticulously tracked the tornado block by block as it aimed for his house, where Melissa was in their underground shelter. KOCO had one of the best Doppler radars on the market, and Lane had kept his cool as best he could as he'd watched the center of the tornado pass within a block of his house. But no radar was perfect, and he had no confirmation about the fate of his wife or their home. He kept stepping off camera, sending her texts and trying to call her, but she wasn't picking up. He tried the neighbors. There was no response. His producers started to try to reach his wife too, but cell service in Moore appeared to be out, and as the minutes ticked by, Lane grew more and more anxious.

Chance Coldiron, who lived a few blocks from Lane, finally got through to the station. He didn't bother to hide his anxiety about the destruction he had just witnessed. "That tornado came down just right along Fourth Street or moved just south," he told Lane on live television, a tone of resignation in his voice. "I lost my house, I'm pretty sure. Maybe yours is gone."

Lane's heart began to race; he felt himself propelled by a mix of adrenaline and disbelief. He knew he wasn't the only one who had something personal at stake. He thought of all the people who were watching him, worried about their own families in the path of the storm, and he willed himself to keep composed, to be "in the zone," as he put it. But he was only human, and as he dashed back on camera, his voice was a little more breathless, his body language a bit more jumpy. Off camera the studio, which has been a busy hive of activity only seconds before, had grown eerily quiet and still. Everyone was staring in shock at Lane, marveling at how well he was keeping it together. They had never seen anything like it—not even when the station itself had been hit.

With the tornado grinding its way east toward Midwest City, KWTV began showing more footage of damage on the ground in Moore. Watching the feed, England's heart sank. The camera shot was from

Santa Fe Avenue, just west of Plaza Towers, and it looked like a war zone. The four-lane street was impassable, blocked by snapped telephone poles and downed power lines. People were running frantically toward houses that looked as though they had been hit by bombs. It barely resembled a neighborhood street. The reporter on the ground announced that a police officer had confirmed that at least one elementary school had taken a direct hit, and children had been inside. It was the nightmare scenario that everyone had feared.

By then the station was airing footage of the damage in Moore side by side with Gardner's live feed of the tornado. On the right side of the screen the storm seemed to come almost to a dead stop, swirling in place like a top over a section of mostly empty farmland just west of the lake. Again it appeared to weaken—but England was still wary. Slowly the funnel shrank in size, even as uprooted trees and bits of houses continued to sail in the air half a mile in every direction around it. From Gardner's vantage point, the tornado began to move almost in slow motion as it gradually transformed into a tiny funnel. For several agonizing seconds it undulated back and forth like a dancing cobra as it very deliberately lifted off the ground and inched back up into the dark clouds—moving ever so slowly, as if choreographed to heighten the tension.

At KWTV people in the studio were literally holding their breaths, wondering if the deadly vortex would lash out again like a venomous snake. By then the tornado had been on the ground for forty minutes, traveling nearly 15 miles from Newcastle straight through the most populated parts of Moore. England had no idea exactly how big the funnel had been, but he knew from the radar that the storm had been more than a mile wide at moments, with winds exceeding 200 miles per hour. If those stats held up, it would register as one of the strongest tornadoes on record and would give

Moore the dubious distinction of being the only city to have been hit twice by such devastating storms.

England wanted to believe that the tornado had finally lifted, but he knew how tricky storms could be. Just because one funnel had gone back up into the clouds didn't mean another one wasn't coming. He didn't trust the storm, and he told viewers in its path to remain on guard because they were still in danger. Meanwhile the radar lit up with other storms stretching a long diagonal across the state from the south toward Wichita Falls, Texas, up toward Tulsa—right along the Interstate 44 corridor. The forecasts had been mostly accurate. Strong storms had erupted to the south, just as the early projections had stated, but nothing like the monster that had just hit Moore. England's early hunch that the worst of the weather would hit close to Oklahoma City had been dead on. He wished to God that he hadn't been right.

An hour south Howard Bluestein and his team of researchers from the University of Oklahoma were positioned right where the initial forecasts had said the worst storms would hit, but so far it had been a series of dead ends. Though he loathed the idea of pursuing a tornado in an urban environment given all the traffic from amateur storm chasers, Bluestein had nonetheless felt a tinge of disappointment as he and his team had watched the storm that would hit Moore begin to blow up on radar. The storm had developed incredibly quickly, more so than most tornadoes, and it could have been a good research opportunity. Still, it had become so big and violent that his mobile Doppler, positioned 50 miles away, had picked up some limited data on the storm. Few people in the world knew more about tornadoes than Bluestein, but as he sat in his truck listening to initial news reports of widespread destruction in Moore, he could only think of how little he truly understood them. Like everyone, he was perplexed by the same mystery: What made Moore so unlucky? It was a question he wasn't sure science could answer.

In the sky over Moore, Jim Gardner and KFOR's Jon Welsh hovered in their helicopters, waiting to see if another tornado would drop to the ground. After a few minutes they broke away, racing to pick up the storm's trail of destruction and follow it back to the west side of town. From the sky they had seen only hints of what the storm had done—through intense power flashes and gigantic pieces of debris that had flown through the air.

Welsh flew toward his house, off Fourth Street, where his wife and kids had ridden out the storm in a cellar. He was relieved to see it was still standing. But his relief quickly turned to remorse as he began to see massive destruction beneath him. He flew over Highland East Junior High, only a short drive from his house, where the gymnasium had been wiped from the slab. In the surrounding neighborhood houses had been flattened into giant piles of bricks and wood. On Interstate 35 Welsh saw cars that had been picked up and tossed like toys. Some were flattened and fused together, as if they had been crushed for scrap metal at the dump. Only an hour earlier Moore had been lush and green—in the full flush of spring. But now the lawns and foliage had been sucked away, and from the sky everything that remained appeared to glow with a tint of slick, burned red. The tornado had covered everything with a thick coat of muddy red earth.

Welsh continued west, narrating for his viewers what he could see of the buildings that had been heavily damaged or destroyed. The hospital was gone. The post office was damaged. A bank was completely wiped away. He flew into a heavy band of rain that made it almost impossible to see at moments, but before the camera could catch up to what he was seeing, Welsh, who had worked so hard to keep his cool even when the storm was threatening his own family, suddenly gasped. "Look at that school! Look at that school, guys! Oh my God!" Welsh cried as the helicopter's camera, its lens blurry with rain, aimed toward the blasted-out remains of Plaza Towers Elementary. "I don't know how to explain it, how to describe it. . . . This is terrible. This is war-zone terrible. This school is completely gone."

Unlike others tracking the storm that day, Welsh did not use those words lightly. He knew what a war zone looked like. It had not been so long ago that he had been flying combat missions over Baghdad, but even that had not prepared him for what he was seeing now. He became emotional as he watched tiny figures, kids, emerging from the rubble of the school and running into the arms of people sprinting from all directions toward the flattened building. As he hovered above Plaza Towers, Welsh glanced out his left window, where, a few blocks away, he saw Briarwood Elementary, which had also been decimated by the storm. Guiding his aircraft closer to show viewers another horrific scene of destruction, Welsh could not hide the anguish in his voice. "As a parent," Welsh said, his voice choking, "this is kind of hard to report on."

Gardner, his counterpart at KWTV, was also struggling to contain his emotions. He was no stranger to disasters. In California he had covered wildfires and mud slides and the terrible aftermath of earthquakes. He had flown over the damage from the May 3 tornado and dozens of other storms since, but he had never seen anything as heart-wrenching as this. As he circled over Plaza Towers, Gardner could barely speak. "This is, uh . . . This ain't good, that's for sure," he said, his voice choked up. As he focused on a group of people frantically digging at the remains of the school, he tried to continue but couldn't. "I'm sorry," he said, his voice thick and shaky. "It's gets a little hard to talk here."

As the helicopters hovered in the sky above, Robert Romines was inside the collapsed building at Briarwood, where he'd been helping to pull kids and teachers out. He had never seen destruction like this. The building looked as though a bomb had blown it apart, and as he climbed over collapsed walls, he could see heavy steel beams that had been designed to hold up the roof bent and snapped like tiny twigs. Around every corner he worried about what he would find. How could anyone survive something like this? But again and again he and the rescue workers found tiny miracles—kids wedged tight into corners that somehow had been spared. The scene was so chaotic that they could only occasionally hear shouts for help. Outside the sky had grown dark again, making it difficult to see in the ruins. They didn't have flashlights, only the faint light of their cell phones, which they shined inside the collapsed classrooms. It was so dark in parts of the destroyed school that the only way Romines detected pockets of trapped kids was when they smiled at him. They were covered in mud from head to toe like soldiers in war, but what little light there was reflected off their tiny white teeth. He had never been happier to see anybody in his life.

After a while Romines made his way back to the parking lot, where Shelly McMillin came to tell him that it appeared that everyone in the school had been accounted for. Though rescue workers were doing another scan of the school, just to be safe, it appeared that, aside from a few serious injuries, everyone had made it out alive. Romines couldn't believe it. He turned back and stared at the school in shock. The building was so badly decimated that he wondered how anyone could have made it out alive. It was nothing short of miraculous.

But his sense of relief was only momentary. He had still not heard from his wife, and word suddenly came that the school administration building had taken a direct hit. With everyone at Briarwood accounted for, he and Jeff Horn ran to their truck and headed back east to check on their colleagues and on Highland East Junior High, near the administration building, which had also been hit. Cell service was still spotty, but they knew from another staffer and from reports on the radio that the tornado had also struck Plaza Towers. After seeing what had happened at Briarwood, how everyone had walked away from that leveled building, Romines allowed himself to believe that everybody had made it out at Plaza Towers too. He did not dare think otherwise.

CHAPTER 21

3:45 P.M. TO 6:00 P.M., MAY 20

Jennifer Doan had lost all concept of time. She had no idea how long she'd been buried in the darkness of the rubble. Sharp pain continued to shoot through her body, and she increasingly found it difficult to breathe. She began to wonder how much longer she had left and whether anyone was coming. She tried to shout, but she could barely gather the breath to raise her voice, and even then she wondered how much could be heard beyond the pile of concrete that imprisoned her.

She could still feel just one of her students—Porter Trammell, who was growing more anxious by the second. He began to cry and scream, and she tried to keep him calm, telling him that someone was coming for them—though she didn't know if it was really true. Every time he moved, Doan felt a sharp pain go through her body. She knew she was hurt badly, but what exactly was wrong she had no idea. She feared for the life of the baby inside her. Part of her wanted Porter to be still, so that she could preserve her strength and her breath. Who knew how much oxygen they had left? But at the same time she feared the moments when he became too quiet. She was terrified of what the silence meant, and of the fate of her other students, whose muffled cries had slowly faded away in the minutes after the storm. Doan could deal with the pain of the boy fidgeting if it meant knowing he was still with her.

A few feet away Emily Eischen and Shelly Calvert, who had also taken shelter in the hallway with their classes, were considering their options for getting out with their kids when they heard footsteps scrambling on the debris above them. It was a group of men, Lindy Simpson among them, and as the rescuers peered over into what had essentially become a pit, the women were relieved. They tearfully motioned down the hall, pointing to the wall where they believed that Jennifer Doan and the third graders were buried. The rescue workers first wanted to clear out the kids who weren't trapped, and the only way out was to lift them up and over a concrete wall, where they would then be passed along a human chain down the mountain of debris. The women began handing the kids over, lifting them up until it was their turn to escape.

When Eischen emerged from the pit, she found herself in a world she no longer recognized. Everything was gone. It was as if an atomic bomb had been dropped and had blown everything to bits. The air smelled strongly of gas, and just yards away she saw a giant fireball that she soon recognized was a house engulfed entirely in flames. As the human chain of volunteers began to help her down the pile of debris, she burst into tears, but then she saw the faces of her students and she knew she'd have to steel herself. It was her responsibility to get the kids to safety, and as she reached the ground, she led them to the parking lot, which had been wiped clean of cars. Everywhere panicked parents were running up looking for their kids. Some were reunited quickly, but others wandered around, screaming their children's names in the most anguished voices she'd ever heard. It was like a terrible dream. Suddenly, in the distance,

Eischen saw her husband running toward her, and when he reached her, she threw herself at him, embracing him like never before. She didn't want to let go, but she needed to get her students to safety. Together they began marching down Eagle Drive toward the Abundant Life Church, which had been designated as a place for parents to go to find their kids.

At KOCO Damon Lane had still not heard from his wife. When the tornado lifted, he turned over coverage to his colleagues as he frantically began calling and texting her, praying that she would respond. He kept receiving an "All circuits are busy" message—service was still down. He couldn't reach his neighbors either, and he had not heard from Chance Coldiron, who had dropped off the storm chase to try to reach his own house, which he believed had been hit. Lane glanced up and saw helicopter footage from one of the rival stations on a nearby television monitor, and his heart dropped. The damage in Moore was horrifying. Highland East Junior High, less than a mile west of his house, had been hit.

Lane suddenly felt helpless. Though the tornado had lifted, the storm was still threatening, and he knew his job wasn't over. He walked back on camera, realizing he had never given the all clear to viewers in Moore. It was now safe to come out of the shelters, he told them, but he cautioned them that the city had been hard hit. The world they would emerge into might be dramatically different from the one they had left just an hour before.

Lane felt something take over. He began to talk directly to residents of his adopted hometown, speaking with the air of a coach who refuses to let his team give up on itself. "Moore, I know we have just gone through one incredible situation. We will recover. Okay? I know,

Moore, there's a lot going on right now. . . . We *will recover.*" Lane had been speaking off camera, and suddenly he marched back in front of the weather map and looked directly into the lens as if he were peering directly into the eyes of viewers at home. "I am very familiar with Moore. It is *my home.* It is where I have called home for the last four years," he continued, an edge in his voice. "I know we have gone through this before, and we will come back stronger than *ever before.*"

Lane's spontaneous pep talk seemed as much for himself as for his hometown, and while he fought to maintain his composure, his voice began to waver a bit. "Again, it's a place that I call home," he said. "The tornado passed, it looks like, just one street north of my house, so you can certainly imagine the emotions I am running through right now." Lane gave one last warning for the storm as it continued east before going back off camera to try his wife again. The studio was dead silent.

At Plaza Towers the atmosphere became more chaotic by the minute. There was mass confusion about who had been evacuated and where they had gone. Because of how quickly the tornado had risen up and how frantically parents had been trying to check out their kids, there was no official record of how many students had been left and who they were. The teachers knew, but only in their heads, and they were scattered all over the property. Amy Simpson was going over her own mental checklist of whom she had seen and whom she hadn't. She knew her prekindergartners and kindergartners were out of the building. She'd personally led them and many of the first graders to safety, including three boys who had been pinned underneath Karen Marinelli, who had been badly injured when a wall collapsed on top of her. Like Linda Patterson and other teachers at the school,

Marinelli had borne the brunt of debris that very likely would have killed her students. Now she lay on a backboard in the parking lot waiting to be transported to the hospital. Her pelvis appeared to be broken. Simpson prayed she was going to be okay.

On the other side of the building she had seen the fourth, fifth, and sixth graders—including Janice Brim and her students, who had been rescued from the tiny printer closet where they had taken shelter. There were some cuts and bruises, but again all of the kids appeared to be okay. And just minutes earlier many of her second graders had been rescued one by one from the demolished back building—handed down the pile of debris as parents loudly cheered, grateful to see their kids alive.

The only students Simpson had yet to see were the third graders. She could not say for sure how many kids were left because she'd been unable to make it to the back building before the storm had hit. In her heart she knew she'd made the right decision to race back to her office to be close to the intercom when the tornado hit, enabling her to issue that final warning to all of her staff and students. But she couldn't help but feel pain and regret. If only she'd seen them, she'd know exactly who was missing. She knew all of her students. She loved them as her own, and she felt a deep pain within, thinking that somewhere, deep inside that pile of rubble, they were scared and injured or worse.

The scent of natural gas began to perfume the air, and Simpson began to worry that there was going to be an explosion. She directed her teachers to walk their remaining students down the block to Abundant Life Church. But there were several miscommunications among police, parents, and other Moore Public Schools officials, who sent frantic family members to another church to look for their kids—causing even more chaos and heartache.

Dark and confusing rumors had begun to circulate about the fate of the kids at Briarwood and Plaza Towers. Some television stations and social media began repeating unverified reports that kids had been evacuated from the schools on buses ahead of the storm—which wasn't true. The entire Moore school system had been on lockdown. Another station reported an unconfirmed rumor that kids at one of the schools were trapped in a storm cellar that was quickly filling with water—also untrue, since neither school even had a storm shelter. Others began offering numbers of students who had been killed or were missing. No one was available to refute the reports and they began to circulate widely. Phone lines were down and administration officials were largely unreachable—and most had no idea what was happening on the ground. The entire city was in chaos.

At Plaza Towers the reported number of missing children began to escalate. It went from twenty to thirty kids to as many as seventy-five unaccounted for. Nobody seemed to know where the numbers had come from, though Simpson believed that rescuers might have been double counting estimates provided by Eischen, Calvert, and the other teachers who had been evacuated from the back building. She couldn't say for sure because there was no official count of who had been in the school at the time the tornado hit. It was all a frustrating guessing game. Her only reliable measure at that point was the number of anguished parents who stood around what remained of her school, waiting and hoping for their kids to emerge. Some had tried to climb into the rubble and had started to dig themselves, but police and firefighters had kept them back. No one knew what they were going to find.

By then several dozen police and firefighters from all over the region, including some who were technically off duty, had converged on Plaza Towers and the surrounding neighborhood. There weren't enough backboards to go around, so they began grabbing broken doors and flat pieces of lumber to carry the injured away from the school and nearby houses, where people were frantically looking for survivors. Up and down the block police used spray paint to mark houses. Some were simply marked with an *X*—symbolizing that they had been searched. Others included a number—when someone had been found dead. Many bodies had been found, but there was no way yet to recover them. Ambulances could barely make it through the streets.

Down in the pit of the school's back building, Lindy Simpson and several other men were beginning to pick apart the pile of debris that had buried Doan and her third-grade students. The men were tearing at it from two sides—with a group on the north and another on the south. Seeing the looks of pain and fear on parents' faces, Simpson wanted to do everything she could to help them find their kids, and she positioned herself so that she could physically see who was coming out of the debris so as to quickly help families reunite with their children. All she wanted was for this horrible nightmare to be over. She hoped for more miracles like those she'd seen, when kids had emerged from beneath walls and cars injured but alive, but from the look of concern on her husband's face, she began to fear for the worst.

Shortly before 4:00 P.M. Damon Lane finally got a text message from his wife. Melissa was okay. Their fence had been blown down, and there was minor damage to their house, but it was still standing. The radar had been right. One street to the north, houses had been blown away. "It looks like a war zone," she told him. Back on air, Lane was noticeably less anxious than he had been only a few minutes before, but as reports rolled in about possible fatalities and widespread damage in Moore, he felt anguish for his city. "We would love it if we did not have to ever have to go through things like this. This is horrible," Lane declared. "I tell you what: Even as a meteorologist, I wish that we could control the weather." But nobody could do that, not even Gary England.

Deep in the rubble, Jennifer Doan sensed movement in the darkness above her. She called out for help, trying to project her voice despite the pressure on her chest, which made it hard for her to breathe. Finally someone responded. "We're here," she heard a man say. She hoped she wasn't dreaming. "Porter," she called out to the student next to her. "Hang on. Hang on. They are here for us." The boy didn't respond, and for a moment Doan worried it was too late. But as the debris began to shift, she felt him move. He was still alive. She had no idea how much time had passed. It felt as if they had been buried forever. She had started to believe they might not make it, but now there was hope not only for her but also for her students. There had to be a chance they were still alive. Around her Doan felt the pile shifting. The pressure was getting lighter. Suddenly, next to her, she felt workers lift Porter out of the hole. She heard him whimper. He was alive. A few seconds later the rocks around her head began to shift. A tiny ray of sunshine suddenly pierced the darkness, and then there was an opening. Doan used all the strength she had to thrust her hand through it, and someone grabbed it tight. "We're going to get you out," a voice told her. Doan was overwhelmed with emotion. "We're right here," she said again and again. "We're all right here."

At the edge of the pile Amy Simpson stood anxiously watching as rescue workers lifted Porter Trammell out and passed him down the long line of helpers. His blond hair was wet, and he was covered in scratches, but he was alive. She'd seen a few more kids before him carved out of the rubble, looks of fear on their tiny faces. They were banged up, but most looked as though they would recover. And every time a new child emerged, everyone on the scene erupted in cheers, trying to keep spirits up. Suddenly Simpson saw Doan lifted up. She was braced on each side by rescue workers, who gently carried her out of the debris. She couldn't walk, and her left hand was pierced by a giant piece of rebar. They carried her to the parking lot and laid her on a backboard, where Simpson and her colleagues ran up and began to comfort her. Someone called her fiancé, Nyle, but they couldn't reach him. Cell service was still out.

By then the pain was so great that Doan began to fade in and out of consciousness. She looked up at the sky and noticed it was a bright blue. She had never seen the sky so beautiful. It betrayed no hints of the horror that had been unleashed only an hour or so before. She thought of her unborn child and hoped the baby was still alive. As she turned her head, she saw the rescue workers place another one of her students, Kai Heuangpraseuth, on the ground nearby. He was covered in mud and pieces of rock, and his eyes were closed, but suddenly he turned to her and asked if he was okay. Doan had never been so happy to know that someone was alive.

Deep inside the rubble Lindy Simpson and other rescue workers were frantically digging. Their efforts were mixed with hope and heartache. For a few minutes every child they found alive was followed by one who was dead. Buried beyond Doan they found another girl, tangled in a mess of steel rebar but alive. Digging deeper, they found three more kids, all wedged together, still crouched in their tornado positions underneath the rock of the collapsed wall. Two were alive; the third was dead. Nearby they dug out two more little girls, who appeared to be holding hands. But it was too late. They were gone. Some of the rescue workers were overcome and forced to step away to regain their composure. Many had dealt with fatalities before—some from the previous tornadoes that had hit Moore. But they had never seen anything as terrible as this.

At the base of the pile Amy Simpson watched as several more banged-up kids were pulled out over the next several minutes—including three more from Doan's class. But then nothing. By then the number of rescue workers gathered outside the back building had easily tripled. Again and again police officials pressed Simpson on how many kids she believed might be left. By then there were only a handful of parents left. Four were at the scene, and she knew of two or three more families who had raced to the hospital thinking their children might be there. She told workers it had to be fewer than ten still inside the building, but her answer was greeted with skepticism. In the crowd she continued to hear wild estimates—as many as fifty kids still missing. But Simpson insisted it couldn't be true. She would have seen more family members. Even if the roads were blocked or they had been injured, as a mother herself she knew that nothing would stop parents from trying to get to their kids.

As she argued with police, some of the remaining parents began to approach her, anguish etched in their faces. "Where is my baby?" a mother tearfully asked her. Simpson's heart ached. By then they had started to push the crowd farther back from the pile. She'd overheard someone say it was now a "recovery mission" rather than a "rescue mission." As the wife of a firefighter, she knew exactly what that meant. As her husband reappeared at the top of the pile, the grim look on his face told her everything she needed to know. Her kids were dead. It was her worst nightmare come true. She felt so helpless, and as she surveyed the frantic faces of the few remaining parents, she longed to do something, anything, for them.

Simpson walked to what remained of the back building and began to climb up the mountain of debris, her sandals slipping on the jagged pieces of rock. No one stopped her, and when she reached the top, she peered over into what used to be the second- and third-grade hallway and saw a glimpse of a blanket covering something on the ground. A body? Suddenly she felt a hand on her arm yanking her back. It was Lindy. "I want to see," she told him. She wanted to identify the kids for their parents. It wouldn't bring them peace, but at least it would be an answer. "You don't want to see this," he told her. "You don't want that image in your head." Simpson, who had tried so hard to keep it together, suddenly lost it. She began yelling at her husband, who, along with another officer who had approached, tried to explain what the protocol would be moving forward. She was so angry, she barely listened. She didn't care about the rules. All she wanted to do was help those parents. "I am sorry. I love you, but your rules suck," Simpson told her husband.

Ambulances were still unable to make it into the neighborhood, so volunteers loaded Doan into the back of a four-wheeler, driving her half a mile to the Abundant Life Church, where she was transferred into the back of a pickup truck that would drive her to an ambulance. In the back of the truck a nurse began to cut her clothes away, and though she was dazed from the pain, the teacher was conscious enough to be horrified at being so exposed in front of people she did not know. She could see a total stranger in the truck bed opposite her, a man who was injured too. She had never seen him before, and she was never to see him again. Within minutes she was being off-loaded into an ambulance, and she told the EMTs that she was pregnant. "Eight weeks," she said. They told her they wouldn't be able to find out the health of her baby until she was at the hospital.

Back at Plaza Towers Doan's fiancé, Nyle, had just arrived. He had raced from Edmond when he saw footage of the tornado nearing Moore and had made it as close as he could to NW Twelfth Street before abandoning his car in the gridlock of traffic heading south into the city. He sprinted the last 2 miles, frantic to find his fiancée. When he finally made it to the neighborhood, he turned the corner and saw the rubble of Plaza Towers. He feared the worst. How could anyone have made it out of that building alive? But somehow she had, and soon he was rushing to his car and then on to the hospital to meet her.

In the emergency room at the OU Medical Center in Oklahoma City, doctors told Doan she had a fractured sternum and spine. But there was good news: Despite all the trauma her body had been through that afternoon, an ultrasound still detected her baby's heartbeat. By then Doan had been installed in a giant body brace to keep her still. The only movement was on her face, where tears began to flow down her cheeks.

Back in Moore the grim news that kids were likely dead at Plaza Towers was beginning to circulate—though the numbers were still wildly off. A few yards away from where Simpson and the families stood, Lance West, a veteran KFOR reporter, went live with what he'd just been told by a source on the scene. At least two dozen kids were dead inside the school. He could barely get the words out before he started to sob.

Less than a mile away Robert Romines had driven over to the city's main firehouse off Telephone Road. He had been to Highland East Junior High, where the gym had been wiped out but there had been no major injuries. Next door the administration building was a total loss, but no one had died. He had been unable to find his boss, Susie Pierce, the city's outgoing superintendent, and he'd come to the firehouse, having heard she might be there. But Pierce was nowhere to be seen.

As he started to walk out the door, Romines was stopped by Robert Crain, an old high-school friend who was the city's assistant fire chief. "Robert, are you okay?" Crain asked him. Romines told him he was still in shock, but he thought they were going to be okay.

Crain gave him a concerned look. "Have you been to Plaza Towers?" he asked.

Romines froze. "No," he said, an edge in his voice. "Why?"

Crain put a hand on his shoulder and suggested he'd better sit down. Romines's heart began to race, and he felt sick. He suddenly knew what was coming. He took a seat.

"How many?" he asked, trying to keep his composure.

Crain paused. "Fifty-one," he finally said.

Romines felt as if the air had been sucked from his lungs, and for several seconds he sat there and said nothing. Crain asked if he needed anything. "Just give me a minute. Just walk away and give me a minute," Romines told him.

Crain stood up and stepped away, and as he did, Romines leaned over, put his face his hands, and began to cry.

CHAPTER 22

NIGHTFALL AND THE CHURCH

As night fell at Plaza Towers Elementary, scores of additional rescue workers descended on the twisted remains of the school, including military search teams from nearby Tinker Air Force Base. With the power out in much of Moore, massive floodlights running on portable generators were positioned around the perimeter, lighting up sections of the site like a Friday-night football game. Cast against the pitch-black darkness of the neighborhood, the effect was eerie and haunting as the lights cast shadows that made the already horrific ruins look even more grotesque. The dull thuds of sledgehammers pounding again and again into the jagged slabs of concrete and brick pierced the night, competing with the distinctive sizzle of the welding torches that crews were using to cut through thick pieces of steel beams left torn and twisted by the storm.

The air was warm and moist and still smelled of natural gas and disturbed earth. And now, as workers broke apart the school piece by piece looking for more bodies, an ugly, stale scent began to rise up with giant plumes of dust. On the mountain of rubble that surrounded what used to be the back building at Plaza Towers, where the second- and third-grade classrooms had been, a line of rescue workers snaked down the side, passing down buckets of debris one by one. Near the base of the pile a handler walked with a search dog trained to sniff out bodies, alive or dead. It was one of several canines meticulously combing through the scene. Occasionally a deep howl would come from one of the dogs inside the school, and activity would come to a dead stop as workers ran to dig and see if the dog had found something or someone. But repeatedly it was a false alarm.

As the hours ticked by, another sound began to echo through the night, this one more horrific. It was the anguished screams of some of the parents of the missing kids. A yellow police line now kept them from getting too close to the debris, but some paced nearby, calling out the names of their children in the hope that their voices might stir something deep within that giant pile of rubble. And when they weren't shouting toward the building, they were yelling into the surrounding darkness. Maybe the tornado had sucked their children away and spit out their bodies in spots that hadn't been noticed yet. Storms were known to suck up young kids and drop them, alive, someplace else. It had happened on May 3, 1999, when a ten-month-old baby had been torn out of her mother's arms by the tornado. Feared dead, the little girl had been found more than a hundred yards from her house, facedown but alive, in a muddy ditch. Everybody remembered "Mud Baby," as she had become known, and fourteen years later parents here clung to the hope that maybe, just maybe, they would have their own miracle.

A few yards away Amy Simpson stood and listened to their grieved cries. She was covered in mud, and there were still pieces of insulation stuck in her long blond hair from when the roof of her office bathroom had been ripped away. But she didn't notice any of it. Her entire focus was on the parents whose babies were missing. Around her she heard the rescue workers speak of missing bodies and the potential for more children concealed inside the obliterated building. But she was certain there were only seven left, all third graders. She knew who they were from the families on the scene and the word of others who had gone to the hospital searching, just in case. Simpson knew there were bodies in the school, and she knew, just by looking at her husband's face, that these children were gone. But still she could say nothing. Officials on the scene wouldn't let her. It wasn't protocol, they said. She hated protocol. Protocol only seemed to be causing the parents more pain.

Simpson's heart ached as she heard the parents' tormented cries, but there were no tears. That invisible cloak of whatever it was that had helped her maintain control still enveloped her, keeping the worst of her emotions in check. Kids were dead. Her school was gone. The absolute worst thing she could ever imagine as an educator had happened. And she had not even begun to consider what other terrible things the tornado had done to her city. The neighborhood around her was in ruins. She knew that many kids at her school, even if they had survived, had probably lost everything else. Some of the parents had no homes to return to, but she knew it didn't matter. It was just stuff that could be replaced, as long as you had your family. Simpson didn't cry. She couldn't. Not yet. There was too much to do.

Even as she kept vigil outside the ruins of the back building, the tiny bodies of the children who had died had already been moved to another part of the school. One by one they had been carried into the demolished remains of what had been the school cafeteria. They were covered in blankets and guarded by several police officers. The state medical examiner's office was on the way with body bags. Seven of them. Blue, rubbery capsules that were designed for adults, not children. And they were bringing more. Wild numbers continued to circulate about the number of missing, and since there was no official list of who had been at school and who had checked out early, rescue workers planned to dig through the night.

Well before the sun had gone down, bickering had started between local police and firefighters and state officials over how to handle the identification of the children's bodies. Some suggested bringing the parents into the school, but that seemed treacherous, given the damage to the building and the fact that there was no power. And it also seemed especially cold. Should the parents see their kids in that kind of setting? Others pressed for the children to be taken to Oklahoma City, where the identification could be made at the medical examiner's office—but that led to a debate over how to get the parents there. Others wondered if the bodies should be moved somewhere closer, to another building in Moore. But where? Most of the town was without power.

The debate dragged on for hours. By then Moore officials had called in Jack Poe, a retired Oklahoma City police chaplain. At seventy-two he was a gruff but gentle bear of a man who had worked some of the state's worst tragedies, including the 1995 bombing of the Alfred P. Murrah Federal Building in Oklahoma City. The five-thousand-pound truck bomb, which blew off the entire northern front of the building, had killed 168 people, including 19 kids—most of them toddlers in a day-care center positioned right above where the bomb had been detonated. It was the worst terrorist attack on domestic soil until 9/11, and Poe still frequently thought about the families who'd lost relatives in the bombing, especially the parents of the youngest victims. Even though most knew the worst had happened, given the proximity of the bomb, it had still been one of the hardest days of his life telling parents their children were gone.

When he'd retired from the Oklahoma City Police Department,

Poe, who had moved to Moore, had agreed to work on a volunteer basis when his new hometown needed him. He lived right next door to Amy Simpson. Her husband and kids had ridden out the storm in his storm shelter, and when Lindy Simpson had raced to Plaza Towers, Poe and his wife had watched his son and daughter until Simpson's parents could come pick them up. Poe had hoped he wouldn't be called into service that night, but after seeing how big the tornado had been, he had an ominous feeling that he would.

Poe arrived to a chaotic scene. Moments of tragedy and destruction almost always were muddled and confused, but this one seemed especially frantic and disorganized. No one knew exactly how many kids had been in the school, and reports were all over the place about how many kids were missing. Simpson, whom he knew and trusted, told him that she was sure it was only seven kids because there were only seven families still looking. But others raised the question of parents who were perhaps buried in the rubble of their own homes or couldn't get to the school site. It was complete turmoil. Both he and Simpson knew what the parents still did not know, or at least had not been formally told: Their kids were dead.

By 10:30 P.M., officials on the scene suggested that the parents relocate down the block to Abundant Life Church to await word of their children. The church had no power, so they sat there in the dark, waiting and waiting. By then the parents were starting to become angry. Why had there been no word of their kids? What was going on? Why had they been told nothing? Officials were still uncertain how to move forward with the identifications, but they realized they needed to at least begin the process. Poe was tasked with telling the parents they needed to help compile identifying details about their kids—the color of their hair and their eyes, birthmarks, and what they had been wearing to school that day. If some had pictures, they'd take them. As Poe broke the news, some of the parents began wailing in anguish while others became angry. Why? Why had this happened? one father asked. Others simply stood there in shock, too stunned to say anything. For the first time they realized it was no longer a rescue operation.

One mother approached Simpson with tears in her eyes. "I don't know what to write, Mrs. Simpson," the woman said in a stunned voice. Simpson knew most of her students by their names and faces and had seen most of them at school that day. She began describing the kids to the shocked parents, who wrote down the information on an official form that had been handed out. No one carried hard photos of their kids anymore, so Simpson used her iPhone to take pictures of their iPhone pictures of their kids, which she gave to police to give to the medical examiner. The little sister of one of the victims had her school yearbook, which she loaned to the medical examiner's office to help them identify the missing kids. The little girl did not know her yearbook was going to be used to identify the bodies of her older sister and her classmates. It broke Simpson's heart, but still she did not cry.

At the OU Medical Center Jennifer Doan woke up in her hospital bed. She was in a massive neck and back brace because of the injuries to her spine. She and her fiancé, Nyle, had finally been reunited, and her baby was still alive, which was a miracle considering her injuries. She wanted to know about her students at Plaza Towers, but no one would tell her. Nyle had unplugged the television in her room. He did not want her to worry.

Twenty miles away Erin Baxter, a kindergarten teacher at Plaza Towers, was at her home in Norman when she first saw footage of the tornado that had hit her school. For hours she had avoided it, but finally, as the local television stations entered their eighth hour of uninterrupted storm coverage, she watched a replay of the storm as it approached her school. She was horrified, and inside she felt the suffocating fear all over again, the worry that the storm was going to take her life away. Baxter quickly flipped off the television. When she tried to go sleep, she couldn't. Every time she closed her eyes she saw the tornado all over again and was overcome by fear. She could barely bring herself to sleep for the next three weeks.

Around midnight there was still no word from officials on the scene at Plaza Towers. By then the police had commandeered a bus and driven the parents to the First Baptist Church, right off Interstate 35 on the north side of town. It had long been a symbol of strength in the community, a gathering spot after every storm. The church had taken a direct hit during the May 3 tornado, but aside from damage to its steeple, it remained standing. Some had come to see it as an example of Moore's resilience in storm after storm.

Amy and Lindy Simpson followed the bus in his truck and sat waiting with the families for another ninety minutes. By then several other Moore Public Schools officials, including Susie Pierce, were at the church. The building was somber and quiet, but it was busy. In the main auditorium some of the pews were filled with sleeping people, Moore residents who had lost their homes and had nowhere else to go. Disaster-relief agencies were setting up in the parking lot. Everybody knew what to do. This wasn't their first tornado in Moore.

The Plaza Towers families had been taken into individual private rooms, where they were being comforted by church staff and other local pastors who had driven in from all over the region to help. While they still had not been told of their kids' fate, Poe had been on the phone already, dealing with what he knew would be the most difficult task the parents would face: burying their kids. He knew that many of the parents didn't have the money to cover the cost of a funeral, and he'd started calling around to old friends to see who could handle helping to bury the children. Quickly, without even knowing the numbers, several funeral directors offered to handle the task for free.

Ten blocks away at City Hall, Steve Eddy and other city officials were still at work in the basement. It was a hum of professionalism. They'd been through this before, and even in the darkness city employees were out removing debris from the roads and trying to get traffic lights working again. None had paused to mourn or question why another deadly tornado had hit Moore again. It was their job to get the city going again, and that was their primary focus.

Around town scores of police had been dispatched to the hard-hit neighborhoods to guard against potential looters. Already people from outside Moore had been arrested trying to ransack damaged houses. Some residents weren't taking chances. They'd set up tents in the front yards of their demolished homes, taking turns sleeping and guarding what they had left—even as more thunderstorms were predicted in the morning.

Eddy was calm and unflappable. Unlike in 1999, when he'd driven around the city feeling panicked and wondering how they would ever rebuild, he was absolutely certain without even knowing the full scale of the damage that Moore could rebuild. Part of him could not believe another tornado had wiped out his city again. But the contracts were already signed for crews to pick up debris. They even had replacement tornado sirens ready to install. It was still spring, after all.

Eddy had barely had time to think of the storm in personal terms. He hadn't yet talked to his wife, but he knew she was okay. A disaster coordinator with the Red Cross, she'd been out of town that day. She'd tried to call him but hadn't been able to get through. But somehow Eddy's daughter, who lived in Washington, D.C., had managed to reach him on the phone and posted an update on Facebook telling rest of the family her father was alive.

The only thing nagging at Eddy was the unknown of how many people the storm had taken. All night he'd heard different numbers—as low as ten, as high as seventy. The rumors of what had happened at Plaza Towers were especially unsettling. At one point he'd heard fifty-one kids were dead. As he prepared to go home for the night, a new number hit the news wires: as many as ninety-one dead in Moore, according to the medical examiner's office, including twenty kids. Even as he felt it was his job to be a rock for his city, Eddy couldn't help but feel a wave of despair. He knew his city could physically rebuild, but he wondered if Moore could survive the emotional blow of having lost so many children.

At the church Simpson watched as Poe and other local police officials went into the rooms and talked to the parents. She thought they were finally being told the terrible news of what had happened at the school. But around 1:30 A.M. the families were sent home with the news that authorities would know more in the morning about the fate of their kids. Simpson could not believe they were still being forced to wait. It made no sense to her.

On the way home she and Lindy drove past massive areas of destruction, including the demolished Moore Medical Center and the collapsed neighborhoods off Interstate 35. She stared out the window, lost in thought, thinking of how happily the day had started and how horribly it was ending. She knew that she needed rest. But there was now so much to do. She had no idea if the families of the lost kids would need her, but she wanted to be there in case they did. She wanted to check on her injured teachers, including Doan. And then there was the question of what to do about graduation. That night, she knew she wouldn't sleep. How could she after a day like this?

Twenty miles to the north Gary England was awake too. After hours at the station he was finally at home, but his mind was still going. He had already watched some of the coverage of that afternoon, weighing what he had done right and what he could have done better. Now he was at his computer, checking on the storm-projection maps and reading the headlines. As he finally padded down the hall to go to bed, his mind was dominated by the same haunting questions: How many people had died? Had he done everything he could have to save them?

CHAPTER 23

MAY 21

Search teams worked throughout the night at Plaza Towers and in the devastated neighborhoods around Moore, desperately searching for signs of life in the destruction. Shortly after midnight it started to rain on and off and the air became muggy and thick, a sign that another storm was coming. This added a frantic edge to what by now most considered to be a recovery operation, though some still held out hope for miracles.

Down Interstate 35 in Norman, Rick Smith and the meteorologists at the National Weather Service had been up most of the night. While there had been a momentary reprieve right after the tornado hit, the bad weather had raged on to the south and east well into Tuesday morning. At 2:30 A.M., nearly twelve hours after the tornado developed, Oklahoma was finally free of severe-weather warnings, but it was only a brief reprieve. An hour later a new set of storms with high winds, large hail, and intense lightning erupted to the southwest of the Oklahoma City metro area—sparked by the same explosive combination that had fueled tornadoes the previous two days. While the forecast was not as dire—the likelihood of tornadoes was not high—any storm was sure to complicate the recovery effort.

Smith had finally gone home around 2:00 A.M. He tried to sleep, but he tossed and turned in his bed, unable to stop thinking about what happened just a few miles up the road and what else Mother Nature might have up her sleeve in the coming days. By 5:00 A.M. he was back at his computer anxiously checking the radar, which showed a line of intensifying storms coming very close to the tornado-ravaged parts of Moore. He thought about all the people who were caught outside—search-and-rescue workers, city employees, and residents who had camped out alongside the remains of their homes. Hundreds of journalists from all over the country had by then descended on the scene, including correspondents and producers from the major television networks, who had raced in to cover the unfolding disaster. The major cable news networks had been on air with live coverage from Moore for nearly fifteen hours straight, and with network morning shows about to go live for viewers on the East Coast, Smith began to worry that these out-of-state reporters, unfamiliar with the vagaries of Oklahoma weather, would be struck by lightning. He especially worried about reporters standing near the satellite trucks with their antennas raised high. It was all about getting the best signal, but those antennas could easily be conduits for lightning, and that made Smith nervous. Knowing that many reporters followed him on Twitter, he quickly tapped out a message warning them of the possibility of an electrical storm. "Lightning is close to Moore!" he wrote. "Please be careful!!" It was 5:45 A.M.

Smith wasn't the only one who didn't sleep well that night. The entire region was on edge, jittery and anxious as the city of Moore began to come to terms with the horror left behind. The reported number of dead and missing continued to vary wildly into early Tuesday morning, complicated in part by the chaotic atmosphere at the state medical examiner's office, which struggled to keep track of how many bodies had been recovered and processed and to separate them from the number of missing. For several hours, a spokeswoman continued to confirm for reporters that as many as ninety-one people were dead, but as the sun began to peek through the ominous clouds overhead in Moore, that number was revised down to fifty-one dead—including as many as twenty kids at Plaza Towers.

In Moore, Glenn Lewis, the mayor, stood near the remains of the hospital that had been destroyed and prepared go on air for the first of what would be at least fifty television interviews that day. While the state's governor, Mary Fallin, had arrived on the scene with an entourage of staff and handlers, who managed her schedule and dealt with reporters, Lewis was alone. He went from camera to camera with little break in between, appearing before audiences around the world as the shell-shocked face of a city that had been so cruelly ravaged by yet another deadly tornado. How many were dead? How many were missing? How many were kids?

Lewis had few answers as he stared, almost stunned, into camera after camera, blinded by the bright glare of the lights that lit him up against the horrific backdrop of jagged lumber and piles of bricks that used to be houses and businesses. It wasn't that he was holding back information. Even as the mayor, Lewis couldn't get a straight answer on the death toll. Everybody he talked to had a different estimate—some high, some low.

All he could think about was the kids. Moore had made it through the May 3 tornado and others since, but the town had never lost children like this before. It was unbearable to think of, and Lewis, who was known for his calm, steady leadership, struggled to keep his emotions in check. When a reporter asked him how he was feeling, he choked up. "My city has been blown to hell," he said.

Amy Simpson had been up well before dawn—she barely slept at all that night. Once or twice she'd drifted off, only to awaken just as quickly. Had it all been some terrible nightmare? She so desperately wished to believe it was so, but this was no dream. Seven of her students were gone, and every time she shut her eyes she saw the anguished looks on the faces of their parents, standing outside the rubble of her leveled school, anxiously trying to find their children. Nobody should have to endure such pain, and it killed her as a mother to think of what they must be going through. Finally she gave up and crawled out of bed.

School administrators had scheduled an 8:30 A.M. meeting of principals across the district to figure out how to handle the last few days of the school year. Simpson knew she didn't have to be there, but she didn't once consider skipping it. She wanted to know what was happening, to be an active participant. Given the massive destruction, kids probably wouldn't go back to class—especially at Briarwood or Plaza Towers. But to end the year on such a horrible note seemed wrong, and Simpson wondered if it wouldn't be good for her students and teachers to meet one last time to say good-bye for the year, to establish some sense of normalcy in a situation that was anything but.

She contemplated this as she walked around her house in a fog. Her two kids, Scarlet and Roarke, were still at her parents' house a few miles away in Norman, and she and Lindy had agreed to go there first thing in the morning to pick them up. Already she was starting to feel the early tinges of survivor guilt that would come to haunt her and many others who had walked away from the destruction at Plaza Towers. On Monday afternoon, as she'd stood outside the pile of rubble that used to be the second- and third-grade classrooms, her phone had rung. It was her twelve-year-old son, who was crying and scared. Her parents had driven with the kids over to the east side of town, a few blocks off Fourth Street, where her grandparents lived. The house had been narrowly missed by the tornado, and they'd been forced to park their car some distance away and walk in to pick her grandparents up, because the roads were blocked by debris.

Waiting in the car, Roarke had gotten scared, and he'd called his mother's cell phone in a panic, wondering if something had happened to his grandparents. He didn't yet know the full scale of what had happened to his mother's school and how close he came to losing her. His call had come while Simpson was trying to help parents at Plaza Towers reunite with their kids and to figure out how many children were missing. "You're okay. You're okay," she had said again and again, trying to soothe him. "You're alive! You're okay. I love you!" The call had ended when he finally saw his grandparents coming down the street, and Simpson told him that she had to go. But afterward, as she stood with the anguished parents of the missing kids at Plaza, she was plagued by guilt. Had she been too short with her son? Had she told him she loved him enough? Why had God spared her when so many other families were hurting?

In her heart she knew there would never be an answer. When she arrived at her parents' house that morning, she ran and hugged the kids, embracing them tight, as tight as she could ever remember, trying to feel only gratitude and not guilt. Still, as her kids and parents cried in happiness—her mother, especially, who had been terrified that the tornado had ripped the family apart—Simpson maintained a brave face. She worried that even one stray tear would cause her to fall apart. And there was no time for that, not now.

The Simpsons' house, just south of Nineteenth Street, still had power, unlike many in Moore, but the entire town was without water, so she quickly jumped into the shower at her parents' house in Norman and dressed. She borrowed her mother's car (hers had been destroyed by the tornado) while Lindy took the kids back home, and she drove back toward Moore, navigating the back roads on the east side of town so that she could make it to the staff meeting. Interstate 35 had been reopened, but it was backed up for miles in both directions, in part by gawkers who had come to see the tornado damage. Above, the sky was just as crowded. Helicopters from the local television stations and the National Guard hovered in the air alongside choppers ferrying packs of news photographers, who shot wide-angle aerial photos of the milewide path of devastation. They raced to get as much footage as possible as the clouds grew thick and black, signaling the threat of yet another storm.

Robert Romines had set up shop in the cafeteria at Moore High School, a few blocks north and west of the old administration building, which had been destroyed by the tornado. Moore High was just outside the path of the storm, and it would serve as the temporary headquarters of the district staff for months as officials laid out plans to rebuild their own offices as well as the damaged schools. Most of the computers and vital records dating back decades had been destroyed by the storm. Not only were student records lost but also purchase orders for textbooks and equipment for the upcoming school year. Some records would eventually be salvaged, but many wouldn't. Moore had one of the largest school districts in the state, with more than 23,000 kids, and it often felt like they were starting all over again.

As the staff gathered that Tuesday morning in the darkened cafeteria of the high school, which was still without power, many simply hugged one another and cried. They struggled to comprehend the loss of life and how they would move forward. News reports were still suggesting that dozens of kids were missing, but by then most people in the room knew there were just seven, but even that was too many. How would anything ever be normal again?

As Amy Simpson walked into the room, many of her colleagues turned and stared, stunned to see her there. One by one they lined up to embrace her, marveling at how calm and collected she appeared to be. But even as she hugged her fellow principals and administrators, Simpson's mind was on the parents of the kids who were lost. What were they doing? Did they know? Were they okay? She was operating under the assumption that the families were at the First Baptist Church, where they had been the night before, and she told Susie Pierce that she wanted to be there when the parents were told what had happened to their kids. Simpson knew she couldn't bring them back or change their feelings of loss and pain, but she wanted to be there just in case they needed her, to grieve with them. Pierce told her it was probably best if she wasn't there—that the job of informing and consoling the parents should be left to the chaplain and members of the church, who were better experienced at dealing with traumatic loss. Simpson had little choice but to agree.

As the meeting got under way, she sat there listening to Pierce, Romines, and other colleagues brainstorming about how to proceed in coming days. The skies were dark again outside and suddenly she heard the whine of a siren. Her heart began to race. Was it all happening again? But as she glanced around the room, she saw that none of the other staff were reacting. The siren wailed again. Then she realized it was just the whistle of a freight train roaring down the tracks a few blocks away. It was a sound she'd heard almost every day for the last forty-three years of her life, but the bleat of the siren and the rumble of the train had evoked the horrifying memories of the tornado approaching the day before. Simpson had willed herself to be strong, but the wail of the train had somehow pierced the invisible armor that had enabled her to put her emotions aside. Only at that moment did she begin to realize how traumatized she was.

A mile to the west Moore police had relaxed some of the restrictions around the neighborhoods blasted apart by the tornado, allowing residents to begin to salvage what they could from their battered homes. Some came armed with bright blue tarps, which they scrambled to drape over ripped-off sections of roofs or windows that had been blown out. It was a race against the elements as the wind whipped up and it began to rain again. Some simply stood in front of their devastated homes and stared, wondering how they would even begin to rebuild their lives.

Just south of Fourth Street near Broadway, seventy-four-year-old Barbara Garcia was back in front of her house. Her arms were covered in splotchy red marks, bloody scrapes that she'd incurred as she was picked up in her bathroom and tossed around inside the tornado. While the local weathermen had warned that nobody could be above ground and survive, Garcia somehow had. Her house was a total loss, and she didn't have insurance. But it was just stuff. All she wanted was her dog, Bowser. She hadn't seen her tiny schnauzer since he'd been sucked from her arms that Monday afternoon.

Garcia had stood outside her house in the hours after the storm calling his name to no avail. She knew he was probably dead, but he was all that mattered to her. That morning she found herself again standing in the midst of the destruction calling out his name.

A crew from CBS News happened upon her and interviewed her, asking her to describe what she'd been through. She was telling the reporter about her beloved little dog, who was probably lost to the storm, when a producer noticed a tiny movement under a large slab of collapsed wall and then a little black nose peeking out. "The dog! The dog!" she cried.

Turning around, Garcia cried with joy, "Oh, Bowsy! Bless your little heart," as she lifted up pieces of steel rebar with the producer's help to free the little dog. His coat was dusty and covered in tiny pieces of rock, but Bowser scrambled out unscathed and walked to his owner, who was overcome. "Well, I thought God just answered one prayer to let me be okay," Garcia tearfully told the CBS crew as she rubbed her little companion. "But he answered both of them because this was my second prayer."

By midmorning the state medical examiner's office had determined that the death toll from the tornado had been dramatically overestimated amid the mass confusion in the hours after the storm. Some of the victims had been counted twice—in part because of miscommunication over where the bodies had been taken. While almost all had been transported to the medical examiner's office in Oklahoma City, some of the rescue squads working the scene in Moore thought they had been taken directly to local funeral homes. At Plaza Towers officials had believed until early that morning that twenty kids were dead—even though they had recovered only seven bodies.

The toll was reduced to twenty-four people—ten of whom were children. The youngest victims were Case Futrell, the three-month-old newborn who died in his mother's arms at the 7-Eleven, and seven-month-old Sydnee Vargyas, who had been sucked from her mother's grasp. The body of her four-year-old sister, Karrina, was found by a neighbor buried in the rubble of his home seven houses away. And then there were the seven third graders at Plaza Towers: Antonia Candelaria, Kyle Davis, Ja'Nae Hornsby, Sydney Angle, Emily Conatzer, Christopher Legg, and Nicolas McCabe.

While Simpson and other school officials believed that the families had been gathered back at the First Baptist Church to receive the terrible news, continued miscommunication among the medical examiner's office, the local chaplain, and other officials in Moore caused the news to be broken to some parents in callous ways. Some were called back to the church, but some parents later said they'd learned their children's fate through a phone call from the state medical examiner's office. Your child's body has been processed, an official told one mother. Where should we send the body?

Amy Simpson had just left the staff meeting at Moore High School and was trying to get back to her home south of Nineteenth Street on the west side of town when a colleague called to let her know that the parents of kids who had died at Plaza Towers were about to be notified. After that the names of all the victims would be made public at a press conference that afternoon. The world would finally know what she had known for hours but couldn't say: The worst carnage had happened at her school.

Simpson hung up the phone and continued driving. She longed to go to the parents but understood why she had been instructed not to. Nothing she could say or do would bring their children back. Now all she wanted to do was go home, but even that seemed to be impossible. The entire city of Moore was crippled by gridlock, as cars backed up trying to get into the storm-ravaged neighborhoods. Everywhere she turned there was a roadblock—to the east, to the south, and to the west. The roads that were open were an endless sea of vehicles that seemed to be going nowhere. A 2-mile drive that usually took ten or fifteen minutes at most was now coming close to an hour. She called Lindy and asked him if he had any idea how she could get back to their neighborhood, and as she spoke to him, she could feel all the emotions that she'd so far been able to keep in check start to bubble forth. When she hung up the phone, Simpson finally began to cry. She put her head down on her steering wheel and gave in to a steady stream of hot tears that had been building up since that terrible tornado had savagely taken aim at her school the day before, ruining so many lives. Why had it happened? Why did those kids have to die? All she could do was sit there in traffic and cry.

At the hospital in Oklahoma City, Jennifer Doan kept asking her fiancé, Nyle Rogers, to tell her what had happened to her students. You need to rest, he told her. Don't worry. Her doctors also refused to say anything. Deep down Doan knew the news was bad, but she wanted to hear it. She wanted to know the names. She wanted to know what had happened to the rest of the school. And even though her fractured sternum and spine had immobilized her, she kept asking again and again until her voice was a labored whisper. What happened to my kids?

In the hallway a hospital psychologist advised against telling her. She wasn't ready. She was too fragile. But Doan wouldn't let up. Even though she could barely speak at times because of the pain, she asked everybody who came to visit her, including Amy Simpson—who made her way to the hospital on Tuesday afternoon and was forced to keep another terrible secret.

The next day Simpson came to the hospital again with a list of the seven kids who had died, which she gave to Doan's fiancé and to the doctors. Except for Christopher Legg, a boy from another third-grade glass at Plaza Towers, they were all Doan's students.

Armed with the list, Simpson, Rogers, and the hospital psychologist went into Doan's hospital room, and the teacher quickly realized from the looks on their faces that she was finally going to get the answer she had been looking for. But even then Doan was not prepared. As the psychologist began to read off the list of names, Doan, immobilized in a back brace that barely allowed her to move, began to wail and cry, shrieks of anguish that were heard all over the hospital. Simpson told Doan that the kids closest to her, the ones she had been able to wrap her arms around—Porter Trammell and Xavier Delgado—had both survived, but her sobs only grew louder with the reading of every name.

"They are all mine!" she cried again and again. "They are all mine!"

CHAPTER 24

THE AFTERMATH

Three days after the tornado, under a stormy Oklahoma sky, its first victim was buried. The funeral of nine-year-old Antonia Candelaria was held at a small funeral home in south Oklahoma City, about 7 miles north of Plaza Towers. Tonie, as she was known, was a vibrant spark plug of a girl—a "ladybug," her mother called her—with limitless energy. She was always singing and dancing. She loved country music, and somehow she knew every word to every single song on the radio, whether it was Toby Keith or Carrie Underwood. Her parents wondered if she might be a performer someday. The third grader had signed up to sing in Plaza Towers' annual talent show, scheduled for the last day of the school. She had still been deciding on a song. And then the tornado came.

Her family lived a few blocks from Plaza Towers, and after climbing out of their own destroyed home, her father had sprinted down the road toward the school to find Tonie and her ten-year-old sister, Trinity, who was in fourth grade. He helped pull out child after child from the rubble, eventually finding Trinity, who had ridden out the storm in a bathroom. But Tonie never emerged. She had died on her mother's birthday.

When mourners gathered that Thursday, the heavens opened, unleashing a soaking waterfall of rain that drenched almost everyone as they made their way into the service, where sad country songs played as people took their seats. The program was festooned with tiny ladybugs, and around the room there were photos of Tonie with her round, sweet face and heart-melting smile. Neighbors recalled seeing the girl running and playing up and down the block—her face and arms often covered in a rainbow of chalk dust from the pictures of friends and family and sunny landscapes she'd been drawing on her driveway.

Her only solace, her mother said, was that her daughter had died clutching the hand of her lifelong best friend, Emily Conatzer, nine, who had grown up across the street from their house. As the service began, one by one relatives stood and spoke about the young girl who had been taken too soon while outside a wild storm began to rage. Lightning flashed through the windows and cracks of thunder rumbled the building—cruel reminders of that terrible Monday for the dozens of students and teachers from Plaza Towers still so jittery from their own brush with death. They jumped with every boom of thunder.

Among them was Amy Simpson, who was still trying so hard to keep it together. It was always the children who were the most intuitive. The kids from Plaza came up to hug her waist and looked up at her with concern. "Are you okay, Mrs. Simpson?" they asked in their tiny voices.

"I'm okay," she said, struggling to keep her composure. Her heart ached, and she wanted to cry, but no tears would capture the immensity of the pain she felt. Tonie's service was just the first of seven funerals scheduled for the coming days—some back to back at local churches. Simpson's anguish was compounded by the pain and fear she saw on the faces of the students and teachers who had escaped with their lives. How would they get through this?

As Moore buried the dead and began the arduous task of cleaning up and trying to rebuild, storms continued to roll through central Oklahoma. Gary England was on air at KWTV for every one of them, as he always was, doing his part to be the calm, guiding voice for a region still on edge. But privately England was more tortured than he'd ever been. Every tornado was horrible, every death was horrible, but this was his worst nightmare: A school had been hit and kids had died. In the days after the storm he'd looked at their pictures and watched and read stories about their young lives so full of promise and possibility, and all he could do was wonder if there was something more he could have done.

England thought back to the May 3 storm, which had hit two schools in Moore, heavily damaging Westmoore High School and completely destroying Kelley Elementary. Thankfully, no kids had been killed that day because the tornado had hit after school, but he'd told a few people it was a clear sign that the old advice to shelter in hallways would not be enough if a tornado was to hit during the day—not with the more destructive storms. But now England anguished over whether he should have been more blunt and outspoken about his concerns over the safety of schools. Should he have used his bully pulpit more forcefully? Like his competitors, he'd gone on air hours early that Monday, suggesting the worst storms could hit before school let out and urging parents to plan ahead. A teacher from Briarwood Elementary had contacted him—thanking him because most of her class had left before the tornado hit. She credited this to his early warnings. But all England could do was think about those kids at Plaza Towers and the others who had died. Could he have done more to save them? Had he failed somehow? It was those same questions that had always haunted him, but now they were even more pronounced. Why were so many people dying?

England counted down the days of May, praying that the tornado that hit Moore would mark the end of a terrible storm season in Oklahoma. But on May 31 the unthinkable happened. West of Oklahoma City, a storm developed that was even bigger than the Moore tornado. As it neared El Reno, a tornado at least 2.6 miles wide dropped to the ground—the widest twister ever recorded. England had never seen a storm like this, and as it lurched unpredictably over the wide-open farmland, he saw things he'd never seen on radar before as it abruptly changed direction and developed tornadoes within the tornado. It was hell on earth, and he began to fear for the lives not only of his viewers but also of his team of storm chasers, who appeared to be getting way too close to the monster funnel and resolutely ignored his calls to pull back.

In the days after the tornado hit Moore England had yelled at his team—including Val Castor, KWTV's veteran storm chaser, who also happened to be one of his closest friends. The frustration had been building up for months. He angrily warned them they were getting too close to the storms, taking too many risks, and getting too amped up on air. They were scaring people by yelling and screaming, he complained, and something bad was bound to happen if they became too panicked. He ordered them to calm down and to be safer, reminding them that they weren't invincible and that no footage was worth dying over.

But on that Friday, as another monster twister dropped down just west of Oklahoma City, some members of his team, seduced by the thrill of the chase, ignored his orders and again seemed to be taking too many risks. It was terrifying to England, who had never seen a storm like this before. "This storm will kill you," he declared to viewers, though he hoped his own staff was listening.

At one point Castor and David Payne, England's heir apparent at KWTV, who was out chasing that day, began yelling over each other as the storm began to intensify around them, and England lost his cool. "You guys listen to me," he told them sternly. "You are not in a good position. This thing is very close to you. You do not need to get that close. You're in the circulation!"

"It's not moving, though," Castor interrupted.

"Well, let me tell you," England shot back, sounding like an irritated father scolding a misbehaving son. "You may think it's not moving, but it is moving. We can see it on radar. . . . Goodness gracious. It's just absolutely unbelievable."

By then all the stations in Oklahoma City were in wall-to-wall live coverage. On KFOR Mike Morgan was becoming increasingly panicked. As the tornado grew larger and larger, he repeatedly advised viewers in the path of the storm who couldn't get below ground to drive away from the storm. "Go south," he said. What Morgan didn't know was that roads were already clogged with traffic, cars full of people still on edge after the Moore tornado. Soon the roads all over the region were gridlocked by people trying to outrun the latest tornado, which, unlike most twisters, abruptly changed direction several times—finally heading southeast toward Oklahoma City and Moore. Along the way eight people were killed when their vehicles were swept up into the storm—including a mother and child whose car was sucked off Interstate 40. Morgan was vilified—even though England and others had often advised viewers to drive out of the path of the tornadoes if they had enough warning time to get away. While he later said he cried over what had happened, he didn't apologize for his advice, telling viewers in a Facebook message that he would never stop giving viewers the information they deserved to be safe from potentially deadly storms.

Morgan wasn't the only one traumatized by the El Reno tornado. That night, after the storm narrowly missed hitting Moore again, England stood in the weather center at KWTV stunned by everything that had happened. Two of the strongest tornadoes on record had hit his viewing area within a span of less than two weeks. Part of him was angry—mad at his storm chasers, who had almost lost their lives by getting too close. (He didn't yet know about the deaths of Tim Samaras and his storm-chasing team, who had been killed in the storm.) He was upset about the tone of the coverage—not only by his team but also by other stations, which he blamed for hyping the storms and scaring people into a panic.

That night Jim Gardner, the station's helicopter pilot, had panned over the landscape ahead of the tornado, and all England could see was the glow of headlights of cars trying to go south. He wanted to yell in frustration. Why would people do that after everything that happened? Cars were the most dangerous place to be in storms. What was wrong with these people? He just couldn't believe it. By then word had come in that some had died in their cars on the highway. England shook his head, pained at a tragedy that he believed could have been prevented.

Around him his team of young meteorologists continued to work, monitoring the weakened storms as they moved east—just in case they intensified again. He recalled the hours earlier in the day when his staff, many fresh out of college, had seemed almost giddy at the bad weather that was coming. He didn't blame them. He had been like that once too, caught up in the excitement of the weather and what it would do. That was the odd thing about storms. No one wanted them to do terrible damage, but at the same time, as a meteorologist you did want the weather to be interesting. But he felt many of his protégés still didn't understand how truly terrible the storms could be. They didn't yet feel the intense pressure, the burden of trying to keep viewers safe—at least not in the painful, obsessive way that he did. They did not know what it was like to be the man everybody counted on to save them or what it felt like when people died. The anguish of the storms, the weight of deaths didn't yet keep them up at night, but it would. Going up against Mother Nature was still a thrill for them—the young, foolish ones, he called them—but lately he had come to feel it was no longer fun.

With the studio still abuzz England quietly walked back to his office and picked up the phone and called his wife, Mary. He had once thought they might have to wheel him out of the station into his grave because he loved his job so much. But something had changed that night. It was not yet 8:30 P.M., and though he'd usually stick around for the 10:00 P.M. newscast and beyond that to watch the tapes and analyze their coverage, he had no interest in doing so that night. "Come get me," he told his wife in a quiet, exhausted voice. "It's over." He said good-bye to his staff but said nothing else. The next day he called the station's owner, David Griffin, and gave notice. England retired six weeks later into an off-air job in weather development with KWTV and never looked back. The era of Gary England as the reigning weather god of Oklahoma television was over. He would never have to confront a tornado again—at least not in front of a camera.

When the storm that produced the El Reno tornado finally died out on the evening of May 31, it did, as many had hoped, mark the end of Oklahoma's spring tornado season. But something strange happened. While storms still rumbled through occasionally, May 31 marked the last time in 2013 that a tornado warning was issued anywhere in the state. The next tornado warning didn't come until April 2014, nearly a year later. It was a new record. Not since 1986 had there been such a long lapse of time between tornado warnings in Oklahoma. While most Oklahomans were grateful, the long dry spell puzzled Rick Smith and the other meteorologists at the National Weather Service, where, in an unusual move, grief counselors had been brought in to talk to staff overwhelmed by the stress of that deadly tornado outbreak over the last two weeks of May. They were professionals who had long ago mastered the ability to keep their cool and separate their emotions from their job of keeping people in Oklahoma safe, but that series of storms had been too much.

It had been an unusually active year for tornadoes in Oklahoma in 2013. There were 79 tornadoes in the first six months of the year—more than in any other state in the country except for Texas, which reported 81 for the entire year. But nationally it had been a slow period for tornadoes. Most years more than 1,000 tornadoes are reported in America. But in 2013 there were just 898—one of the lowest years on record.

The statistic mystified Smith and scientists like Howard Bluestein, who noted that there seemed to be a trend in tornadoes. Every season with a huge outbreak of deadly weather seemed to be followed by, for lack of a better word, a drought. Smith and Bluestein had no idea why the weather behaved like this—why some storm years were more active than others. Maybe it was climate change or maybe it was just bad luck. It was another reminder of the mystery of the tornado. "The last frontier of atmospheric science," Bluestein called it. That season took a toll even on Bluestein, who was troubled by the deaths in Oklahoma. He had known Tim Samaras and the other chasers killed by the El Reno storm. Like him, they had dedicated their lives to trying to unlock the mystery of tornadoes. He tried to focus on how much Samaras had contributed to the science of tornadoes. He was a hero within the meteorology community. That he had been killed by the thing he had invested decades in trying to understand seemed especially cruel, and it was yet another reminder to Bluestein of how dangerous and ruthless tornadoes could be.

In Moore city workers began clearing debris from the blasted-out neighborhoods within five days of the May 20 storm. They were helped by thousands of volunteers from all over the country who descended on the city to help residents rebuild as quickly as possible—many church members who had been moved by the city's unlucky streak and wanted to help. By late June, a month after the storm, the land around Plaza Towers Elementary resembled a muddy, rocky moonscape, wiped clean of the remains of the demolished school and homes that had once stood there. People from outside Oklahoma were stunned at how quickly things were moving—especially compared with places like the Jersey Shore, where the ruins of many homes destroyed by Hurricane Sandy in October 2012 were still standing largely untouched many months after the storm.

Steve Eddy, Moore's city manager, gently reminded people that his city had been through this before—five times now. Of all the lessons he'd learned—and by now there had been many—he believed strongly that the quickest way for the city to find its way back to normalcy was to clear the slate and rebuild anew. While many looked at the barren landscape with anguish, pained by everything that had been lost in the terrible storm, he tried to focus only on the positive. He pushed people to look forward, to focus on rebuilding the city even stronger.

That summer the city council approved some of the toughest building codes in the country, establishing guidelines that required houses to be rebuilt with reinforced walls and windows that could withstand winds of at least 135 miles per hour. That would not have been enough to protect homes in the path of the May 20 tornado, which packed winds of at least 200 miles per hour, but it was the best they could do aside from building homes made entirely of concrete, with no windows and heavy steel doors. In the weeks after the tornado some had proposed building homes exactly like that in some of the devastated neighborhoods, but Eddy and other Moore officials quickly rejected the idea. Nobody wanted to live in a town where the houses looked like crypts.

Always the professional, Eddy focused less on why and more on what to do now. But his mind was occasionally consumed by the question of why Moore had been struck again, and when the city resumed its weekly testing of tornado sirens every Saturday at noon, even he found his heart racing a bit, the ominous whine a reminder of that horrible Monday.

Slowly his own life got back to normal. He had barely seen his wife in the month after the storm. He was busy at City Hall, and she worked at the Red Cross, which was overseeing disaster efforts. At church a few Sundays after the storm, their pastor had made them both stand up before the congregation to finally publicly congratulate them on their marriage, which had happened in Hawaii three weeks before the tornado. "Their honeymoon," the minister said, without a trace of irony, "was a disaster."

Within days of the tornado, Moore Public Schools administrators announced plans to rebuild Briarwood and Plaza Towers. This time, however, each would be rebuilt to include a massive safe room able to shelter as many as 1,400 people. With reinforced concrete walls ten inches thick, the new shelter was said to be able to withstand the winds of an EF5 tornado like the one that had hit on May 20. Moving forward, every new school in Moore would include such a shelter, officials said—thanks in part to a grant from FEMA. But existing schools in Moore and in much of Oklahoma would still be unprotected, in spite of a public outcry that the state should add shelters to protect kids in case another tornado like May 20 happened again.

While polls found incredible public support for shelters, proposals that would have allowed the state to issue bonds or raise sales taxes to pay for them were stymied in the state legislature by conservative lawmakers, including Governor Mary Fallin, who felt it should be up to individual cities to determine if they wanted to invest taxpayer money in protecting schools from tornadoes. Not every city, she said, was as prone to tornadoes as Moore seemed to be.

The political opposition mystified officials in Moore. School administrators began to try to figure out how to pay for more shelters out of an already tight budget, and in the meantime Mayor Glenn Lewis and other city officials began urging residents to install their own shelters at home. By the summer there was a waiting list of upward of six months in Oklahoma City and Moore to install a tornado shelter. Companies couldn't keep up with demand. Local television and radio stations, which used to give away cars during contests, soon began giving away storm shelters instead.

Even as Moore slowly began to rebuild, it was the wounds beneath the surface that took far longer to heal. Those who had survived the tornado—especially the kids and teachers at Briarwood and Plaza Towers—struggled to get back to their normal routines, but they were haunted by what had happened. Scores of grief counselors descended on the city—closely monitoring the children who had been inside the schools for any signs of trauma. In some ways it was the educators who struggled the most—adults who truly understood in a way the kids couldn't the horror of what had happened that day and what had been lost. They were tortured by memories of the storm, which were stirred up by any little thing—a shift in the wind, the testing of the tornado siren on Saturdays. Even the smell of coming rain—which used to be so soothing—now triggered terrible memories.

Many of the teachers went for weeks without sleep, unable to close their eyes without being transported back to that day. They vividly remembered how the tornado had felt and sounded as it began to rip apart the building around them. They remembered the screams of their students and emerging into the Armageddon of the neighborhood afterward. Many of the teachers participated in group counseling sessions—listening as their colleagues spoke of their anxiety attacks and described how haunted they were by questions that would never be answered. Why had this happened to them, to their school? Moore was a city of faith where many trusted and believed in the Lord's will, but still they wondered, why had God allowed such a terrible thing to happen to innocent children?

Jennifer Doan had been released from the hospital a few days after the storm, and for most of the summer she wore a brace as her fractured spine healed. She needed to have surgery for her injured hand, which had been pierced by steel rebar, severing many nerves. But she delayed it because of her pregnancy and other injuries. Though she was in intense pain, she refused to take medication, fearful that it could hurt her baby. But in many ways she felt numb without the drugs, as if she were walking in some haze of a terrible nightmare.

Her mind kept going back to that day in the back hallway. She felt guilty for being alive when seven of the kids who had gathered around her were not. She tried to feel normal, to feel excited about the baby. It was a boy, she'd learned. But on many days she found it hard to muster enthusiasm for life, even though she knew she had so much to live for—her two young daughters; her fiancé, who had stayed at her side through every terrible moment; and her soon-to-be-born baby son. But she struggled to deal with the memories of the storm and the guilt she felt at not having protected her students. Amy Simpson and others told her she had done everything she could. "God makes our choices for us long before," Simpson had told her. "You had no control over what happened." Doan tried to accept it, but her mind would flash back to that day, buried under the rubble, where she had listened to the sound of the children's cries slowly fading into total silence, and she couldn't help but blame herself.

A few days after she was released from the hospital, Doan had gone back to Moore for a memorial service for the children who had died, but after that she had stayed away, worried about what being in Moore might stir up. While the other teachers had leaned on one another, Doan had kept to herself, grieving on her own. Over the summer she finally visited the site where Plaza Towers had been. The remains of the school were long gone, and it was just flat earth being prepped for the construction of a new school that would open for the 2014 school year. It was surrounded by a chain-link fence covered with teddy bears and other memorials left behind by visitors from all over the world who had come to pay their respects. Just beyond the fence were seven crosses, each bearing the name of a child who had died. Doan stood there and cried.

On the way back to Edmond, where she lived, Doan pulled over at a tag agency in Moore. She needed to renew her driver's license, and on her way into the building a woman stopped her. She recognized Doan from the news, and she gently pulled the still-recovering teacher into a hug. "You're such a hero," the woman told her. "What you did for those kids . . . You are a hero." Doan tried to be polite, but she found herself unable to speak. She knew the woman meant well, but the encounter only reminded her of how much she felt like a failure.

Her job was not only to educate her students but also to keep them safe. That had been her assignment that Monday, what the parents who had dropped their children off at school had trusted her to do. She had gone over and over it with her counselor. How could she be a hero, she wondered, if kids she was supposed to be protecting had died? She couldn't stop blaming herself.

A few months later Doan and Nyle Rogers married, and that December she gave birth to a healthy baby boy. She named him Jack Nicolas—his middle name after Nicolas McCabe, the student who had been just out of her grasp in the back hallway at Plaza Towers and had died.

In the months after the tornado Amy Simpson had thrown herself into trying to help her students and teachers recover after the storm, often putting their needs above her own. With Plaza Towers destroyed and a new facility more than a year away, Simpson and her students were moved temporarily into the older wing of a junior high school across town while Briarwood held classes at a local church.

For Simpson the list of things she had to do was overwhelming, from ordering new textbooks to making sure they'd have enough desks. The school district had issued a waiver to families displaced by the storm, and she worked to ensure that every kid who wanted to be back at Plaza Towers that fall would be. While about 80 percent of the students had decided to return, some families—including a few who had lost children on May 20—had opted to move on, to turn the page and begin anew someplace else. It made Simpson sad, but she understood. Some of her teachers had decided to transfer to other schools too—hoping to make a fresh start.

The summer she had looked forward to was consumed by the aftermath of the tornado. Even when her family went on vacation to Texas for a weekend, her cell phone rang at all hours of the day with calls from teachers and parents considering how to approach the new school year with kids who were still assimilating the trauma of what had happened. Simpson was a big believer in routine and normalcy as a way of healing—and going back to class, she hoped, would be a big help. But she agonized over how to address the tragedy that had hit their school. She wanted kids to talk about their feelings about the tornado and losing their classmates, but how should she handle the emotions that would ensue? The city had assigned extra counselors to keep an eye on the kids. They were planning special classes, including art therapy to help the children deal with their fears about the weather and memories of May 20. But what would happen when the storms came again?

As Simpson focused on her kids and teachers and making sure

everything was going as smoothly as it could for the upcoming school year, she was also confronting her own emotional roller coaster. While she had kept herself from breaking down in those early hours after the storm, in the months afterward it seemed as though the tears would never stop. She was consumed by guilt. Had she done everything she could to protect the kids who had died? Had she handled everything as well as she could have in the hours after the storm? She'd heard from a teacher that some of her colleagues were mad at her for her demeanor after the tornado had hit, for how calm she'd been. All she'd tried to do was be strong, but some of her staff had apparently taken it the wrong way, believing she had been too stern with them or cold.

Simpson used to love storms. Now she hated them. And even though she'd lived in Moore her entire life and knew the city tested the storm sirens on Saturdays, she now jumped every time she heard them go off. Sometimes, for no reason at all, she just started to cry. Her two kids soon grew impatient with it all. "The tornado again?" her son Roarke would say in an exasperated voice. It was just another layer to the guilt Simpson felt about everything, especially her own children. She worried she was being a bad mother, because she was so torn up inside. She felt guilty for how the tornado had consumed their lives and ruined their summer. Most of all she felt terrible for getting irritated with her son and daughter when they acted up. They were kids being kids, and she was a mom being a mom. There was nothing abnormal about it. But afterward she was consumed with guilt, thinking of the parents who no longer had their kids. She found the guilt suffocating at times, but still she pushed on. She had no right to complain when others were suffering so much more.

On some days Simpson went alone to visit the graves of the children who had died. She had been so angry with Lindy for keeping her from climbing into the pit of the demolished back building in the hours after the tornado to help identify the bodies of the kids who'd been killed. She'd wanted to help the parents who were in misery, but now she was grateful that he'd held her back. She could imagine them as she'd last seen them—happy and joyful and bouncing around without a care in the world. She had always loved her husband, but after the tornado their relationship had grown even stronger. Before the storm, at Christmas, she'd often caught him staring off into the distance, lost in thought as their kids tore into presents. After the tornado she talked to him about the guilt she sometimes felt looking at their kids, and he confessed that in those lost moments he'd been thinking about his own experiences as a firefighter, when he'd tried to save a child but it had been too late. He'd felt guilty for the happiness he felt when others had lost so much—the same feeling his wife now felt.

As the summer went on, Simpson practiced what she called her "happy face," the one she used around her kids and the children at Plaza Towers. Sometimes it wasn't so hard. Before the new school year began, the community united around the school and threw parties for the kids who had survived the storm, trying to keep their spirits up. There were trips to amusement parks and basketball parties with members of the local NBA team, the Oklahoma City Thunder. And the gifts kept coming well into the school year, warehouses full of books and new school supplies that would last years. The kids, many of whom came from poor backgrounds, had never been given so much. It was like Christmas every day.

Simpson was thrilled to see them so happy. But it wasn't enough to stop the pain or curtail the fear she felt about what the next storm season would bring. They would be crouched in the hallways again the next spring if another storm came. There was nowhere else to go until they moved into the new building. But someone had gifted the school hundreds of tiny football helmets—armor to protect the kids' heads if the walls somehow came crashing down again.

While she improved by the day, the tears still flowed from time to time without warning, and by October her son told her that he'd had enough. He was tired of hearing her talk about the tornado and of seeing her cry. Simpson again felt guilty, realizing that her own kids, in some ways, had been victims of the storm too. They came to an agreement: If he felt she was going on and on too much about the tornado or was too sad, all he had to do was say, "Ten-twenty"—short for October 20, the day of their talk. Over the next few weeks her son didn't hold back. "Ten-twenty!" he'd tell her, and immediately Simpson would snap back into focus. As with her students at Plaza Towers, she realized that it was the kids who were the strongest after the storm while the adults were a mess. In private moments she sometimes wondered if the tears would ever stop.

EPILOGUE: MAY 20, 2014

On a windy Tuesday morning one year after the tornado, the people of Moore gathered on a barren patch of land just west of Interstate 35 where the hospital had once stood to mourn the people who had died. Dignitaries from all over the state were there, including the governor, Mary Fallin, and the local congressman, Tom Cole, whose own home had been narrowly missed.

An honor guard slowly marched up to a tiny stage positioned in front of a fire truck, and there was a long moment of silence, interrupted only by the whoosh of cars passing on the nearby highway. Finally there was a slow tap of a bell—one toll for every victim who had died. It rang twenty-four times for the people who had been killed on May 20, 2013—and once more for Kathryn Bagay, a ninety-year-old grandmother who had succumbed three months later to head injuries she'd suffered when the tornado tore apart her house.

The mood was somber, and many wiped away tears throughout the service. Several clutched photos of their relatives who had died—a sister, a mother, an uncle, a son. All taken too soon. It was the first time out of all the tornadoes that had hit Moore that the city had held a ceremony like this. It was an affair that was held as much to remember the ones who were gone as to remind the people here that they had survived. Somehow, in spite of everything bad that had happened, the people of Moore were still standing.

Surrounded by tiny red flags that read, "Moore Strong," the dignitaries broke ground on a new medical center—one that would be even better than the one that had been destroyed. A gleaming, 120,000-square-foot, glassy structure standing five stories high, it would be the tallest building ever built in Moore. "Our Devon Tower," Glenn Lewis joked, referring to the tallest skyscraper in the state, which loomed fifty stories high over nearby downtown Oklahoma City.

While there was still much rebuilding to do, it was startling to see how far Moore had come. Just to the west, neighborhoods that had looked as though they'd been leveled by an atomic bomb were starting to rise again—packed with brand-new homes that were often twice the size of the ones that had been there before. All were accompanied by new storm shelters that peeked slightly out of the ground. Many of these were positioned right in the front yard, front and center, as if daring another storm to come.

Farther to the west, the new Plaza Towers and Briarwood Elementary Schools were nearing completion. They sat in the middle of what was still largely a construction zone—packed with workers who had come from all over the country to rapidly rebuild. Some were undocumented, though nobody here said a word—not even in the middle of red-state America, where many argued against amnesty for illegal immigrants. But Moore had always been more tolerant, more welcoming in that respect. It was just the way people here were—and they were grateful to anyone who would help them get their city back to normal again.

While some residents had moved on, most had chosen to stay—determined not to let Mother Nature run them away from the city they loved. Some moved to other parts of Moore, but many rebuilt homes right in the same spot where they had lived before. "I could never live anywhere else," a woman named Kristy Rushing told me as she prepared to move back into her home across the street from the newly rebuilt Plaza Towers. Her husband and two of their five kids had barely escaped with their lives on May 20, and in the days afterward, as her family grappled with having lost everything save a few pictures and mementos, Rushing had vowed to never return to Moore. It was too risky. But then, eleven days later, they'd had to flee for their lives again when the El Reno tornado took aim at a relative's home where they were staying as they tried to figure out their lives. Scared and crying and wondering how such a nightmare could be happening again, Rushing had realized that no matter where they went, they were at risk of some disaster. "You can't control Mother Nature," she told me. Still, she admitted to feeling anxious every time the wind blew. Everybody did—especially the people who had been in the path of the tornado.

A few days before the anniversary I went to see Jennifer Doan at her home in Edmond. She was in the nursery rocking her new son Jack, a tiny baby with an infectious grin who was now almost six months old. As we sat at her dining room table, Doan talked in a quiet, sometimes quivering voice about what the last year had been like for her. There had been good days and bad days. She knew she would never forget, never really heal fully, and she wondered if she would ever feel normal again, if she would ever be able to hear the rain or a gust of wind and not feel a jolt of fear shoot through her body. Spring used to be her favorite time of year. Like everyone here, she had loved the storms. But now even a small crack of thunder made her a wreck. Her husband, Nyle, closely monitored the weather on his phone, and when anything erupted, she would put on headphones and turn the music all the way up until it was over. She did the same thing on Saturdays when they tested the emergency sirens around the city. Doan had an alarm set on her phone a few minutes before testing began to remind her to put them on. Still, she had never considered leaving Oklahoma. "This is where I live," she told me.

Doan longed to be back in the classroom. She missed being around kids. Being a teacher was her calling, and she was angry at the possibility that the storm could take that away too. Doctors were still unconvinced that she was emotionally ready, but she saw it as a final, vital step in healing. A few weeks later she was given permission to go back to work the following fall. She was going to teach third grade at a newly built school in Moore—South Lake Elementary—where Amy Simpson, her principal at Plaza Towers, was being transferred. Like the new Plaza Towers and Briarwood buildings, South Lake had been built with a storm shelter.

Simpson had mixed feelings about her new job. It was an honor to be asked to open a new school in Moore—a rare opportunity to truly build something from the ground up. She was hiring every new teacher and helping to decide on colors and logos and everything else. But her heart was with Plaza Towers, and she wondered how she would feel not being near those who understood in a way others simply never would what it was like to survive a tornado and deal with the loss of life. As I spoke to her on the eve of the anniversary, Simpson was still looking forward to the moment when she could get through a day without crying.

What gave her the strength to move on was the kids, she said. Everyone had been anxious about how they would adapt in the months after the storm, and while there had been bad days—some kids still wore headphones on gusty days or grew anxious at the sight of dark clouds—it was the children who proved to be the most resilient. "It's the adults who are a mess," she told me.

I saw what she meant a few days later. On the afternoon of May 20 Simpson invited me as her guest to a gathering to mark the anniversary of the tornado at Plaza Towers. The school system had decided against participating in the larger remembrance ceremony earlier in the day or holding something equally public—worried about the impact on the kids.

Across town Briarwood held its own ceremony. Students, teachers, and parents happily paraded from their temporary school at a church a mile east to the site where a new school was rising up to replace the one that had been destroyed by the tornado. At Plaza Towers Simpson and her colleagues had decided to hold a celebration of life. It would not only honor the seven who were lost but also acknowledge the ones who had survived and had triumphed over a tough year.

Before the ceremony anxious parents had made their way into the tiny auditorium, where they took their seats. They worried about how the ceremony would go. There would be a slideshow featuring photographs of the children who had died, followed by a moment of silence. But they worried: Would it be too much? Would it be too traumatic?

Soon the kids marched in, led by their teachers. They were happy and chattering. It was a school pride day, and the students wore shirts covered with slogans like "Oklahoma Strong." On stage Simpson began the school assembly as she always did, asking the students to recite the Plaza Towers creed. And then she launched a slideshow that featured pictures of the kids' year. There were shots of teachers giving hugs to beaming students and of the classes posing together with local celebrities who had come to visit the school, including Damon Lane, the weatherman from KOCO, and the Thunder Girls, the dance team from the local NBA team. Simpson had designed a soundtrack for the pictures, which included songs like "Happy" by Pharrell and "Roar" by Katy Perry, which the kids danced to and sang along with as if they had not a care in the world.

A few seconds later they were all rapt and still as the school held a moment of silence for the victims of the storm. On the screen the pictures of the seven who had died slowly flashed in succession, followed by an image of a burning candle. On stage Simpson wiped away tears. A few feet away I watched a teacher dab at her eyes with a tissue, and as she did, a tiny little girl next to her looked over and grabbed the adult's hand in hers and squeezed it, the child trying to comfort the adult.

Afterward I stood outside talking with others who had come to the school that day to remember. Among them was Jack Poe, the city chaplain, who told me that he hoped to never go through another day like May 20. It had been one of the worst days of his life, seeing the parents of the kids killed in such anguish. "Thank God, the weather has been good to us this year," he said, peering up at the clear blue sky.

And it was true, the weather had been good—unusually good. Usually the stormiest month of the year, that May had been strangely quiet. Up to that point there had been only five tornadoes in the entire season—the strongest being an EF2 tornado with winds upward of 135 miles an hour that hit in the northeastern corner of the state, near Arkansas. By the end of 2014 Oklahoma reported just sixteen tornadoes for the entire year, the lowest number of storms ever recorded since records had been kept beginning in the 1950s. A record-breaking year of strong tornadoes followed by almost nothing, and scientists had no idea why.

As quiet as the weather was, the people of Moore would never stop eyeing the sky with unease. They knew another storm was coming. Maybe not this year, but someday. "We hope that this will never happen," Mayor Glenn Lewis told the crowd that morning at the anniversary service. "But . . . this is Moore, Oklahoma, and we're probably going to have another tornado someday."

And so it goes in Oklahoma, where people have long been accustomed to living at the mercy of the sky.

ACKNOWLEDGMENTS

I knew that writing a book would not be easy, but this was much harder than I ever imagined, in part because the subject was so close to my heart. As a journalist, you always want to get something right, but with this book, I felt intense pressure to write the best story I could about my home state and its unique and sometimes dangerous relationship with the weather. This book would not have happened without the willingness of so many people to talk about what they went through on May 20, 2013. I am especially grateful to people in Moore, Oklahoma, who shared their stories of that day and beyond, even when it was incredibly painful for them. They are truly heroes, exhibiting the kind of bravery and resilience that we all should aspire to.

This book would also not have been possible without Joy de Menil, my amazing editor at Viking, who never gave up on me, even on the darkest days of this project—and there were many. From day one, Joy understood this story and why it was important to tell, and words do not do justice to how incredibly grateful I am that she stuck with me even when I had doubts about myself. Thank you so much to Joy and everybody at Viking for taking a chance on a first-time author. It is such an honor to have this book produced by an imprint with such a storied literary history—dating back to *The Grapes of Wrath*, another tragic tale of Oklahomans and the weather.

A huge thank-you goes to out to my agent, Howard Yoon, who had faith in me and in the story and worked tirelessly to find the best publisher, even when many were skeptical that readers would be interested in a story about the weather in a state most people have never visited. He played the role of agent, editor, cheerleader, and, at times, therapist, and saying "thank you" simply does not seem to be enough.

Behind every author is a cadre of friends, the support network that keeps you going on the good days and the bad. I would especially like to thank Sarah Schumacher, who I thought hated me when we first met more than a decade ago in Washington, D.C. At first, she was my roommate, but over the years she has become so much more—closest friend, a sister, my family. There is no one in my life more important. She has been there for me through everything—love and heartbreak, new jobs, new cities. While I was writing this book, Sarah was producing something amazing, too: her beautiful daughter, Matilda, who I know will grow up to be as smart and unique as her mother. I am so grateful every day that we are friends. I would also like to thank Sarah's husband, Dan Ribaudo, and Michael Philip Fisher and Matthew Konopka. They are not only incredible friends, but they are also the best karaoke partners anyone could ask for.

One of the amazing things about covering the White House or a presidential campaign is not just being on the front row of history, but the close friendships you develop with other reporters. I first met David Greene in Waco, Texas, when we were both covering George W. Bush. He was with National Public Radio, and I was with

Newsweek. We instantly bonded over the feeling of how lucky we were to have jobs that took us to far-flung cities all over the United States and the world. We found every karaoke bar in every presidential primary state, where I would hold up my cell phone close to the stage so that he could serenade his wife, Rose Previte, back in D.C. with "Mandy" by Barry Manilow. Over the years, David and Rose became two of my most beloved friends. In 2013, David, who was in the middle of finishing his first book, encouraged me to write my own and put me in touch with his agent, Howard. This book wouldn't have happened without David or Rose, who, in the middle of opening her own restaurant in D.C., somehow found the time to give me pep talks on hard days.

I am lucky to have had many people in my cheering section. Chris Laible spent hours listening to me talk about the weather or working through ways of how to structure the story. And when I was locked away writing, he chimed in with supportive texts and e-mails. Katie Connolly and Jonathan Schleifer texted me photos of cute weenie dogs to cheer me up when I struggled to write some of the more emotionally fraught sections of the book. And I likely wouldn't have written the book at all had it not been for the early support of Justin Sullivan, who often had more faith in me than I had in myself. I hope that I have encouraged you as much as you've encouraged me.

A big thank-you to Megan Liberman and Dan Klaidman, my editors at *Yahoo News* who gave me the time and support I needed to write the book. Thank you to Beth Fouhy, my former editor, who quickly deployed me to Moore that May as we watched the tornado on television in our offices in New York. Beth allowed me to go back to Oklahoma and do more reporting later that summer, which became a key part of the foundation for the book. Thanks also to Kelli Grant and especially to Liz Goodwin, an amazing reporter, colleague, and close friend whose unwavering faith, support, and advice helped me get through tough periods.

Thanks also to Sara Murray, Josh Haner, Khue Bui, Jennifer Sondag, Charley Devilbiss, Cecilia Jen, Cara Laverty, and Eric Pfeiffer.

I would also like to thank my mother, to whom this book is dedicated. She was a single mom who raised me on a paltry salary at a time when Oklahoma's economy was in peril, and looking back, I still don't know how she did it. But my mother was always a survivor. She came from a family that was so poor that they wore dresses made out of flour sacks to school. She devoured books and wondered about life beyond the farm in an era when girls were raised to think that finding a husband was their main career pursuit. One of my mother's first jobs was working in an oil field—an industry that was not exactly packed with women. Any bit of adversity that came her way, she picked herself up and kept moving. Like any mother and daughter, we've had our tough moments, but I know everything I have accomplished in life is thanks to her. I love you, Mom, and thank you—especially for encouraging me to love the weather.